THE RISE AND FALL OF
BABYLON

THE RISE AND FALL OF
BABYLON

GATEWAY OF THE GODS

ANTON GILL

METRO BOOKS
NEW YORK

CONTENTS

INTRODUCTION

The study of Mesopotamia, Ancient Iraq, Assyria, Babylon, the Ancient Near East – several names exist for the subject – is a new one. Although a handful of early European travellers wrote memoirs of their journeys through the country, noting the sights they saw, it wasn't until the 19th century that a systematic study began. Claudius James Rich's *Narrative of a Journey to the Site of Babylon in 1811*, caused a stir and fired the imagination. Rich's adventures inspired Byron to write a play, and aroused the curiosity of Victorian scholars and explorers. Although venturing into areas both dangerous and tough, Englishmen had all the confidence that comes from knowing that they belonged to what was then the top nation, and their expeditions were backed by a strong currency. In the mid-19th century, men such as Henry Layard and Henry Rawlinson made great strides in advancing our knowledge of the cities, culture and languages of the ancient and hitherto forgotten peoples of Mesopotamia. French and Italian scholars also involved themselves. There was collaboration. Occasionally there were squabbles. The greatest collections today are to be found in the British Museum in London, the Louvre in Paris, the Vorderasiatisches Museum in Berlin, and – until recently – the National Museum of Iraq in Baghdad.

At the end of the 19th century, with world power shifting, the Germans took a hand. Robert Koldewey tirelessly worked at Babylon for 17 years and the fruits of his labours today adorn the Vorderasiatisches Museum in Berlin. A few years later, after the First World War, it was the British again, notably at work excavating Ur – the most ancient city to have been unearthed – in the 1920s. Another interruption was caused by the Second World War, but thereafter work continued intermittently until 1991 and the outbreak of the Kuwait War (the Second Gulf War). Since then, matters have been effectively at a standstill, the Iraq War of 2003 having disastrous consequences for archaeological sites in Iraq, and for Iraq's important museum and library collections.

Given the chequered nature of Assyriology (the generic name for the study of this ancient civilization) and the fact that it has never been able to progress smoothly, it is hardly surprising that it is not only a new science, but one in which relatively few facts have been established. The Mesopotamians were almost as lavish in recording their history and day-to-day life as the Ancient Egyptians, so much so that thousands of clay tablets lie in storage in museums still waiting to be catalogued, let alone published; but much more of their culture has been wiped out by time, and they had no native stone to build with, so their monuments could not withstand, as the pyramids have, the abrasion of time.

Because of this, I have to begin with a warning. You will find, if you read further than this book on the subject, that although there is general agreement among experts, the devil is in the detail. Interpretation of events, when events took place, where they took place, transliteration of names, the identification of artefacts – all are subject to different opinions and ideas. A young and growing discipline, which has recently taken a very hard knock from an unnecessary war, Assyriology is an exciting field to be in; but it can be a confusing one.

In the use of names, I have tended to adopt those in most general use and most familiar to a general reader, but I have not followed the general Bible spelling of Nebuchadrezzar's name. His name serves as a good example of what I mean. Correctly transliterated (for the sake of accessibility, I am avoiding diacritical marks in this book) it is 'Nabu-ku-dur-ru-u-sur'. In the Bible, the writers of Daniel and Ezra call him Nebuchadnezzar. Only the pro-Babylonian prophet Jeremiah employs the correct name (used by most modern scholars): 'Nebuchadrezzar'. Elsewhere, for the sake of ease of recognition, I have used Belshazzar not Bel-shar-usur, Neriglissar not Nergal-sharezer, and so on, wherever possible. I have used the Akkadian names for the gods, where necessary adding the Sumerian name in parentheses.

In terms of events, interpretation of buildings' use, interpretation of ritual, and so on, I have tried to follow the consensus of modern scholarship. Archaeologists such as Koldewey and Woolley, let alone their Victorian predecessors, were pioneers. Most of their findings are still valid; some are debated, some have been corrected, but their books, as indeed some of what you will find on the internet, should be approached with a little caution. Victorian scholars like E. A. Wallis Budge often employ transliterations of proper names far from modern usage; and there is a lunatic fringe which confuses history, the Bible, and pseudo-mysticism to muddy the water further – try S. D. Baldwin's *Nebuchadnezzar's Panoramic Vision of the Six Kingdoms of the World*, written in the 19th century, as a sample – but this at least is recognizably off the wall.

So, while I have aimed for consistency and a clear line, never forget that this is a period of history yet fully to be understood. Kings who appear important may only seem so relatively, simply because we have more information about them than others, and the same goes for events. But nothing can detract from the interest of Mesopotamia's long and ancient history, nor from its claim to have created almost all the machinery of modern bureaucracy and society – with it, we are presented with a distant mirror, to borrow Barbara Tuchman's phrase, in which we are able to discern ourselves.

Of necessity, the vast majority of dates, and all those defining periods, are approximate. Dates referring to kings are regnal years.

HALF TITLE *Low-relief sculpture of a bull, from the Processional Way leading to the Ishtar Gate in Babylon.*

TITLE PAGE *Early Western scholars examining an Assyrian rock sculpture, from* Discoveries in the Ruins of Nineveh and Babylon *(1853) by the British archaeologist Austen Henry Layard (1817–94).*

PROLOGUE

The Land between the Rivers – or Mesopotamia as the Greeks named it – is often seen as the cradle of our civilization. Regarded by many as the original of the Garden of Eden, the twin rivers of the Tigris and the Euphrates enabled and encouraged from very early on in our history the settlement of land, and the transition from hunter-gatherers to nomadic pastoralists to fixed farming communities in a relatively short space of time.

The area covered by Mesopotamia is that, roughly, encompassed by modern Palestine, Syria, Iraq and Kuwait, though the most important centres lay in what is now Iraq. The first identifiable people to have inhabited it – living in the southernmost province near the shores of the Persian Gulf – were the Sumerians, who emerged, we are not sure from where, soon after the beginning of the third millennium; but there is ample evidence of a well-developed culture which preceded them. In time they were replaced as (and this would be a pattern that would repeat itself several times) more primitive but more forceful peoples – usually nomadic pastoralists – moved in, either by force or by infiltration. They were attracted to the rich alluvial soil which enabled a man to settle, grow crops, harvest predictably, and become prosperous; even to have the leisure to enjoy artefacts created for no other reason than to give pleasure.

As time passed, the Sumerians were superseded in turn by the Akkadians and the Amorites, who established dynasties in southern Mesopotamia. To the north, with the emergence of the powerful Shamshi Adad, during the reign of Hammurabi in the south, the Assyrians did the same thing, from their base at the city of Ashur. Over many centuries, power shifted from one to the other of these peoples, as one or the other at times ruled all Mesopotamia and beyond. At other times, they existed side by side in fragile alliance, and at all times they faced threats from their neighbours, particularly the peoples to the north and east. And in the meantime cities became kingdoms which sometimes – rarely – became empires, only to fragment back to kingdoms and city-states again, as the millennia rolled by.

One feature that provides consistency in this complex picture is that the essential system of ethics, and the essential pantheon established by the Sumerians, though adapted over time, was always adopted by each wave of newcomers; and although the Sumerian language ceded to Akkadian as the common tongue, little else changed. Babylonian and Assyrian were dialects of Akkadian, both shared the same gods, though different emphasis was given to their importance, and over time they developed a shared, or at least overlapping, history. From Hammurabi's day, that is, from the early second millennium, the city of Babylon became the cultural and religious centre of Mesopotamia, and whatever vicissitudes befell it, it retained that standing until the end.

From this tangled web a handful of great men emerge. The best known to us, mainly from stories in the Book of Daniel which some of us learned at Sunday School, is Nebuchadrezzar. We know about his dreams, which Daniel interpreted - on one occasion having to guess what the

> ❛By the waters of Babylon, there we sat down
>   and wept when we remembered Zion.
> On the willows there we hung up our lyres.
>   For there our captors required of us songs,
>   and our tormentors, mirth, saying, "Sing us
>   one of the songs of Zion."
> How shall we sing the Lord's song in
>   a foreign land?
> If I forget you, O Jerusalem, let my
>   right hand wither.
> Let my tongue cleave to the root of my mouth,
>   if I do not remember you, if I do not set
>   Jerusalem above my highest joy. ❜
>
> PSALM 137; 1-6

dream actually was before doing so – and we know about the giant figure of gold, silver, bronze, iron and clay, and about the burning fiery furnace which did not consume Shadrach, Meshach and Abednego; and about the madness of the king, when he roamed the wilderness eating grass, letting his hair and nails grow long. From the Book of Revelation we know about the woman dressed in scarlet and purple, riding on a scarlet beast with seven heads and ten horns, and full of blasphemous names – a woman, the Bible continues,

> *bedecked with gold and jewels and pearls, holding in her hand a golden cup full of abominations and the impurities of her fornication; and on her forehead was written a name of mystery: 'Babylon the great, mother of harlots and of earth's abominations. And I saw the woman, drunk with the blood of the saints and the blood of the martyrs of Jesus.'*

And of course everyone knows about the Tower of Babel, from that handful of verses early in the Book of Genesis.

One wonders what can have excited such vituperation, and when one looks at what really happened, one begins to understand what caused it, though it should be remembered that Daniel was written in the Second Century and Revelation around the late 60s AD. What is important for now is that these works, and other books of the Hebrew Bible and the Apocrypha, have ensured that Babylon has had a central place in the European consciousness and imagination since the early days of Christendom.

Historically, Nebuchadrezzar was the last truly great king of Mesopotamia. His long reign saw a final and magnificent flowering of his culture, which, by his time, had been developing continuously and uninterruptedly for close to 2500 years. In order to understand him, it is necessary to understand his context and his roots.

BELOW The Building of the Tower of Babel (1595; oil on panel, Gemäldegalerie Alter Meister, Dresden, Germany) by Marten van Valckenborch (1535–1612). The Tower of Babel held a powerful fascination for medieval and early modern Europeans, and was the subject of paintings by a number of artists, including Pieter Brueghel the Elder and Abel Grimmer.

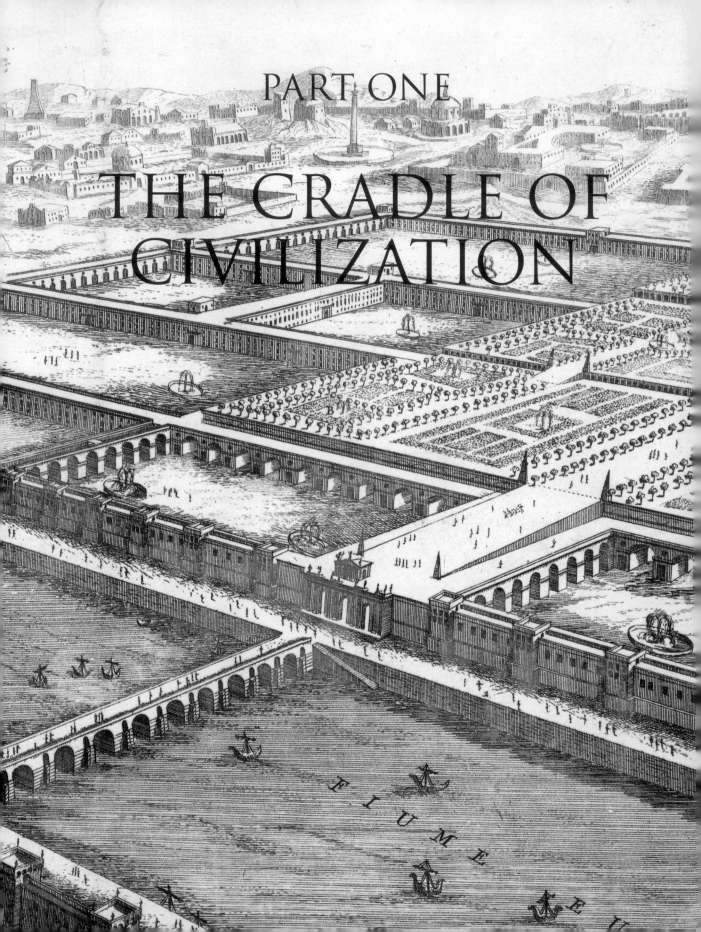

PART ONE

THE CRADLE OF CIVILIZATION

CHAPTER ONE

THE LAND OF TWO RIVERS

T HE NILE, the vital water source of Ancient Egypt, flooded regularly and more or less predictably, once a year, its waters augmented by the annual rainfall in the Ethiopian highlands. The Tigris and the Euphrates, the two rivers that irrigated Mesopotamia, were less certain in their behaviour. They both rise in the mountains of what is now eastern Turkey, and converge to form the Shatt al-Arab river shortly before emptying into the Persian Gulf.

RIGHT *Aerial view of the Euphrates in Iraq. On its 1678-mile (2700-km) course, this major waterway, which has been used for transport and irrigation from ancient times, flows past the historic sites of Mari, Sippar, Babylon, Borsippa, Uruk and Ur.*

PREVIOUS PAGES *This 18th-century Italian engraving (after a drawing by the Austrian architect Johann Fischer von Erlach) gives an impression of the city of Babylon in the reign of Nebuchadrezzar II. The huge temple ziggurat known as the* Etemenanki *(top right) may be the model for the Biblical story of the Tower of Babel.*

To the north, Mari on the Euphrates is some 155 miles (250 km) distant from Ashur on the Tigris, but further south, where the rivers converge, Sippar on the Euphrates is only about 37 miles (60 km) from Dur-Kurigalzu on the sister river. They then diverge again before coming together once more; their estuaries are relatively close to one another. From source to mouth, the Euphrates runs for 1740 miles (2800 km); the Tigris, 1180 miles (1900 km).

The two rivers have different natures. The Tigris (its original Sumerian name, *Idigina*, means 'swift river') is faster, running between higher banks. The more leisurely, meandering Euphrates is sometimes level with its banks, and changed its course often in the past, which frequently spelt disaster for the cities it deserted, as well as necessitating constant repair and redigging of the irrigation canals that depended on it. Over millennia, the rich silt it threw up has buried many of the communities it fed, but the same alluvial soil enabled people to settle and farm in the sure knowledge that the river would always provide for them. The Euphrates' Akkadian name *Puratu* means 'the fruitful one'. The existence of the rivers meant that humans could live, and live well, in the otherwise arid, subtropical climate of the Near East. By 5500 BC farming had spread from the Levant (the eastern Mediter-ranean) and the Zagros Mountains (in modern Iran and Iraq), where there was reliable rainfall, to cover the whole of the Mesopotamian plain.

EARLY CULTURES

The earliest pottery style to have been identified in this region belongs to a group called the Hassuna, who were active in northern Mesopotamia. This people cultivated primitive, hardy cereals, which would originally have grown wild – emmer, einkorn-wheat and barley – the last the mainstay of the area up until the present day. They also domesticated and bred animals – goats, pigs and cattle. (Even their ancestors had learned the value of animal husbandry; the dog was the first animal to be domesticated by humans, as early as 12,000 BC.) Although the Hassuna had developed from tribes of hunter-gatherers, having adopted a settled farming lifestyle, they hunted less than their forefathers, and probably only as an adjunct to their new agricultural activities. Certainly, by the reign of Nebuchadrezzar (605–562 BC), hunting in the area had become more a recreation than a necessity.

The Hassuna, who knew how to smelt lead and copper, are also the first culture known to have produced pottery, fired in purpose-built kilns and decorated with paint. They are also thought to be the first to have used seals, probably to stamp property; an indication of the beginnings of an organized society that recognized the rights of the individual.

The Hassuna were in time replaced in their province by the Halafians, whose presence has been traced to around 6000–5400 BC. This culture shows signs of developing sophistication. They produced high-quality pottery, hand-shaped but crafted with such sureness of touch and symmetry that they could almost have been produced on a potter's wheel, delicate and fine, decorated with abstract borders and central crosses; necklaces of cowrie-shells and volcanic glass, and tools of obsidian and flint. The few examples of their sculpture that have been found are confined to small, votive figurines of the 'earth-mother' type. Here was a people secure and wealthy enough to afford luxury goods, which in turn point to the beginnings at least of a hierarchy, and a ruling class. It is likely that social structure was developing rapidly, and that communities were beginning to split into skilled workers who practised their craft and nothing else, rulers who maintained order, made decisions on behalf of their group, and ensured ample reward and respect for their services, and a rank-and-file of food-providers, farmers and – possibly – hunters.

At the same time as the Halafians but further south were the Samarrans, who were the first known civilization to exploit the Euphrates by developing irrigation canals, a technique that opened the arid plains of southern Mesopotamia up to permanent settlement.

THE UBAID CIVILIZATION

Further south still, and having much in common with the Samarrans – at least in the early stages of their culture – were the people known as the Ubaid after the site where their artefacts were first unearthed. They lived close to the shores of the Persian Gulf, which in those days extended further north than they do today. Tell al-Ubaid is a stone's throw from the Sumerian settlements of Ur and Eridu, the latter originally an Ubaid settlement, which according to the Sumerian King-List was the oldest of all cities. The Ubaid people appeared around 5900 BC and remained a presence until 4300 BC, effectively laying foundations for the Sumerian people, who were to inherit the region from them. Eridu's antiquity is borne out by the fact that it was inhabited until around 2500 BC, but after that very early date fell into disuse, and thereafter was only restored and maintained as a historical shrine, the home of the god of wisdom (and, at that time, also of the sea) Ea (Sumerian: Enki).

Ubaid pottery soon began to supplant local work to the north, for the Ubaids had invented a basic potter's wheel, which enabled them to mass-produce their work and export it. The south, while more stable agriculturally, owing to the rich alluvial soil, did not have the resources of the north – there was no stone, timber good enough to build with, nor were there precious stones or metals. These things the north at least had access to. Trade became an early imperative. The north had more plentiful rainfall than the south; the southern marshes provided beds of giant reeds, used then (and still) for building, and abounded in waterbirds, while the lakes teemed with fish. Where now ruins lie in arid plains, then, either on account of irrigation or an earlier course taken by the river Euphrates, there was vegetation and greenery. All the cities of ancient Mesopotamia were built on the banks of one or other of the twin rivers.

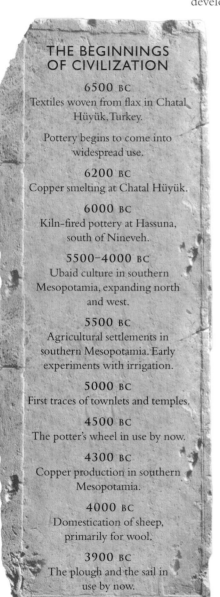

THE BEGINNINGS OF CIVILIZATION

6500 BC
Textiles woven from flax in Chatal Hüyük, Turkey.

Pottery begins to come into widespread use.

6200 BC
Copper smelting at Chatal Hüyük.

6000 BC
Kiln-fired pottery at Hassuna, south of Nineveh.

5500–4000 BC
Ubaid culture in southern Mesopotamia, expanding north and west.

5500 BC
Agricultural settlements in southern Mesopotamia. Early experiments with irrigation.

5000 BC
First traces of townlets and temples.

4500 BC
The potter's wheel in use by now.

4300 BC
Copper production in southern Mesopotamia.

4000 BC
Domestication of sheep, primarily for wool.

3900 BC
The plough and the sail in use by now.

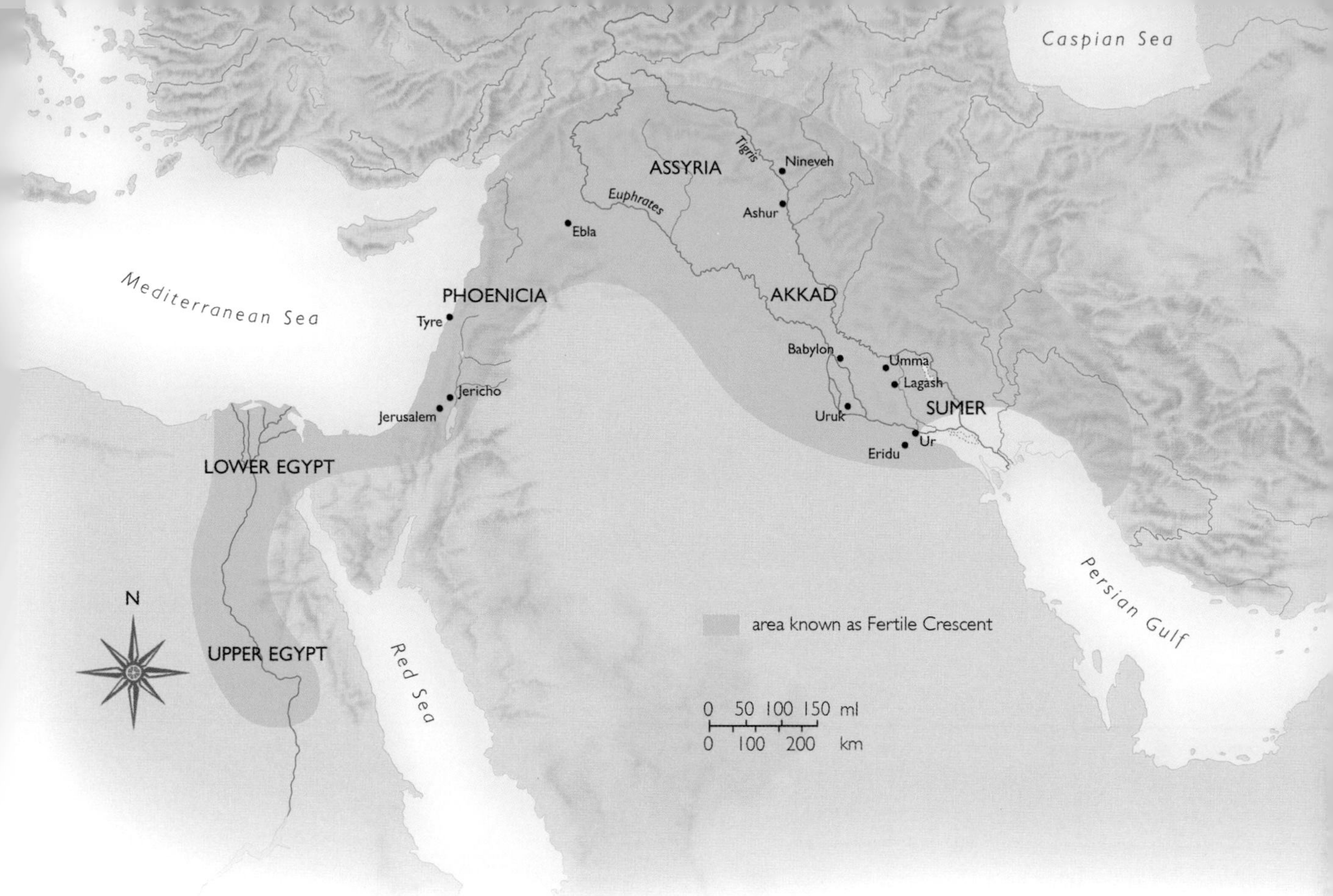

Caspian Sea

ASSYRIA
Tigris
Nineveh
Euphrates
Ashur
Ebla

PHOENICIA
AKKAD
Tyre
Babylon
Umma
Lagash
Jericho
Uruk
SUMER
Jerusalem
Eridu
Ur

Mediterranean Sea

LOWER EGYPT

N

UPPER EGYPT

Red Sea

Persian Gulf

area known as Fertile Crescent

0 50 100 150 ml
0 100 200 km

ABOVE *The Fertile Crescent
in* c.2000 BC, *showing the
principal kingdoms and cities
in the region.*

The Ubaid culture is characterized by the paucity of useful materials such as
stone. Their pottery is not as fine as that of the Halaf people, and its decoration is less
inventive. However, they were resourceful, using terracotta to manufacture sickles,
axes, adzes and knives. Their houses were constructed out of reed mats, with bundles
of reeds for pillars, and sometimes they were reinforced with mud or clay. Similar
structures were still being made by the Marsh Arabs around Basra until very recently,
though it remains to be seen whether or not such traditions have been interrupted
forever by recent wars. Among their most striking artefacts are their sculptures –
slender, standing figurines, usually female, sometimes with a child at her breast. Their
heads are extraordinary – attenuated, rather elegant, but scarcely human, with long
slits for eyes, the nose hardly defined, a long, sloping head, and wide, pouting lips,
decorated with black paint, and sometimes having hair fashioned from bitumen – an
early example of extreme stylization. Bitumen would be used throughout the
Mesopotamian period for a variety of purposes, from decoration, to sculpture to
mortar, its naturally occurring presence an indication of the petroleum which would
provide the area with a mixture of wealth and trouble six thousand years later.

Statuary of this period tended not to depict ordinary people, but gods, goddesses,
and rulers. The temples of Ubaid – already the centres of social and administrative
life – were built of mud bricks cemented with clay. They took the form of a central
cella (an inner chamber) with smaller rooms at each corner. The *cella* contained a
low platform at one end for the god's image, and an altar at the other. Outside, the
walls were decorated with shallow buttresses and niches that caught the sunlight. This
basic form persisted throughout the Mesopotamian period.

The Samarrans and the Ubaids prospered as a result of their efficient management
of the rivers. Their resources were great, their populations expanded. Organized

INVENTIONS THAT CHANGED THE WORLD

The potter's wheel was in use in the Ancient Near East by 4500 BC – towards the end of the Ubaid period and at the beginning of that of Uruk. Fine examples of Ubaid pottery exist and pottery, even when broken, provides a valuable dating-aid to archaeologists, because its makeup is so durable. Not only beautifully decorated ware is useful. In the Uruk period (c.4000–3000 BC), humble, bevel-rimmed bowls appeared, made by hand in moulds and produced in vast quantities, perhaps for use as containers for workers' rations, to be discarded after use in the way we throw away the foil containers of a takeaway. But the potter's wheel meant the birth of a real industry, and points to a large demand for better-quality goods. It also points to the emergence of a professional, specialized class of artisan in a society that is beginning to look distinctly modern.

It must have been a short step to turn the potter's wheel through 90 degrees, to create a mode of locomotion. We know that wheeled transport was in use by 2600 BC, and possibly even earlier. In his excavations at Ur in the 1920s, the British archaeologist Leonard Woolley discovered a series of tombs belonging to an élite class. Among many exquisite objects found there, he also noted the remains of heavy, four-wheeled waggons, drawn by oxen whose remains lay nearby. On the so-called Royal Standard of Ur, now in the British Museum and dating to about 2600 BC, similar four-wheeled waggons – battle chariots in this case, are depicted, drawn by teams of domesticated onagers. The wheels are heavy and solid.

The domestication of oxen led in turn to another momentous invention: by 4500 BC, the plough was in use, allowing speedier and more efficient cultivation. Before long, a hopper was added to create the seeder-plough, an even more efficient device that was in use for millennia.

Because the Tigris and the Euphrates did not enjoy the regular annual flood which raised the level of the Nile, systems of irrigation were quickly introduced. There were many different kinds of canal, and the Babylonians had specific words for each of them.

The domestication of sheep around 4000 BC, predominantly for their wool, led to another crucial invention: the loom. The art of weaving dates back to prehistory, and it was an important industry for the Mesopotamians to develop. As the population grew, so did the industry, providing not only clothing for the people, but a valuable export. For all its fertility, Mesopotamia was not rich in minerals or wood or stone, as was Egypt. For these things it depended very much, and from an early stage, on international trade.

ABOVE *This low-relief sculpture of c.668–630 BC shows a palace guard standing by the light, two-wheeled hunting chariot of the Assyrian king Ashurbanipal. Such vehicles first appeared in around 1700 BC.*

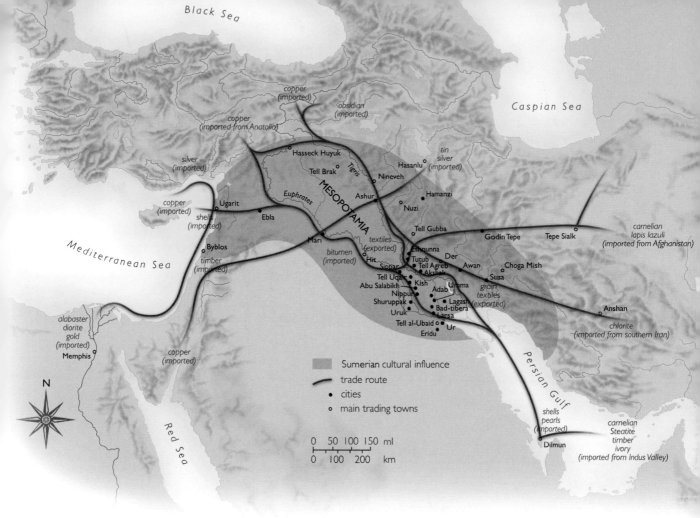

Map showing the following labels:

Black Sea

Caspian Sea

copper (imported)

copper (imported from Anatolia)

obsidian (imported)

silver (imported)

Hasseck Huyuk

Tell Brak

Nineveh

Ashur

tin silver (imported)

Hasanlu

Hamanzi

Nuzi

MESOPOTAMIA

Euphrates

Tigris

copper (imported)

Ugarit

shells (imported)

Ebla

Tell Gubba

Godin Tepe

Tepe Sialk

carnelian lapis lazuli (imported from Afghanistan)

Mediterranean Sea

Byblos

timber (imported)

Mari

textiles (exported)

bitumen (imported)

Hit

Eshnunna

Tutub

Der

Awan

Choga Mish

Sippar

Tell Agreb

Akshak

Susa

Anshan

Tell Uqair

Kish

Adab

Umma

grain textiles (exported)

Abu Salabikh

Nippur

Lagash

chlorite (imported from southern Iran)

Shuruppak

Bad-tibera

Uruk

Larsa

Tell al-Ubaid

Ur

Eridu

alabaster diorite gold (imported)

Memphis

copper (imported)

Persian Gulf

N

Red Sea

shells pearls (imported)

Dilmun

carnelian Steatite timber ivory (imported from Indus Valley)

Sumerian cultural influence

trade route

• cities

○ main trading towns

0 50 100 150 ml
0 100 200 km

ABOVE *Map showing the already extensive trade routes, principal cities, and sources of imported goods in third-millennium BC Mesopotamia, along with Sumer's sphere of influence.*

society followed, either in terms of primitive democracies or in terms of ruler-administrators, who were initially of the priestly class. Farming was an arduous undertaking. Farmers had less leisure than hunter-gatherers, since farming involved periods of intense activity alternating with periods of leisure, depending on the seasons, while there was constant anxiety about whether the crops would succeed. As towns developed, their populations grew, and although most of the town-dwellers were workers on the nearby land (increasingly owned and/or managed by the temple or the palace), living in close proximity to one another brought people a new set of problems: transmitted disease and social friction. The habit, never broken, of tipping rubbish into the street (and the streets were narrow) encouraged rats. In addition, a diet that lacked variety could create nutritional problems, while the repetitive and strenuous nature of farm labour harmed people's health.

Although the south developed faster than the north, it still had to acquire timber, copper, and other materials lacking in the region from Anatolia and Persia, via northern and eastern Mesopotamia. Trade was one way of acquiring such vital commodities. War and expropriation would be another.

LEGENDS OF THE FLOOD

In 1929, the British archaeologist Leonard Woolley (1880–1960) was excavating at the Sumerian city of Ur when he came upon a stratum of clean soil about 2 metres (6.6 ft) deep, which contained nothing. Beneath it was evidence of Ubaid pottery, while above it was Sumerian work. This mysterious layer of clean sand was taken to

THE PEOPLES OF MESOPOTAMIA

Several peoples dominated the Ancient Near East, and it is the complicated interconnection of their shifting periods of power that delineate the history of the period that concerns us.

The Sumerians, who may possibly have been indigenous and who simply gained ascendancy over their rivals settled in the south of Mesopotamia, near the northern shores of the Persian Gulf, replacing an earlier culture which we know as the Ubaid, named after Tell Ubaid, near Ur, where artefacts related to that culture were first discovered. The Sumerians were the first to found true cities, notably Uruk, Ur and Lagash, and to devise such essential tools of administration as writing, administration, politics, laws, justice, education and medicine. They were also the builders of the first ziggurats, and, as their cities became states and rivals, defensive walls. The first Sumerian period of dominance was between roughly 3500 and 2000 BC, and it was during the troubled time of what we call the Early Dynastic Period (2900–2400 BC) that the walls were built. Increasing numbers of bronze weapons were manufactured, and war begins to feature in art. At the same time, social divergence made its appearance with the formation of ruling élites, the emergence of secular rule (power hitherto had been in the hands of the priest-administrators), the appearance of a poor, agricultural, dependent class, and of slavery. Among the élite could now be numbered the *lugal* (literally 'big man', or 'king', and the *sangu* (accountant). The skill of writing was in the hands of specialized scribes, though this period also sees the appearance of creative writing, since the rulers wanted to have their deeds and achievements recorded and glorified for future generations. This is our first consistent indication of man's awareness of himself, of his place in the world, and of a sense of history. People with the leisure to reflect thought about the genesis of the world, human suffering, and the inevitability of death. The high level of their sophistication is attested by the exquisite artefacts dating from around 2600 BC excavated by Leonard Woolley in the 1920s.

The Sumerians laid the foundations for the religious belief, ethical systems, and general cultural and administrative processes for the whole of our period; subsequent conquerors, from less developed cultures, adopted and adapted to what they were taking over. The line was not even broken by the Persian invasion of Cyrus the Great (reigned *c.*590–529 BC) in 539 BC, though that did spell the end of the Mesopotamian Period. Even the Sumerian language survived, though as one used by priests and an élite class, much as Latin and Greek were used in the medieval period and Latin still is in the Roman Catholic Church. It was not destined to survive as a common tongue, and it is unrelated to other languages.

Sumerian came to an end (though it was to revive for a period with the so-called Third Dynasty of Ur) with the invasion from slightly further north by the Akkadian king, Sargon the Great (reigned *c.* 2334–2279 BC), who descended to take control and established the first true empire from his – now lost – city

ABOVE *Gypsum and alabaster statue (c. 26th–25th century BC) of the city superintendent Ebih-il, from the Temple of Ishtar at Mari.*

of Agade, which he established, and which is believed to be close to what would in time become the city of Babylon. Akkadian, a Semitic tongue, became the common language, and under his grandson, Naram-Sin (2254–2218 BC), the empire reached its greatest extent, stretching from the Persian Gulf to the Mediterranean.

But it was not to last. The Sumerian king Ur-Nannu formed a coalition of rebel cities around Ur and established what we call the Ur III Dynasty, which lasted until another wave of invaders, this time the Amorites, descended, possibly from the northwest. The Amorites established themselves in the cities of the south, producing one famous king, Hammurabi (reigned c. 1795–1750 BC), the 'Law-Giver', who based himself at Babylon. Once established as a major city, and despite later sackings and the eclipse of Babylon as the dominant power until 626 BC, it never lost its central importance as the principal religious and cultural centre of Mesopotamia.

In time the Amorites were replaced by another group, the Kassites, this time from the Zagros Mountains, about whom little is known, though they held sway for several centuries. In the meantime the Assyrians had established a kingdom to the north centred on the city of Ashur on the Tigris. Pressure from them and another rival people to the east, the Elamites, finally forced the collapse of the Kassite hegemony, allowing the emergence of a new Babylonian dynasty, resulting in a power-struggle with Assyria, which Assyria finally won. The resulting Assyrian Empire lasted approximately 300 years until it succumbed, in turn, to the Babylonians. The last great king of Mesopotamia, Nebuchadrezzar II, established an empire which way outdid that of his mighty predecessor, Sargon; but if this was Babylon's greatest flowering, it was also its last. With one exception, minor kings followed Nebuchadrezzar's long and illustrious reign, and soon the whole area had been taken over by Persia under Cyrus the Great, almost without a fight.

ABOVE *Ur-Nanshe (or Ur-Nina), the earliest Sumerian ruler whose name is absolutely identifiable, was the first king of the dynasty of Lagash, probably in the first half of the 24th century BC.*

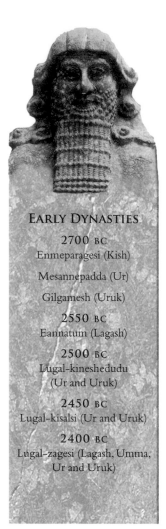

EARLY DYNASTIES

2700 BC
Enmeparagesi (Kish)

Mesannepadda (Ur)

Gilgamesh (Uruk)

2550 BC
Eannatum (Lagash)

2500 BC
Lugal-kineshedudu
(Ur and Uruk)

2450 BC
Lugal-kisalsi (Ur and Uruk)

2400 BC
Lugal-zagesi (Lagash, Umma,
Ur and Uruk)

be evidence of a great flood that had put an end to the Ubaid culture. There are two important versions of the flood story in ancient Mesopotamian literature, the story of Atrahasis, and the flood sequence in *The Epic of Gilgamesh*, in which the hero is called Utnapishtim.

In the Gilgamesh version, the flood is brought down upon humankind because people had bred so successfully that there were simply too many of them, and the noise they made was driving the gods mad. In the Atrahasis myth, a story that reflects real life, the junior gods rebel, because they are fed up with the work of canal clearance and maintenance they have been forced to undertake. In response, the senior gods create mankind to do the work, but mankind flourishes, creating a problem of overpopulation. The gods try to reduce their numbers by various means – drought, famine, pestilence – but mankind always bounces back; in the end, they resort to flood. Like Utnapishtim, Atrahasis is warned by Ea, god of wisdom, and escapes with his family and sufficient livestock and grain to start afresh.

There are several other flood myths, all of which come from roughly the same geographical area – including of course the familiar one from the Old Testament involving Noah. In actual fact, there was no global cataclysm, but there were many local disastrous floods, when the rivers burst their banks and covered the land. In such cases, those who were able would retreat to higher ground, rescuing what they could, and after the flood, they would begin again.

The Sumerian King-List, which should not be taken too literally, lists ten kings who ruled before 'the Flood'. None of these has any discernable basis in history; if they did, they would have to be amalgams of several kings, but even so the length of their reigns is impossibly long. The first, Alulim, is supposed to have ruled for 28,800 years; his successor, for 36,000. However, the cities to which some of them are connected – Sippar, Shuruppak and Larsa, did exist. In passing, it is interesting to note that the number of kings who ruled before the Mesopotamian flood – ten – is the same as the number of Old Testament elders who held sway before Noah's flood. The Old Testament elders also lived for preternatural lengths of time, though not as extravagantly long as their Mesopotamian counterparts: all save one (Enoch, who did not die but was taken away by God), reached the age of about 1000.

In the pre-dynastic period, the Sumerian King-List indicates the passage of power from Eridu to Shuruppak in the north, until the flood which concerns us occurred, after which power is thought to have shifted to the northern city of Kish. It would then pass to Uruk, Ur and Lagash until the Akkadian invasion of around 2334 BC.

Archaeologists other than Woolley have noted the presence of a widespread layer of riverine silt deposits, which left a few feet of yellow sediment in the cities of Shuruppak and Uruk and extended as far north as Kish. The polychrome pottery characteristic of the Jamdat Nasr period (3100–2900 BC) was thereafter replaced with Early Dynastic artefacts.

THE URUK PERIOD

Whatever the cause, around 4300 BC a new power base emerged at the city of Uruk, some 75 miles (120 km) northwest of Eridu along the Euphrates, and it was here that a fresh culture began, bringing fresh developments with it.

The Uruk period covers approximately the millennium from 4000 to 3000 BC. The people, as far as we know, were not outsiders, but the heirs of the Ubaids and other indigenous peoples. But it was as if a page had been turned, for dramatic strides were made – new styles in pottery design, the construction of large cities, the building of sophisticated temples (for example, the Eanna complex at Uruk) and the development of administrative structures. Above all, however, the Uruk period gave rise to the first written records.

LEFT *A marble statue of Lamgi-Mari, King of Mari on the Middle Euphrates, dating from the Early Dynastic Period (c.3000 BC).*

This culture is named after Uruk because it is there that the most extensive archaeological investigations have been made. However, the culture was not confined to that city; indeed, it covered the whole southern province. It is almost certain that Uruk, which covered some 70 hectares (173 acres), was the largest city of its time, and the greatest. Its walls were at least 6 miles (10 km) around.

As the millennium passed, Uruk grew to cover 100 hectares (247 acres), not counting satellite settlements. In addition, the settled area of Babylon as a whole expanded from around 80 to around 210 hectares (198 to 510 acres). Uruk's success was due to its location on a flat plain near the marshes that bordered the shores of the Persian Gulf. Here, by digging irrigation canals from the Euphrates and its minor tributaries, it was possible to cultivate not only cereals, but also to grow fruit trees and date palms, and to breed sheep and goats. The marshes provided fish and waterfowl, as well as grazing for domesticated water-buffalo. With such wealth and security, the population could expand, since there was food in abundance to feed it. Growing prosperity also meant that specialized artisan classes could be maintained, earning their bread not directly, but by selling their skills. There is evidence of weaving 'factories', run by women, and of copper smelting works; finds of bevel-rimmed bowls indicates that there was mass production of 'throwaway' artefacts – the bowls were probably used as ration-measures, or as containers for labourers' meals: in other words, disposable lunch-pails. These proved so popular that they quickly spread, not only over the whole of Mesopotamia, but the surrounding countries as well.

One of the most important developments of this period, demonstrating the response to a need for greater administrative efficiency, is the invention of the cylinder seal, an artefact that epitomizes Ancient Mesopotamia. Stamp seals could only carry limited information; much more could be stored on a small cylinder – most are no bigger than a man's thumb – which could then be rolled over soft clay to leave its impression, as many times as was desired. Ranging in quality from utilitarian to luxurious, cylinder seals were ubiquitous, and were made of stone, faience, baked clay or bone, or (in the high-status artefacts) alabaster, carnelian and lapis lazuli. The information that was carved on these seals was not merely practical: decorative depictions of gods, goddesses, monsters, heroes, animals and buildings abound, evidently carved by specialist craftsmen. This mastery of the plastic arts manifested itself towards the end of the Uruk period in the appearance of the first large-scale relief and in-the-round sculpture. These show clear evidence of great technical skill, indicating that they were the work of experienced and professional artists.

THE GROWTH OF BUREAUCRACY

Since Mesopotamian society was becoming more complex, it needed leaders to organize it, supervise the distribution of food, invigilate payments and barter, and, ultimately, to impose taxes to pay for public services. In the Uruk period this was still the business of the temple; its imposition of a religious ideology in turn engendered a system of ethics and encouraged conformity and acquiescence among the populace. In its role as the centre of the administrative power, it was important that the temple should be, physically, the most imposing building in town. Uruk was wealthy enough to boast not only the Eanna temple complex (Eanna being one of the two districts of Uruk – the other was Kullaba), which had as its centrepiece a limestone temple 75 metres (246 ft) long, but a ziggurat as well. Here, for the first time, columns were decorated by having differently-coloured cones of sandstone, alabaster and bituminous limestone planted in them, bases outwards, to form a pattern of closely-packed coloured discs. Here were found the Uruk Vase, an exquisite alabaster creation dedicated to the goddess Ishtar (Sumerian: Inanna), depicting a procession of naked men bringing farm produce to offer the goddess; and the marble portrait bust known as the White Lady of Uruk (or Warka; see page 136). Until quite recently, both could be seen in the National Museum of Iraq in Baghdad. However, both of these artefacts were looted during the US-led invasion of Iraq in 2003. The vase was badly damaged, as the body was torn from the base. The White Lady was missing for six months before being found, undamaged, in a farmer's backyard.

Administration needs to keep track of itself, and therefore needs records. Cylinder seals were able to convey terse, basic data, such as quantity and ownership, but the recording of more detailed information called for something more complex. The Uruk answer to this was the pictogram, a form of proto-writing in which an object is denoted by a symbol. Next to the symbol a number or numerical value could be placed, and thus a simple form of accounting became possible. This is not a written language, and any literary tradition the Uruk culture may have had, we are ignorant of, as we are of what precise language was spoken. Nevertheless, the pictograms represent the first records. In the first half of the fourth millennium a system of *bullae* was introduced. A *bulla* is a hollow sphere of clay marked with seals and containing stone and clay tokens referring (according to their shape and/or material) to various types of produce, from wheat, say, to goats. The tokens were sealed within the *bulla*, and the seals on its surface guaranteed the contents through the probity of the sealer.

ABOVE *A baked clay artefact (the so-called 'Weld-Blundell Prism', from the Ashmolean Museum, Oxford) containing the Sumerian King-List, which details rulers from 'before the Flood' up to Sin-magir of Isin (c.1827– 17 BC). It is inscribed in cuneiform script, and is thought to have been made in Larsa, Iraq.*

However, since the tokens could not be retrieved without smashing the *bulla*, the practice arose of impressing on the exterior of the *bulla* a note of its contents. Yet this was a laborious system, which gave way to what we would recognize as conventional written records, just as pictograms gave way in time to cuneiform script. This transition occurred in the 600 years from 3100 to 2500 BC, and refinements and improvements to cuneiform would continue down to Nebuchadrezzar's day.

It is unclear what happened in the years leading up to 3000 BC to cause the Uruk culture to go into terminal decline. The main buildings seem to have been razed, possibly as the result of an onslaught by a rival city. One of the several Gilgamesh epics tells of Uruk (of which the hero Gilgamesh was a king), facing attack from the city of Kish. The beginning of the third millennium was certainly a time of great strife and upheaval. It seems also to have been a period in which various cities that had consolidated their power and grown to become city-states, turned on each other, either from necessity or greed, and made war.

CHAPTER TWO

THE EARLY KINGS

CHIEF AMONG THE CITIES THAT emerged in the post-Ubaid period, in the first quarter of the third millennium, around 2800 BC, were Lagash, Umma, and Ur. It is at about this time that we move into history proper, for if artefacts and buildings are the province of the archaeologist, the historian needs written documents to guide him or her to dates and to establish facts. Writing was developing all the time, and from now there is increasing evidence of written records, either on hand-sized clay tablets, on larger 'cylinders' or 'prisms' for important documents and finally on stone steles and boundary markers.

The people of this region whose presence we can confidently date to this period were the Sumerians. The Sumerians may have been an indigenous people, or they may now have emerged as dominant after a period of infiltration. Whatever the truth of the matter, by the time they enter the historical record they are already well-integrated.

In the 1920s Leonard Woolley led an Anglo-American archaeological expedition to excavate the site of Ur. Among many other important discoveries, the expedition uncovered the traces of two early Sumerian dynasties at the city, known to us as the First and Second Dynasties of Ur.

Building methods and artefacts discovered there differed noticeably from what had gone before. For some reason, the regular building-brick (much like our own) employed earlier was now replaced by a brick that was rounded on top, rather like a loaf – the plano-convex brick. It seems an odd, even a bad, design, but it has been argued that if laid in a herringbone pattern, the rounded upper surfaces gave greater cohesion to the mud or bitumen mortar used to bind them. Whatever the case, these bricks, common for a time in the ancient Near East, were in the long term abandoned for a more conventional form.

RIGHT *The famous 'Ram in a Thicket' statuette (dating from c.2600 BC) was part of the treasure trove discovered in the 'Royal Tombs' at Ur by Leonard Woolley. Made of wood and embellished with gold-leaf and lapis lazuli, this artefact was carefully reconstructed before being put on display in the British Museum, where it can still be seen.*

TREASURES OF THE ROYAL TOMBS

However, unquestionably the most exciting finds at Ur were the artefacts that Woolley and his team unearthed in the city's so-called Royal Tombs. While excavating the town cemetery, where they identified a total of 2000 graves, they discovered 16 that were especially grandiose and significant. Among them was a tomb, not unlike the ordinary tombs but larger, consisting of a plain earth pit large enough to accommodate a wooden coffin, as well as providing space on three sides for funerary offerings. Spears were stuck head downwards at the head of the coffin, between which were alabaster and clay vessels. Alongside the coffin, they found two

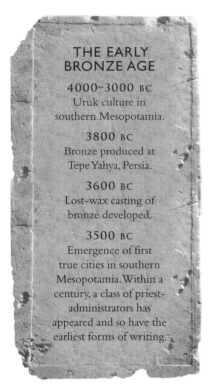

THE EARLY BRONZE AGE

4000–3000 BC
Uruk culture in southern Mesopotamia.

3800 BC
Bronze produced at Tepe Yahya, Persia.

3600 BC
Lost-wax casting of bronze developed.

3500 BC
Emergence of first true cities in southern Mesopotamia. Within a century, a class of priest-administrators has appeared and so have the earliest forms of writing.

gold-mounted daggers, as well as several other daggers of copper, chisels, other tools, about 50 copper bowls, silver bowls, and copper jugs and plates. More spears were set at the foot of the coffin, along with assorted arrowheads. The body must have been richly dressed, for the archaeologists found the remains of a silver belt, a gold dagger and a whetstone of lapis lazuli, three gold bowls, two electrum axeheads, hundreds of gold beads, and jewellery. There was also a superb gold helmet.

The goldsmith's work was of fine quality, and from inscriptions on two of the bowls they were able to identify the corpse as that of 'Meskalamdulag, hero of the Good Land'. He may have been a king, but it is more likely that he was a prince or a very high-ranking military man, since other tombs found at the site were far more impressive.

The sixteen tombs were all slightly different in form, but essentially consisted of a stone-built chamber in which the coffin lay. In an antechamber a number of other corpses, male and female, varying in number from half-a-dozen to 80. All were richly dressed – the women in red, a colour of mourning – and the treasures they had with them were all expensive, being made of gold and lapis lazuli. The remains of waggons and of oxen were also found. Two adjacent tombs, one belonging to a man, identified as Abargi, and another to a woman, Pu-abi, were exceptionally fine. From them Woolley extracted artefacts so sophisticated that at the time even experts dated them to a period thousands of years later. Painstaking reconstruction, much of it supervised by Woolley's wife, Katherine, was required to restore them. They can now be seen, in very much their original condition, in the British Museum; several artefacts from the tombs were also acquired by the National Museum of Iraq and the University of Pennsylvania Museum.

Among these wholly remarkable treasures are an intricate headdress of Pu-abi, a superb statuette of gold and lapis depicting a ram in a thicket, lyres, the so-called Standard of Ur – an inlaid rectangular box depicting scenes of war and peace, whose sides slope inwards towards the top, and which may in fact have been the sound-box of an instrument – and a luxurious inlay-work board-game, complete with dice and counters, whose rules, it was established by comparison with similar ancient board-games, were akin to those of ludo.

The female attendants had headdresses decorated with silver ribbons, but silver decomposes in the earth and what Woolley had found had lain underground for 4500 years. All the archaeologists were able to detect were traces of silver chloride to show where the ribbons had been. But on one corpse they found no trace of silver ribbons. Close to the body, however, they found a disc about 7 centimetres (2.75 in) across, certainly silver, possibly a box, and solid enough to have survived. Yet when he cleaned it he found that it was a tight coil of the silver ribbon, so well preserved that even the delicate edges were distinct. Woolley came to a moving conclusion about this lucky find:

Why the owner had not put it on one could not say; perhaps she was late for the ceremony and had not had time to dress properly, but her haste has in any case afforded us the only example of a silver hair-ribbon which we were able to preserve.

> ❛I will next describe the thing which surprised me most of all in this country, after Babylon itself – I mean the boats which ply down the Euphrates to the city. These boats are circular in shape and made of hide; they build them in Armenia to the northward of Assyria, where they cut withies to make the frames and then stretch skins taut on the under-side for the body of the craft ... Every boat carries a live donkey – the larger ones several – and when they reach Babylon and the cargoes have been offered for sale, the boats are broken up, the frames ... disposed of and the hides loaded on the donkeys' backs for the return journey to Armenia.❜

HERODOTUS: *THE HISTORIES* (c.450 BC)

ABOVE *Another exquisite artefact found in the Royal Cemetery at Ur is the ceremonial Dagger of Meskalamdug (c.2500 BC; shown here is a reproduction at the University of Pennsylvania Museum of Archaeology and Anthropology). The original dagger probably had a bronze blade, though possibly gold, and a silver-and-gold hilt. The pattern of the gold sheath is in fine filigree.*

SARGON THE GREAT
(r. 2334–2279 BC)

Sargon (whose name is probably an honorific – Sarru-kin means simply 'The king is the true one') came from the north down to the more fertile south and crushed the last of the Early Dynastic kings, Lugal-zagesi, of Umma and Uruk. His roots were, if not humble, probably not royal, though this too may have been a propaganda ploy to present him as a man of the people. The Sumerian King-List tells us that he was a gardener who rose to be the cup-bearer (actually a high official) to a king of the city of Kish called Ur-zababa. Another legend, written apparently well after his time, indicates that his mother was a high-priestess (and they were always aristocrats, if not princesses), but that he didn't know who his father was, though his father's people came 'from the steppes'; and that his native city was Azupiranu. Moses-like, he was placed in a basket by his mother after she had borne him in secret, and placed on the river to float where fortune might take him. He was found by a drawer of water named Aqqi (the word means '*I drew out*'), who brought him up. His fortunes rose through the goodwill of the goddess Ishtar, '*who loved me*'.

Whatever his origins, Sargon established himself as the supreme ruler. Revered for two thousand years as the ideal monarch, and hailed as 'the coming man' of non-royal birth who could forge his own destiny and rise by his own merit, he was the first ruler who could truly be called king of a kingdom. His dynasty was handed down through his direct heirs. His grandson was one of the other truly great kings of Babylon.

Under Sargon, Akkadian became the dominant language of the country, supplanting Sumerian, and Sargon's monument inscriptions (in cuneiform) are in that tongue. He was the first to found his own city, Agade or Akkad, the site of which is now lost, but which most experts believe to have been close to Babylon itself, then an insignificant village or townlet.

OPPOSITE *The first golden ages of Mesopotamia and the Levant; map showing the extent of the kingdoms and empires of Sargon, Shamshi-Adad and Hammurabi. Akkad's old enemy Elam is in the east, while beyond it lies the Marhashi region – ultimately to be the cradle of Babylon's nemesis, Cyrus the Great.*

What precise fate met the attendants buried with Abargi and Pu-abi (who may have been rulers, or, if not, certainly pre-eminent among the nobility) is uncertain. When discovered, the bodies lay in orderly rows, and the presence of small copper bowls by each one, plus a cauldron in the room from which they may have been served a lethal draught, may suggest a ritual suicide of the chief acolytes of the principal deceased. However, it has also been suggested that these people were themselves eminent in their society, and had arranged before their deaths to have their bodies buried close to their chiefs. But there is nothing in contemporary texts to suggest that retainers were killed, or killed themselves, at the death of their employers, and the graves discovered by Woolley lack any contemporary written references. Nor have similar burial sites yet been unearthed in the region. What is certain is that the plethora of rich, expensive and imported goods – gold, lapis, and so on – and the high level of craftsmanship, point to an extremely affluent society. These tombs date to about 2600 BC, perhaps a century or two later. Ur was enjoying a peak of prosperity at that time, lying as it did near the Gulf, and operating as an important trading centre. That trade over long distances was already well established

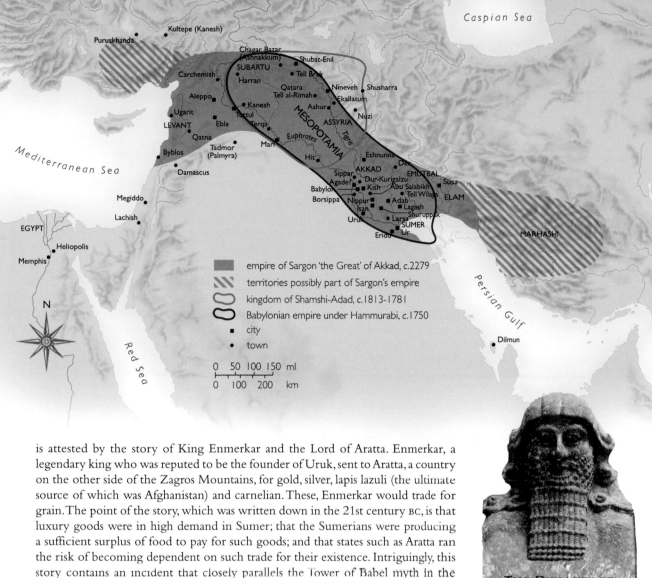

empire of Sargon 'the Great' of Akkad, c.2279
territories possibly part of Sargon's empire
kingdom of Shamshi-Adad, c.1813-1781
Babylonian empire under Hammurabi, c.1750
■ city
• town

0 50 100 150 ml
0 100 200 km

is attested by the story of King Enmerkar and the Lord of Aratta. Enmerkar, a legendary king who was reputed to be the founder of Uruk, sent to Aratta, a country on the other side of the Zagros Mountains, for gold, silver, lapis lazuli (the ultimate source of which was Afghanistan) and carnelian. These, Enmerkar would trade for grain. The point of the story, which was written down in the 21st century BC, is that luxury goods were in high demand in Sumer; that the Sumerians were producing a sufficient surplus of food to pay for such goods; and that states such as Aratta ran the risk of becoming dependent on such trade for their existence. Intriguingly, this story contains an incident that closely parallels the Tower of Babel myth in the Hebrew Bible.

THE RISE OF RIVAL CITIES

In the meantime, less blessed cities were breeding tougher people. To the northeast of Ur, across the narrow plain that separated the Euphrates from the Tigris, the cities of Umma and Lagash were engaged in a long-standing border dispute over a swathe of particularly good farmland. Squabbles and little wars over such matters were not uncommon, and as was often the case, this one was settled by arbitration in the end, reflecting the way the gods reached their decisions (though of course the stories of the gods are in reality reflections of man's behaviour). But territorial ascendancy remained an imperative, and about 2340 BC a leader appeared in Umma called Lugal-zagesi. He conquered the king of Lagash, one Uruimingina, by all accounts a reformer and a liberal, and took control of his city. Lugal-zagesi, an energetic man and clearly a great warrior, was to boast that in the end he controlled the entire region, from the Gulf to the Mediterranean – 'made all nations wait upon him, made everyone from where the sun rises to where the sun sets submit to him'. He certainly took control of all central Mesopotamia, including Ur, and perhaps as far north as Eshnunna, ending for a time – and in the event it would be a long time – the

THE DYNASTY OF AKKAD (THE SARGONIDS)

2334-2279 BC
Sargon (the Great)

2278-2270 BC
Rimush

2269-2255 BC
Manishtushu

2254-2218 BC
Naram-Sin

2217-2193 BC
Shar-kalisharri

•

2141-2111 BC
Gudea ruled in Lagash

TRANSPORT

By 2700 BC, the city of Uruk, then the largest in Mesopotamia, had a population of 50,000; and the country had established trade routes linking it with Egypt, Palestine, Cyprus, Anatolia, Lake Van (in Turkey), Lake Urmia (in Iran), down the Persian Gulf to Dilmun, and beyond to India. Lapis lazuli was imported from Afghanistan, timber from the Lebanon. The development of transport had long since become an imperative.

Even after the invention of the wheel, the sledge was still preferred, especially for hauling heavy loads. Sledges were drawn by oxen or onagers (a large domesticated wild ass; they may also have been crossbred with donkeys to produce a kind of mule). Goods were also carried by river and sea, the sail having been invented by 4000 BC.

Merchants often employed professional hauliers and agents to handle their goods, with legal indemnity in case of loss. Long-distance haulage was often done by donkey caravan.

The introduction of the horse in c.2000 BC was a dramatic innovation. Originally domesticated some 1500 years earlier in the Ukraine, the horse is thought to have been introduced into Mesopotamia by the Hurrians, a people who possibly originated in Armenia but who were certainly living in northern Mesopotamia as well, and were moving south to the attractive fertile plains by the middle of the third millennium. The full potential of the horse appears not to have been realized at first; an advisor to King Zimri-Lim of the city of Mari (1782–1758 BC) indicated that no high-born person would be seen dead riding one, in a letter to his master: '*Let my lord preserve his royal dignity. Let my lord not mount on horseback but ride in a chariot with mules.*'

The light, two-wheeled chariot first appeared around 1700 BC. By then solid wheels had been supplanted by spoked ones. The speed of the horse also meant that burgeoning city-states could communicate far more easily with each other via mounted courier.

The other animal that revolutionized transport, opened up new trading opportunities, and was also useful in war, was the camel. However, this did not appear in Mesopotamia until very late (c.1000 BC). Its introduction brought the first contact between the Arabs and the communities of the Ancient Near East, though they were initially treated as enemies. Yet by the reign of Nabonidus, the last king of Babylon, in the sixth century BC, nomads regularly used camels to cross the great deserts and enter Mesopotamia. Indeed, Nabonidus himself relocated his court across the desert to Taima (modern Tayma), which by then lay within the bounds of the Babylonian empire.

BELOW *This scene, from the Standard of Ur, shows merchants with a team of onagers pulling a heavy, four-wheeled wagon, the first form of wheeled transport.*

independence of the city states with their little kings (*lugals*) and governors (*ensis*). But Lugal-zagesi himself only managed to hold on to his small empire for a couple of decades. He would then be swept away by an invader from the north.

SARGON OF AKKAD

Few events in the long history of Babylon happened overnight – most changes were gradual, sometimes almost imperceptible. The Akkadians, the next people to rule the country, may already have been a presence there; Lugal-zagesi himself may have come from Akkadian stock. But it was with the conquest of the Akkadian ruler Sargon (r. *c.* 2334–2279 BC), and his establishment of a brand new city, Agade, that the face of Mesopotamia truly changed.

Sargon was not of royal descent; he probably rose through the ranks to hold high office, a cup-bearer or perhaps a *shagina* (general), and then usurped whichever leader he served. We are told that he found work as a gardener, but that probably meant that he was in charge of the maintenance of irrigation canals.

Whatever his origins, once in power, he was able to give free rein to his ambition, and he did so with astonishing success.

Sargon the Great, as he is remembered, is the first recorded major conqueror in history. Along with his successors, he managed to build what was the first empire (Egypt, which had all the resources it could ever need to hand at home, never had great territorial ambitions outside its own borders, which it protected fiercely).

The Akkadian empire was almost to match the extent of any subsequent Mesopotamian empire. Only those of Ashurnasirpal and Nebuchadrezzar, around 1500 years later, surpassed it. Not only did Sargon manage to subdue all the Sumerian city-states, and put an end to Sumer as a major political power, he and his successors also took over the entire Tigris-Euphrates basin and expanded into

ABOVE *Illustration by A. Forestier (from* The Illustrated London News, *23 June, 1928) reconstructing the scene Leonard Woolley envisaged at the entombment of the aristocratic people whose sepulchres he excavated at Ur, dating from about 2600 BC. Heavy four-wheeled carts similar to those in the image opposite can be clearly seen, with their solid wheels, but this time they are drawn by oxen.*

NARAM-SIN
(r. 2254–2218 BC)

Naram-Sin was the grandson of Sargon. Under him the Akkadian empire grew to its fullest extent, stretching from the eastern shores of the Mediterranean to the northern shores of the Persian Gulf. Following the precedent set by his grandfather, he styled himself 'King of Kish', partly because claiming kingship of that ancient city conferred validity on one's status, partly because the word punned with the Akkadian kishshatum – 'the entire inhabited world'.

Under Naram-Sin the neighbouring eastern country of Elam, always a thorn in Babylon's side, was subjugated, at least for the time being; he put down two major rebellions by coalitions of cities that resented his hegemony. Under his dominion, art flourished and developed. The lost-wax process of bronze casting, long believed to have been a Greek invention, was in use by his time, and may even have been in existence considerably earlier.

However, Naram-Sin seems to have fallen prey to hubris. He was the first king to deify himself; a stele in the Louvre celebrating one of his victories shows him atop a mountain, trampling his enemies, and wearing the horns of godhead (admittedly only one pair, the insignia of a minor god: important ones had at least four).

ABOVE *Fragment of a victory stele of Naram-Sin (from the Museum of Fine Arts, Boston, Massachusetts). He was the first ruler to be known as 'King of the Four Quarters'.*

But it was enough. Additionally, he piled treasures into the temple of Ishtar at Agade, while neglecting the great national temple of Ellil at Nippur. Ellil's oracle fell silent as a result. Ishtar herself took fright at this, abandoned her sanctuary and withdrew her protection. Warnings were issued to Naram-Sin in a dream, but he ignored them. Nemesis could not be far off.

This dismal tale is told in a Sumerian poem, 'The Curse on Agade'. Historically, governing an empire stretched to its limits was too much for the centralized administration, and history turned the page. Naram-Sin's successor, Sharkalisharri, managed to keep things together for about 25 years after his father's death, but it was a losing battle. The gods had decided to punish Babylon. They unleashed the Gutians upon the now-civilized Akkadians. The Gutians, pouring in from the northeast, were a savage people, human in form only, but with faces of apes, and endowed with the savagery of dogs. Chaos and anarchy descended on the country. During the decades marking a Gutian presence in the land, there was a high degree of confusion (though they themselves established a mini-dynasty of which we know little). *'Who was king? Who was not king?'* laments the Sumerian King-List, perhaps overstating things a little. But whatever the case, the great era of the Sargonids was at a close.

neighbouring countries, quelling Elam in the east, the Levant in the west, and as far north as Subartu, perhaps even pushing as far as the Taurus mountains, well into Anatolia. Sargon was careful however of placating those who lived in his new power base. He presented the captured Lugal-zagesi in a neck-stock before the national god, Ellil (Sumerian: Enlil) at the religious and scholastic centre of Nippur. In time he would be among the first monarchs to employ the strategy of diplomatic marriage.

He also installed his daughter as high-priestess of the moon god, Sin (Nanna), at Ur: creating what would become a traditional appointment for the king's eldest daughter. This daughter, Enheduanna, was extremely cultivated and creative, and has an important claim to fame as the first writer in history to be identified by name. She wrote in Sumerian, and was the author of, among other texts, several hymns to Ishtar (Inanna). She also introduced a personal note into her work; her writing shows evidence of a refined form of cuneiform script.

Sargon's commemorative inscriptions (saved for us by a punctilious scholar of later Mesopotamia who copied them all, with their provenances – the original steles have been lost) tell us that he went on to win 34 battles, and to take 50 city rulers prisoner. One especially notable feature was the focused nature of his empire: Sargon concentrated on controlling important trade centres such as the cities of Mari and Ebla. In the latter city, some 22 kilograms (48 lbs) of Afghan lapis has been found by modern archaeologists. To the northwest, Sargon controlled the cedar forests. By controlling Elam in the southeast, he also held sway over the land trade routes leading to Afghanistan and India.

His empire encompassed what was for the people of the time an unimaginable expanse, and after its collapse, 200 years later, its reconstruction became the ambition of many subsequent rulers, especially the Assyrians. The name of Sargon, and the (now lost) city of Agade passed into legend, and their names were invoked as paragons for two thousand years.

AKKADIAN REFORMS AND CONQUESTS

Akkadian – a Semitic language – now ousted Sumerian as the common tongue, though the Akkadians took over Sumerian cuneiform writing, as well as most of

‘Amongst a mass of bronze weapons which did not at the time seem to be associated with any burial we found the famous gold dagger of Ur, whose blade was of gold, its hilt of blue lapis lazuli decorated with gold studs and its sheath of gold beautifully worked with an openwork design derived from plaited grass – the material of which a commoner's dagger-sheath was sometimes made; with it was another object, almost equally remarkable, a cone-shaped reticule of gold ornamented with a spiral pattern containing a set of little toilet instruments, tweezers, lancet and pencil, also of gold. Nothing at all resembling these things had ever yet been unearthed in Mesopotamia; so novel were they that a recognised expert took them to be Arab work of the 13th century AD, and no-one could blame him for the error, for no-one could have suspected such art in the third millennium before Christ.’

SIR LEONARD WOOLLEY: *EXCAVATIONS AT UR*

their customs and beliefs. The Sumerians were absorbed into society, but their language, which was totally different from Akkadian, indeed an isolate – a language like no other – now fell into disuse, except in the temples and the law courts, and for certain rituals and ceremonies. In this way, it survived throughout the Mesopotamian era.

Among the reforms introduced by the Akkadians was the identification of individual years by relating them to some significant event, either of the previous year, or of the beginning of the year in question. There had been systems in place before, such as the identification of the year with the name of a given local official, or dating by regnal years. Unfortunately, very few year-names of this period have been unearthed and only a handful from the very end of the dynasty provide us with any useful information. Other reforms encompassed agriculture. Conquered farmland saw its villages destroyed and everything brought under centralized bureau-cratic control. Grain and oil were distributed in standard-sized pottery vessels; a system of taxation based on produce and/or time committed to public works – maintenance of defensive walls and canals, for example – was introduced. Efficient and even ruthless farming methods paid off and huge surpluses were produced, to be used for trade. Despite the size of the cities, and their importance as cultural and administrative centres, and as power bases, the economy was and would remain entirely based on agriculture, and the bulk of the population was employed in it.

Successors to Sargon

Sargon ruled as an absolute monarch from his capital, but local affairs were left in the hands of the governors of the various cities under his sway. His own rule lasted about 55 years, but by the end of it there were rumblings of dissent in certain parts of the empire. He and his son and successor, Rimush, dealt harshly with these insurrections. In putting down one city alone, he records that over 54,000 men were killed, captured, or sent into forced labour, an indication of the size to which cities had already grown. In all, Rimush's purges accounted for at least 100,000 deaths, and this doesn't count victims of conquest.

An older brother of Rimush, Manishtushu, succeeded him, perhaps ousting him in a palace coup. Following this king's reign of some 14 years, his son, and Sargon's grandson, Naram-Sin, came to the throne. Naram-Sin, who ruled from 2254 to 2218 BC, expanded the Akkadian empire to its greatest extent, and consolidated its power in the region. During his reign, local governors became answerable directly to him, not (as before) to their own individual city gods. There was still dissent, but it was kept under control. In the meantime, ever more land came under the control of the crown.

Naram-Sin was as skilled and as aggressive a soldier as his grandfather. He claimed to have conquered Arman (possibly the Syrian city of Aleppo) and Ebla, while we know that he was active in southern Turkey from a stele found near modern Diyarbakir. In Kurdistan there is still a rock relief showing him leading his army, in a mountain pass near Sulaimaniyeh.

The art that has survived from this time is represented by exquisitely cut cylinder seals in precious stone, but above all by a splendid life-sized bronze head (now in the National Museum of Iraq). Some consider this artefact to be a portrait of the king; it is quite clearly of an actual person, and its execution points to a new naturalism in art. At the same time, in representations on objects, the clean-shaven Sumerians cede to the long-haired and heavily-bearded Akkadians. From now on, a shaven head and chin would identify priests alone; eunuchs were portrayed with a shaven chin only.

LEFT *This bronze bust of an Akkadian king, which was found near the Ishtar temple in Nineveh, is thought to depict Naram-Sin or Sargon.*

PRIDE BEFORE A FALL

Traces of Naram-Sin's fortifications have been found in the north at Nagar (modern Tell Brak), and in the far southeast at Susa. A stele now in the Louvre in Paris depicts the king high on a mountain, trampling his enemies underfoot. If one looks closely at the scene, one can see that the king's crown has an embellishment: a pair of horns sprout from it. This was new. Naram-Sin had conferred godhead upon himself. Admittedly he only awarded himself one pair of horns; major gods had three or four sets; but in the context of historical perspective this was clearly an act of hubris, and one for which he was to pay with his empire.

Hitherto, kings had seen themselves as the representatives of the gods on Earth, and the highest honours they accorded themselves might contain the title 'King of Kish', which betokened 'King of All the World' (Practically speaking, control of Kish meant control of all the irrigation systems down both rivers from there). Naram-Sin had the determinative cuneiform sign for 'god' prefixed to his name in his inscriptions; while his underlings addressed him as 'God Of Agade'. One such inscription runs:

> *Because he had been able to preserve his city in the time of crisis, the*
> *inhabitants of his city asked from Ishtar in Eanna, from Ellil in Nippur ...*
> *from Ea in Eridu, from Sin in Ur, from Shamash in Sippar ...*
> *that he be the god of their city Agade, and they built a temple for him in*
> *the middle of Agade.*

This inscription has a political subtext: many of the cities mentioned, along with their suppliant gods, were ones that had rebelled. On the stele the king is placed well below the symbols of the great god that hover above the peak of the mountain, referring to the sun-god Shamash (Utu), in whose city (Sippar) the stele was erected. But even this step was regarded as excessive.

As so often happens with empires, the Akkadian empire had simply reached its natural limit of growth. It had become too large to police efficiently, and as a new series of rebellions broke out, Naram-Sin's son and successor, Sharkallishari (2217–2193 BC), spent his reign attempting to maintain control. After him, five minor kings in succession continued to fight a losing battle against insurrection, and were finally reduced to ruling nowhere but Agade itself. Divine retribution in the form of a fresh wave of invaders, the Gutians, this time from the northeast, was perceived as the reason for this collapse. The Akkadian empire fizzled out with the death of Shu-Turul in 2154 BC. By then, however, the Gutians were well in control of much of the country, and their first kings almost certainly overlapped with the last kings of Akkad. In time, the city of Agade itself fell into ruin, was covered by the shifting sands and the silt, and today, 4000 years later, it remains lost to us.

The Gutians, about whom we know very little, did not establish an empire. The kingdom they created was based on a handful of cities in the east, and the period that followed the fall of Akkad was one of confusion. '*Who was king? Who was not king?*' lamented the Sumerian King-List, while another later Babylonian document (*c.* 1800), known as the Weidner Chronicle, notes that the god Marduk, furious with Naram-Sin, '*summoned the forces of Gutium against him*'.

The Gutians held sway in the eastern part of the country for perhaps as much as 90 years (the precise length of time is disputed and may have been far shorter). They appear to have kept themselves to themselves, since the Weidner Chronicle continues reprovingly: '*The Gutians were unhappy people, unaware of how to revere the gods, ignorant of the rituals.*' It wasn't long before Marduk was looking for someone to send them packing.

LEFT *The Victory Stele of Naram-Sin, in rose sandstone This detailed view shows Naram-Sin near a mountain top, trampling on his enemies. His helmet carries the twin horns of a minor god. However, such hubris was to get him into trouble with his enemies and detractors, since it was still unusual at the time for kings to identify themselves with deities, even minor ones.*

CHAPTER THREE

THE THIRD DYNASTY AT UR

AMONG THE INDEPENDENT CITY-STATES that emerged after the fall of the Akkadian empire was Lagash, ruled by its *ensi*, Gudea (r. 2141–2122 BC), whom we know from the many inscribed statues of him that have been unearthed. Gudea's ambitions were not extensively territorial, although he did mount an expedition against Elam. Yet the fact that he was able to maintain stability and run a prosperous province is an indication of how relatively little influence the Gutians wielded.

It is probable that by the time the Gutians arrived, Akkad had been so worn down by internal strife, rebellions to the north, and poor harvests, that it took little effort to deliver the *coup de grâce*. Gudea was certainly able to maintain trade routes to the Mediterranean for timber and to the Gulf for imported stone without being bothered by the Gutians; and the many statues in his image, usually carved from expensive diorite, bear witness to his wealth, and he felt confident enough, it has been suggested, to go so far as to elevate himself to godhead.

Expelling the Gutians

But it fell to a Sumerian king, Utu-hegal of Uruk, to drive the Gutians out of the country. Perhaps the Gutians left without much of a fight; in any case, after his victory, which was much written up, Utu-hegal did not hold power for long. The next person of serious historical significance to dominate southern Mesopotamia, from the city of Ur, was Ur-Nammu, who had been governor of Ur under Utu-hegal's kingship.

Ur-Nammu was the founder of what is now referred to as the Third Dynasty of Ur, or Ur III, which lasted for around 100 years. He reigned from about 2112 to 2095 BC, and during that time, using diplomacy as much as military force, reunited all the major Sumerian cities, styling himself 'King of Sumer and Akkad'. His reign saw a return to the use of Sumerian, at least in official documents and correspondence, but Akkadian influence and infiltration was too strong to expunge. It may even be the case that the dynasty of Ur III was ethnically Semitic. Certainly, by now Sumerians and Akkadians had been assimilated into a homogenous population, and most of their culture and tradition had likewise fused. Sargon's daughter had composed her poetry in faultless literary Sumerian; the later kings of Ur III and their spouses bore Akkadian names. However, nothing of the military triumphalism of the Akkadians attached to this final Sumerian dynasty; their inscriptions emphasize piety and learning rather than extravagant victories.

As well as re-establishing a stable kingdom in the south, Ur-Nammu proved himself an avid renovator and reformer, launching an ambitious building programme at Ur, where among other projects he began construction of a massive ziggurat, probably employing the services of alumni of a school of architecture that had been established in Akkadian times. At its base, this edifice measured some 60 by 50 metres (197 x 134 ft), and probably rose to a height of 30 metres (98 ft). Despite its size (even in its reduced state today, it appears massive), the ziggurat gives an impression less of bulk than of lightness, due to the fact that its lines were slightly convex, an

BELOW *Even in its current ruined state, the ziggurat constructed at Ur by Ur-Nammu is an imposing sight. Dedicated to the god Nanna, this huge temple was built in around 2100 BC.*

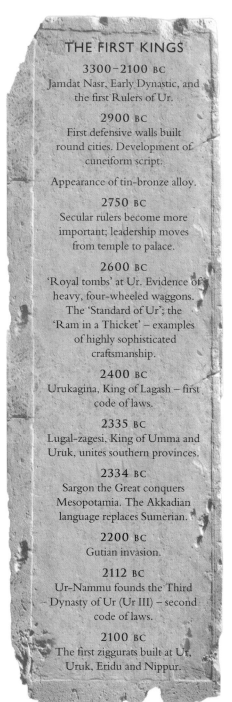

architectural *trompe l'oeil* technique known as *entasis*, which was long supposed to have been invented by the Greeks 2000 years later. Ur-Nammu's ziggurat, restored by Nebuchadrezzar and completed by Nabonidus, remains the best preserved of all such structures to this day.

Ur-Nammu drove the last remnants of the Gutians out of his kingdom, and secured the trade routes. He was particularly involved in canal construction and maintenance, building weirs to control water-levels; he also encouraged sea-borne commerce. He reconstructed the temple of the then national god, Ellil (Enlil) at Nippur and adopted the title, 'King of Sumer and of Akkad', meaning that he controlled northern and southern Babylon. His unfortunate death in battle occasioned hymns lamenting his passing, and songs regretting the work that he had left uncompleted. Later Babylonian scholars tried hard to square such an inauspicious death with such an exemplary life.

THE LONG REIGN OF SHULGI

It was almost certainly his son and successor, Shulgi (r. 2094–2047 BC), however, who was the chief architect of Ur III's success, drawing up a legal code, and expanding the kingdom during his long reign. Shulgi's first two decades were mainly occupied with construction work, but by the beginning of the third decade there is evidence to suggest that he was taking a warlike stance. Much of his military activity – and Shulgi always claimed to be a man of peace – was probably directed against Elam, and concerned with ensuring safe passage through the passes of the Zagros Mountains, which the land trade routes to Afghanistan and India followed. Another reason for mobilization of troops was to secure the frontiers, which were under constant threat from outlying peoples attracted to the rich farmland of Mesopotamia.

During Shulgi's reign, there appears to have been little or no rebellion within his kingdom, a state of affairs that reflects his strong and efficient administration and his appointment of loyal governors answerable to him. Travellers and merchants could journey safely along all his roads, on which he had established rest-houses at regular intervals. To assure himself of the priesthood's support, he toured all the important shrines and temples in his kingdom, but also placed them under state control and exacted taxes from them. By now, ultimate power had passed from the temple to the palace.

Several hymns in Shulgi's praise survive, commemorating victories and celebrating his greatness – one has him running heroically from Nippur to Ur and back – some 200 miles (320 km) – some of the time through a violent storm. The hymns attest his popularity, not least with the priesthood, an important political faction that it was always prudent to assuage. The fact that Shulgi, relatively early in his reign, was able to assume godhead (as Naram-Sin had done) without exciting opprobrium, bears witness either to the hold he had on his people, or to his popularity, or both. Shulgi even claimed divine descent. Yet given what we know of his character, it is possible that political expediency rather than hubris prompted these declarations. He was not the only Ur III king to be associated with divine parentage, and he was not the

only one – though the relationship was emphasized in his reign – to be regarded as the 'husband' of the goddess Ishtar (Inanna). Interestingly, during the Ur III period, Ishtar herself is cast in a nurturing role; under the Akkadians, her warlike qualities were stressed. As her husband, the king associated himself with the goddess' cosmic partner, Tammuz (Dumuzi), the good shepherd.

Yet leaving aside myth, and political or propagandistic manoeuvring, Shulgi was still a great leader, fit to join Sargon and Naram-Sin as one of the hero-kings in later popular Babylonian tradition.

Shulgi is not only presented as a good and wise king, but as an educated and cultivated man. Apparently, he was top boy at school (the *edubba*, literally, 'tablet house') – such a level of education was rare even for a Mesopotamian king – and acquired a command of cuneiform and mathematics. He was skilled in the use of weapons, and a brilliant huntsman; his prey included lions, bulls, boar and wild asses. At the same time, he had an interest in conservation: he would never kill young

ABOVE *Found in fragments during excavation of the sacred precinct of the moon-god Nanna in Ur, the rose sandstone stele of Ur-Nammu depicts various scenes, including the one above showing the king (left) making an offering to the deity.*

ZIGGURATS

Nothing is more emblematic of Ancient Mesopotamia than the ziggurat, the great stone stepped pyramid composed of solid mudbrick and faced with high-quality baked brick. Most have now crumbled to ruins, but their influence and their importance is inestimable.

Ziggurats were not tombs, but temples. It is believed that, in a flat land, they served as artificial mountains, reaching to the gods, and that their upper platforms held shrines to their city's tutelary deity; *ziggurat*, an Akkadian term, simply means 'building on a raised area'. They rose in square or rectangular levels, each one smaller than the one below, in a succession of sometimes seven platforms, accessed by outer stairways which in some cases were so arranged as to oblige the climber to make a circuit of each platform before reaching the staircase which would take him or her to the next level. The ziggurat at Dur Sharrukin (Khorsabad), built around 710 BC, may have had a spiral ramp leading to its top, each platform painted a different colour.

The first ziggurats were built at Ur by Ur-Nammu, *c.*2112–2095 BC, and must have involved a vast investment of manpower, as well as architectural and mathematical exactitude in their design. All the major Mesopotamian kings built them, making them the centrepieces of their cities and the focus of their temples. Nebuchadrezzar the Great's ziggurat at Babylon was one of the most massive, having seven tiers and a temple to Marduk at its summit. Even under the shadow of the great threat from Persia, the last king of Babylon – Nabonidus, a great antiquarian, historian and preserver of his country's traditions – lavishly renovated Ur-Nammu's ziggurat at Ur, and made his daughter priestess of the Moon-god, Sin, whose temple it supported.

The common practice of rulers restoring ziggurats built by their forebears was continued in modern times by Saddam Hussein (1937–2006). The Iraqi dictator revived memories of the principal emperors, such as Hammurabi and Nebuchadrezzar the Great, even imitating the latter in having many of the bricks used in his partial (and ill-advised, some argue) reconstructions of the ziggurats at Ur and Babylon stamped with his own name.

The ziggurat's form was known in early modern Europe, through the Biblical Tower of Babel and through the writings of such early historians as Diodorus and Herodotus. The image of the Tower of Babel has always exerted a powerful fascination on the popular imagination, and in art, especially through the two famous paintings by Pieter Brueghel the Elder (1525–69) and a romantic illustration by the 19th-century engraver Gustave Doré. The ziggurat inspired the design of the tower in German director Fritz Lang's 1927 film, *Metropolis*. Its architectural form influenced European and American architecture from the 1920s through to the Palace of the People in Bucharest, the Secret Intelligence Service HQ Building in London, and the headquarters building of the California department of General Services in West Sacramento. Frank Lloyd Wright's Guggenheim Museum in New York is a dramatic development of the same theme, inverting the form.

BELOW AND INSET *The ziggurat at Choga Zambil (ancient Al-Untash), Iran, built by the Elamite King Untash-Gal (1265–1246 BC). Records indicate that this temple complex was built with the profits from trade around the region. The resonance of the ziggurat form through the ages is shown in modern examples such as the MI6 building in London, which was constructed in the early 1990s.*

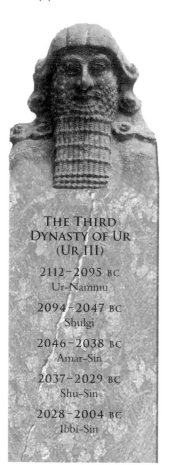

THE THIRD DYNASTY OF UR (UR III)

2112–2095 BC
Ur-Nammu

2094–2047 BC
Shulgi

2046–2038 BC
Amar-Sin

2037–2029 BC
Shu-Sin

2028–2004 BC
Ibbi-Sin

animals or mothers with young. He was (as we have inferred) a fast runner, so swift that he could outrun a gazelle. In addition he was an exceptional musician and linguist, composed songs (both words and music), and had even mastered extispicy, the art of reading entrails to divine the future.

Even if we take much of this with a generous pinch of salt, everything historically points to a firm and conscientious ruler, who developed and improved what his father had started and who was genuinely interested in implementing a formal legal system. The idea of being a protective father to his people was the core ethos of Mesopotamian kings: '*I did not deliver the orphan to the rich man, the widow to the mighty man, the man with one shekel to the man with one mina, the man with one lamb to the man with one ox.*' Gudea had already legislated to allow women to inherit and own land in their own right; Shulgi likewise promulgated laws to protect women's interests. In a divorce case, the wife, if she had married as a virgin, received one silver mina as compensation. A former widow who had remarried would get half a mina; but in the case of a couple who split up without having been married, the woman got nothing. Criminal physical injury was usually punished by a fine rather than by the principle of 'an eye for an eye', although murder, rape and robbery carried the death penalty. Property and abuse of responsibility for land-management were also covered by his Code, as was the management and handling of slaves.

THE ADMINISTRATION OF UR

Between them, both kings, father and son, re-established the system that had worked so well in the past, of appointing governors to manage the cities under their sway, and centralizing control of canal maintenance and lines of communication between the various provinces of the kingdom. Foreign trade was revitalized, the harbour at Ur was restored and expanded, copper and other raw materials were imported in exchange for finished goods such as textiles, and silver brought down from the north. The key to it all lay in their administrative ability. Ur III left us tens of thousands of clay tablets that treat every aspect of life in the minutest detail, from the death of a single domestic animal to the number of men in a given canal-clearing crew. Sadly,

> **'**• If the wife of a man followed after another man and he slept with her, they shall slay that woman, but the male shall be set free.
>
> • If a man divorces his first-time wife, he shall pay her one mina of silver.
>
> • If a man is accused of sorcery he must undergo ordeal by water; if he is proven innocent, his accuser must pay three shekels.
>
> • If a man's slave-woman, comparing herself to her mistress, speaks insolently to her, her mouth shall be scoured with one quart of salt.
>
> • If a slave marries a free person, that slave is to hand over the first-born son to his or her owner.**'**

CLAUSES FROM THE LAW CODE OF UR-NAMMU

GUDEA
(r. 2141 – 2122 BC)

The Gutians took over several city-states and may have been the principal power in the region, but they never took over the Sargonid empire, and plenty of independent city-rulers existed alongside them. One of these, best-known to us from the large number of statues of himself which have come down to us, was Gudea, who styled himself ensi, or governor, of the city of Lagash. A serious, confident-looking man, wearing a businesslike skullcap and simple, circular crown, cleanshaven (and therefore looking much more Sumerian than Akkadian), hands folded neatly in that uncomfortable way so many Babylonian statues depict, dressed in a toga which left the right shoulder bare, he looks the image of the bureaucrat-administrator. He may have controlled several smaller cities from his own power-base. He is thought to have clashed with the Elamites, but things were prosperous and secure enough for him to build a temple, the Eninnu, dedicated to Ningirsu, the city's tutelary deity and a god of rain, irrigation and fertility. He looks like a planner, not a warrior, though: one of his statues shows him with a kind of blueprint on his lap. From the inscriptions on his statues, we learn that he was proud of such

achievements as the restoration of the Eanna, the major temple of Ishtar, as well as several other smaller temples.

Content to be a quiet ruler, seeking peace over war, consolidation over expansion, he saw his role principally as a good shepherd to his flock – one of the principal hallmarks of responsible kingship in Babylonian thinking.

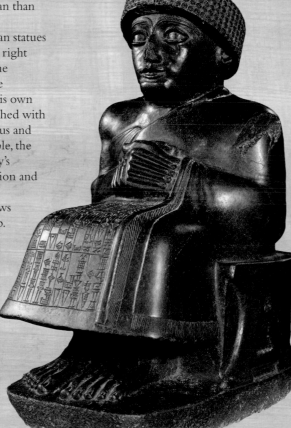

RIGHT *One of the many statues of the successful builder-cum-administrator ruler of Lagash, Gudea, an early exponent of the cult of personality. Dating from c.2130 BC, this artefact is made of a granite-like rock known as diorite (Louvre Museum, Paris).*

many of the tablets have been unearthed illegally, sold irresponsibly to private collectors and dispersed around the world. Even so, enough evidence remains for us to form a very clear picture of what went on.

Payment for labour, canal-maintenance, farmwork, boatbuilding, weaving – was in the form of oil, grain, bread, onions, fish, and, above all, beer; the quality and various types of the latter, and its production, were very strictly controlled, sometimes from the highest level. One text indicates that a princess was 'Comptroller of Beer'.

So the new kingdom prospered. There was little fighting, and the arts, always a good indicator of stability and wealth, reached new heights of sophistication. Beautiful necklaces of agate and carnelian, the stones almost certainly imported from India, survive, as do luxury cylinder seals of rock crystal. Luxury foods were imported for the wealthy, and paid for in humbler local produce.

More sinister is the impression conveyed by administrative records dating from around the mid-point of Shulgi's reign, which hint at a quasi-totalitarian bureaucracy, backed by accountancy of a quite frightening exactitude. To cope with this, writing was standardized and the system of weights and measures rationalized. There is some evidence of private enterprise, and plenty to attest the existence of workshops employed by temple and palace authorities in the manufacture of textiles, leatherware, joinery, masonry, stonecutting, jewellery and pottery. Yet the vast majority of people were employed in herding huge numbers of sheep, goats and cattle (flocks and herds

'O Father Nanna, that city into ruins was made ...
Its people, not potsherds, filled its sides;
Its walls were breached; the people groan
In its lofty gates, where they were wont to promenade, dead
  bodies were lying about;
In its boulevards, where the feasts were celebrated,
  scattered they lay.
In all its streets, where they were wont to promenade, dead
  bodies were lying about;
In its squares, where the festivities of the land took place,
  the people lay in heaps ...
Ur – its weak and its strong perished through hunger;
Mothers and fathers who did not leave their houses
  were overcome by fire;
The young lying on their mothers' laps like fish were
  carried off by the waters;
In the city, the wife was abandoned, the son was abandoned,
  the possessions were scattered about.
O Nanna, Ur has been destroyed, its people have
  been dispersed!'

A LAMENT FOR THE CITY OF UR, WHICH FELL TO THE ELAMITES
AT THE END OF UR III

RIGHT *Known as 'The Woman with the Shawl' (c.2130–2150 BC), this portrait sculpture in expensive steatite of an unidentified aristocratic young woman comes from Telloh (ancient Girsu).*

of up to 350,000 head have been recorded), and in growing grain. Grain for private sowing could be 'borrowed' from the temple or the palace granaries, but at 20 percent interest. Borrowing from private moneylenders – the fathers of modern banking – cost a great deal more: the going rate was an extortionate 33.5 percent.

FREQUENT INVASIONS

Ur extended its influence as far as Mari in the northwest – Ur-Nammu made a diplomatic marriage with a daughter of that city's king to cement relations – and northeast as far as the Hurrians, who lived in a region between Lake Van and Lake Urmia. But once again the pattern was repeated, and by the time of the reign of Ibbi-Sin (2028–2004 BC), a fresh threat presented itself. This time, the hungry outsiders, were the Amorites, driven from their native lands by extensive droughts.

To the people of Ur III, the Amorites were, if not as bad as the Gutians, primitive and unwholesome:

> He dresses in sheepskins; he lives in tents in wind and rain; he doesn't offer sacrifices; he lives rough on the steppes; he digs up truffles and wanders about; he eats raw meat; he has no fixed abode; and when he dies, his burial lacks ritual.

The Amorites came to be regarded with suspicion and, finally, fear.

After Shulgi's death in around 2047 BC he was succeeded in turn by two of his sons, Amar-Sin and Shu-Sin, who incidentally followed their father's example in having themselves deified. By the time Shu-Sin came to the throne in about 2037 BC the Amorites were beginning to infiltrate the kingdom. A few years into his reign, however, it must have become clear that they had a more aggressive intention than simple immigration, for it is then that we hear of Shu-Sin's construction of a great wall, north of Sippar, between the banks of the Tigris and the Euphrates, to keep these unwelcome foreigners out. Records indicate that the wall, which was named 'That Which Keeps Out The Amorites', was planned to be 167 miles (270 km) long, but whatever the size of the actual structure, it was ineffective. During the reign of Ibbi-Sin, Shu-Sin's successor and the last king of Ur III, the Amorites ceased to be just a dangerous nuisance and, operating in organized armed units within the country, became a definite threat.

Ibbi-Sin spent his long reign fighting a losing battle against decline. The collapse was gradual but unrelenting. As the Amorites gained control over more and more of the land, the cities of Ur III became isolated from each other, communications broke down, massive inflation occurred – the price of grain rose to sixty times the norm between the seventh and eighth years of Ibbi-Sin's reign alone. In the end, the king commanded little more than the city of Ur alone, but it was not the Amorites who dealt the final blow, but the Elamites, the old enemy who, sensing the weakened state of the rival kingdom, broke free of it and dispatched an expeditionary force with which to take and raze the city. Ibbi-Sin was captured and taken back to Susa as a prisoner.

It was left to a king of the city of Larsa, Ishbi-Erra, to throw the Elamites out of the country. He established a successful dynasty at Larsa which lasted from 2017 to 1794 BC; and not far away, at the city of Isin, another dynasty, founded by King Naplanum, was equally successful over a similar period, from 2025 to 1763 BC; but the last essentially Sumerian hegemony over Babylon was at an end, and it was the Amorites, who finally established themselves at the city of Babylon in 1894 BC, who controlled much of the rest of the country. From now on, Babylon would be plucked from obscurity to a central position which the city would hold, not always in terms of power but always in peoples' minds, throughout Mesopotamia for the next 2000 years.

LEFT *The struggle to expel the Elamites from Mesopotamia was a long and bitter campaign. The conquest by Ashurbanipal's warriors of an Elamite city with towers and fortified walls is shown on this stone bas relief (c. 7 BC) from the royal palace at Nineveh.*

CHAPTER FOUR

KINGS, GODS AND THEIR CITIES

Naram-Sin's elevation of himself to divinity set a precedent in Mesopotamia, although his example was by no means universally followed. Kingship had always been regarded as a sacred responsibility, but the king had hitherto been regarded as the representative of the god of his city. This all changed when the king ruled more than one city.

There were many gods in the Mesopotamian pantheon, each with his or her particular allotted task. Some gods had no direct contact with human beings, while others had quite intimate, informal and even sexual contact with them. But apart from their specific duties, linking them with anything from war to weaving, many of the gods, and especially the principal deities, were closely associated with particular cities. From the earliest times, they were thought to dwell in their cities, and the king (or occasionally *ensi*) of a given city was their representative. The king and the deity were closely identified with one another, and if anything were done to displease the deity, giving him or her cause to abandon the city, it was believed that its fate was sealed. Tied in with this was the habit conquerors had of taking away the city's images of their god and erecting them in their own town. The Elamites did it to the Babylonians, the Babylonians to the Assyrians and vice versa, and each of the latter two to any foreign power they overran.

Although human, a king might claim legitimacy of rule through descent from the gods, but he was always bound by a responsibility towards his subjects, and on that he was judged. Significantly, at the annual Spring Festival, he would be ritually stripped of his insignia and humiliated by the chief priest, which not only acted as a reminder to him (and his people, for the ritual was a public one) to maintain an essential humility, but may also be seen as a throwback to the days when a city (or tribal) leader was elected on his merits alone. The king had to bear in mind that he wielded power on the sufferance of his people. In time, this observance became no more than mere ritual, but originally it carried real force: the more pain the king endured in his humiliation, the better pleased the local god would be. At the same time, the Spring Festival could not take place without the physical presence of the king; and it was a bad omen if it was not held.

RIGHT A statue fragment from Telloh portraying Gudea – king of Lagash c. 2143– 2124 BC – as a patron of building works. This detail shows the ruler's hands folded somewhat awkwardly (in a pose typical of statuary of this period), while on his lap lies a city plan or 'blueprint'. The image has a clear propagandistic purpose – the script on Gudea's kilt contains a litany of his many achievements.

RULING BY DIVINE ASSENT

The king had three main duties: he was the city's link with its god, the organizer of the daily work of the city – especially its agriculture – and the strategist who led his people successfully in war. After the start of the second millennium, the practise of kings deifying themselves ceased – if they were deified at all, it was after death – but their close links with the gods always remained. His very office, it was believed, had been ordained by the gods and had originally been 'lowered from heaven', as a gift

bestowed on mankind. By extension, the king himself may have been endowed by the gods, even before birth, with his regal qualities, a concept familiar to the pro-Babylonian prophet Jeremiah, who wrote early in his long book of the Hebrew Bible: '*Before I formed you in the womb I knew you, and before you were born I consecrated you ...*'

From the great Amorite king Hammurabi to the last Babylonian king of all, Nabonidus, a period spanning over one thousand years, kings always claimed to have received their remit from the gods; even interlopers and successful rebels like Nebuchadrezzar's father, Nabopolassar, claimed to have been '*summoned by Marduk*', and to be '*well-loved by Ea*'. Even so, the king had to justify the gods' approval by his behaviour.

Alongside his three principal duties, the king had to maintain the prosperity of his city, city-state, or country, which meant being a good businessman as well as a good estate-manager. He was also responsible for the maintenance of the canals, both for transport and irrigation, he had to arrange granaries to store grain in years of surplus against years of drought, war, epidemic or flood; and he had, certainly from Ur-Nammu's time and perhaps earlier than that, to draw up a legal code. (We know that the Code of Ur III was formally the work of his son Shulgi, but it is highly unlikely that some form of legal system was not already in place during his father's reign.) Implicit in all this was the central role of the king as a good father to his people, a good shepherd to his flock. If his conduct pleased the gods, he would be blessed with a long reign, military success, a complacent people, many heirs, and good harvests. If it did not, then he could expect a correspondingly short reign, blighted by a rebellious people, no heirs, failed crops, military defeat and death in battle. The Assyrian king, Sennacherib (r. 704–681 BC), was so appalled by the fact that his father met just such an inauspicious death that he left campaigns to his generals. Kings could be seriously alarmed by the threat of such setbacks, and in times of trouble this led to a curious and (for the Mesopotamians) rather barbaric custom: if the priests should by any chance divine unfavourable omens, or if things were actually beginning to go badly, the king and his consort might go into retirement for a period. Since the well-being of the land, so the convenient argument ran, was tied up with the king's person, he had to be protected. But somebody had to stand in for him and draw off the menace – a scapegoat, in other words. This person, selected by a process which is not clear, became substitute king, and 'ruled' with all the appurtenances of monarchy, including his own consort, but enjoying no actual power, until the danger had passed, whereupon the substitute king and his consort were killed.

THE AMORITES

2034 BC
The Amorites begin to move into Mesopotamia.

2004 BC
The Elamites sack Ur.

2000 BC
Domesticated horses introduced.

1894 BC
The Amorites found a dynasty at Babylon.

1792 BC
Hammurabi ascends the throne of Babylon. Third code of laws. Establishment of an empire covering much the same area as Sargon's.

1700 BC
Introduction of the two-wheeled, lightweight chariot with spoked wheels.

1595 BC
The Hittite king Mursilis sacks Babylon. Babylon enters a 'dark age'.

RIGHT *Detail from the podium of Shalmaneser III (r. 858–824 BC), from the Ekal Masharti, or Hall of the Throne. On the right, Shalmaneser shakes hands with Marduk-zakir-shumi of Babylon, marking their alliance. Behind Shalmaneser is a eunuch attendant bearing weapons and other equipment.*

CHECKS AND BALANCES

The king was helped in his work by the traditional perception that man had been created to do the gods' work. Since he was the gods' representative, religion – always a useful tool for social organization – demanded of his subjects that they do his will. Mesopotamian kings were not therefore much criticized, but unlike their Egyptian counterparts, who were gods incarnate and whose humbler subjects were not even allowed to look at them, they were not regarded as infallible. Pharaohs may from time to time have fallen victim to palace coups; Mesopotamian kings not only had that possibility to contend with but could not rule out popular rebellion either. Moreover, if a rival should stage a successful coup, that in itself was deemed to legitimize it, since it was reasoned that the gods would not have allowed it to succeed

THE MESOPOTAMIAN PANTHEON

The gods of the Ancient Near East were many and various. Although the pantheon developed early, and its basic structure remained unchanged, at times different gods held the ascendancy, notably Marduk, originally an agricultural deity, whose city was Babylon, and Ashur, the principal god of the Assyrians. The dominance of any one god was usually due to the dominance of his or her city or people. Marduk came to subsume within himself the 50 gods who made up the group known collectively as the Anunna. Each god or goddess was associated with a city, though in the earliest times there were also gods who represented natural phenomena, seasonal weather and geographical features, such as rivers or mountains, and many of these survived as minor deities. These included (using their Sumerian names) Ennugi, god of canals, and Enbilulu, god of the Tigris and the Euphrates. A later addition, who became increasingly important as society became more sophisticated, was Nabu, the god of writing.

ABOVE *Drawing of a Kassite relief sculpture, depicting the god Marduk with the serpent-dragon associated with him at his feet.*

There is much disagreement about the overall structure of the Mesopotamian pantheon, as different gods borrowed or shared the same attributes and consorts in various places at different times. In one myth, for example, Marduk is credited with the creation of mankind rather than Ea (to give him his Akkadian name; in Sumerian it was Enki), who is responsible for this act in an earlier creation epic. In another, the important goddess Ishtar, whose husband in Babylonian mythology is Tammuz (Sumerian: Dumuzi), appears as the wife of Ashur. However, a basic plan of the cosmos can be delineated.

The primordial element was water, which was divided into Apsu, sweet water, whose gender was male, and Tiamat, salt water, whose gender was female, and who also represented the blind forces of primitive chaos. The Earth itself was a round plateau or disc that floated on the Apsu, surrounded by mountains that held up the skies. From a union of Apsu and Tiamat came Mummu, the vizier of the gods, and two serpents, Lakhmu and Lakhamu. A union of the serpents created Anshar, the sky and masculinity, and Kishar, whose city was Kish, and who represented femininity and the Earth. These two engendered An (Sumerian: Anu), the upper heavens, whose city was Uruk, and whose consort was Antu. Their children were the goddess Bau, the life-giver; Ellil (Enlil), the god of the air, whose city was Nippur and whose consort was Ninlil, the 'Lady of the Open Field'; and Ea (Enki), whose city was Eridu. Ea was the god of wisdom, magic, and the source of sweet water. In the early myths, he is credited with having created mankind, and with 'taming' Apsu, who ceased to be a personified entity. His consorts were either Damkina or Belet-ili (Ninhursag – the 'Lady of the Mountain'). An, Ellil and Ea – sky, Earth and water – formed the first major triad of the gods; and it was Ea who had most to do directly with the affairs of men.

LEFT *Another portrayal of Marduk's dragon, in a bronze sculpture from the late Assyrian period (c. 800–600 BC).*

Ea had three daughters: Ninkasi, the goddess of brewing (the ancient Mesopotamians were very fond of their beer); Ninsar ('Lady Greenery') and Uttu (the spider or weaver). In another myth he is the father (and Damkina the mother) of Marduk, the great god of the Babylonians, and Bel (or Baal), another aspect of the air. Ellil and Ninlil also had three children: Ninurta, god of war and of the plough, whose city was Lagash; Nergal, god of disease, and Sin (Nanna), the important god of the moon, whose city was Ur. Sin's consort was Ningal ('Lady of the Reeds') and their three children were Shamash (Utu), the important god of the sun and of divination; Ereshkigal, goddess of the underworld, and Ishtar (Inanna), the highly important goddess of love and war, whose city was Uruk, but who was also associated with Nineveh and Arbela. Sin, Shamash and Ishtar formed the second great triad of the gods. Shamash and his consort, Aya, had two children, Kittu (justice) and Misharu (law). Ereshkigal was

twice married, firstly to Gugalana, the Great Bull of Heaven, who was killed by the demi-god and hero, Gilgamesh, and secondly to Nergal, by whom she had a son, Ninazu, the god of healing. Ishtar had many lovers – in this, she is reminiscent both of Aphrodite (Venus) and the Hindu deity Kali – but her husband was Tammuz (Dumuzi) another agricultural deity, whose death caused Ishtar to go down to the underworld to seek him. In some versions of the myth he returns, while in others he has to stay in order that she may be allowed to return. Associated with Adonis, Tammuz also makes one think of Persephone, since his 'death' and 'rebirth' became an annual event marking the end of the harvest and the return of the spring, respectively. The underworld itself, sometimes called Kur, was a gloomy place, 'the house of dust', where the souls of the dead were condemned to feed on mud and clay. There was no concept of heaven, though the gods dwelled in a great hall, Upshukina, or in Dilmun (a kind of Mount Olympus) a paradise beyond the seas usually associated with what has become modern-day Bahrain.

Finally, there were the younger generation of gods, the Igigi, led by Ellil; and the Uttuku, spirits and demons who were subdivided into Ekimmu (evil) and Shedu (good). 'The Seven' – serpent-like beings – were the worst of the Ekimmu. Heroes included Utnapishtim (also known as Atrahasis), the ancient Mesopotamian Noah, and the only mortal (with his wife) to be accorded immortality; the famous, semi-divine Gilgamesh, Adapa, who broke the wings of the South Wind and was by mischance cheated of the gift of immortality, Etana, who flew to heaven on an eagle's back to seek a cure for his infertility, but failed; and Enmerkar, who founded the city of Uruk. Enmerkar has been identified with Nimrud, and one legend associates him with the building of a great tower (like Babel) and a consequent confusion of languages, this time visited on man by Ea. The very early Sumerian King-List mentions Etana, Enmerkar and Gilgamesh as actual kings, and there are grounds for supposing that the latter two did actually exist historically, though the deeds of the real people, lost in time, cannot be thought to parallel those of the legendary ones.

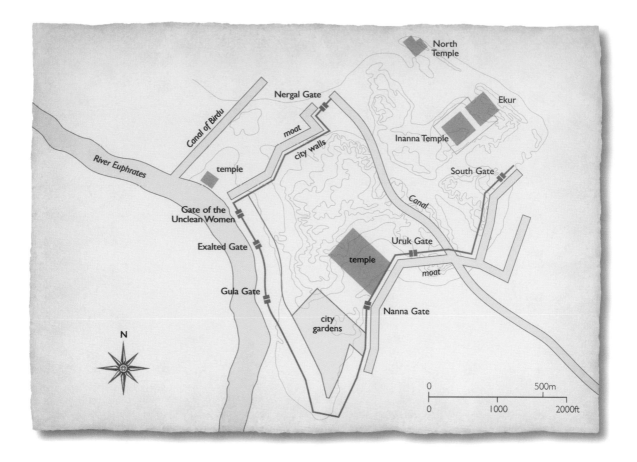

ABOVE *City plan of the settlement at Nippur. One of the most ancient of all Babylonian cities, it was dedicated to worship of the Sumerian god Enlil.*

had the usurped monarch not deserved it. For most of Mesopotamian history, these devices were useful checks on any nascent megalomania in a ruler, and in fact, though the Assyrian kings in particular could be savage in putting down any rebellion in a client state, and kings like Rimush did not tolerate any form of uprising, evidence of domestic tyranny is rare.

In any case, the king could scarcely be an autocrat and survive, for his power was subject to several formal checks, which became ever more apparent with the passage of time. Firstly, areas of the kingdom were always inhabited by nomadic pastoralists whose regions were effectively autonomous; secondly, the kingdom was traditionally made up of strong cities under governors who, although appointed by the king, wielded considerable power in their own right – this was compounded by the fact that the governors not only often came from important local families with great influence in their region, but were also free to form alliances with each other; thirdly, by the first millennium, the citizens of many cities, notably Babylon itself, enjoyed tax exemptions and other advantages, such as freedom from military service. In addition, these cities were also wealthy enough to assert their independence once more, if they so chose. When the Assyrians controlled the whole of Mesopotamia, they had to deal with uprisings in the south quite frequently, and outbreaks of local rebellion recur throughout the history of ancient Mesopotamia. Moving punitive forces over long distances could take time, and although the introduction of the horse in around 2000 BC meant that hard-riding couriers made communication faster, distance often acted to the advantage of dissidents.

Centralized royal control increased over time, with the growth of little states, and then kingdoms, and, from time to time, empires. But the essential unit of authority remained the city. Even when subsumed within a larger polity, a city did not lose its traditional importance, identity or function. Two cities of particular interest merit discussion here.

NIPPUR – CENTRE OF CULTURE AND RELIGION

Nippur (modern Niffar) was one of the earliest to be established. It lay midway between the Tigris and the Euphrates, probably on a now-vanished tributary of one or the other, and halfway between Sippar to the northwest and Ur to the southeast. Located on the frontier between Sumer and Akkad, it was of national importance as a religious centre and as a centre of learning. Its tutelary deity was Ellil (Enlil), god of the air and one of the most important in the pantheon. Its principal temple, the Ekur, was dedicated to him, but the city was also home to temples to other important deities including Ishtar (Inanna), the goddess Gula, consort of Ninurta, and Sin (Nanna).

The city existed as an Ubaid settlement from as early as the sixth millennium. Ur-Nammu built the Ekur and its ziggurat, perhaps on the site of an earlier shrine, for Mesopotamian tradition maintained that once a temple had been constructed, it could be renovated, built over, improved, but not replaced. The Ekur was the chief shrine of Mesopotamia before Marduk replaced Ellil as the national god. However, another temple of great significance was that dedicated to Ishtar, which functioned at least from the Uruk epoch to the post-Babylonian Parthian age (nearly 4000 years), during which time it was restored no fewer than 22 times. The city itself lasted until about AD 800, though during its long history it suffered intermittent periods of abandonment and/or decline, for example from the 18th to 15th centuries BC, from about 1150 to 800 BC and during the first century AD. Nippur revived in the eighth century BC and prospered especially during the reign of the Assyrian king, Ashurbanipal (669–627 BC). At its height, the city covered 150 hectares (370 acres), with the ziggurat alone measuring 57 x 39.5 metres (187 x 130 ft) at its base. In common with all important cities from the third millennium onwards, Nippur was protected by a massive encircling wall.

Nippur's importance as a cultural, academic and religious centre grew primarily from its central position in the land, but was also based on its traditional role as the place of assembly for electing a common ruler (though this practice had long since ceased). Yet this 'tradition' may have been an invention of the Ur III rulers for propaganda purposes: Ellil/Enlil was the chief god of the land; Nippur was his city; a man declared king there had the right (at least in theory) to be regarded as king of the land. Priests were the custodians of this and other 'traditions', and Nippur remained a city run by temple authorities. There were about 26 temple complexes in all, including the four major shrines, rivals for royal bounty (Naram-Sin got a posthumous bad press from the priests of the Ekur when he favoured the temple of Ishtar/Inanna). The complexity of the city's organization meant that a significant percentage of the population was involved in administration, and had to be literate. Scribes in Nippur maintained the Sumerian literary tradition long after the language itself had fallen from general use, and a number of schools were founded in the city to teach and conserve it. However, it wasn't just about maintaining ancient traditions. Scribes also learned how to compose formal inscriptions for steles, while the demands made in mathematics were daunting; in one text, for example, a teacher asks his students:

ABOVE *A typical 'peg' figure in cast copper, showing a multi-horned (and hence powerful) god. Figurines such as this were buried in the foundations of buildings to attract good luck. Measuring some 29 cm (10 in) high, this example from Girsu is dedicated to Ur-Baba of Lagash (22nd century BC).*

ABOVE *A limestone relief from Telloh (c.2550–2500 BC; Early Dynastic Period) commemorating the building of a temple to Ningirsu and Nina by Ur-Nanshe, Prince of Lagash. Top left, the king carries a hod full of bricks on his head. Below right, he is seen at ease on a throne, holding a beaker. Behind him, a servant holds a flask. The smaller figures are the king's children and other family members. All are ritually dressed in woollen kilts. The plaque would have been hung on the temple wall by the hole in the centre.*

Do you know multiplication, reciprocals, coefficients, how to balance accounts, administrative accountancy, how to allocate salaries and wages, divide property and delimit shares of fields?

Nippur's reputation for learning was well-known nationally, and occasionally satirized, but the citizens were so proud of their scholarly reputation that at least one comic tale hints that even the vegetable sellers there spoke Sumerian. Other tales celebrating Nippurean native wit include the celebrated 'Poor Man of Nippur', in which a humble and downtrodden inhabitant called Gimil-Ninurta manages thrice to outwit and punish an avaricious and gullible mayor.

THE RISE OF ASHUR

Some 280 miles (450 km) north of Nippur, on the banks of the Tigris, lay the city of Ashur. Using the river for cultivation, navigation, and as part of its defensive system, Ashur was the first capital of Assyria, a country which took its name from the city. Ashur established its identity under the Amorite Shamshi-Adad (1813–1781 BC), who carved out a kingdom encompassing most of northern Mesopotamia. Ashur was already an important mercantile centre, with strong links to Anatolia and Persia.

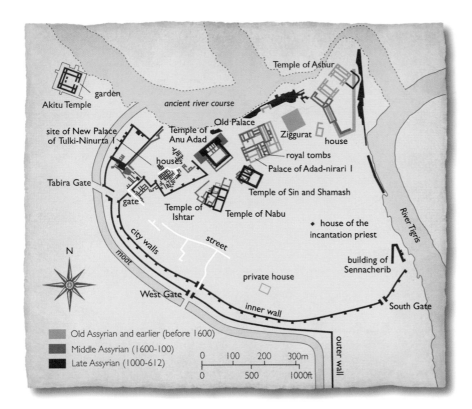

Temple of Ashur

garden

Akitu Temple

ancient river course

site of New Palace
of Tulki-Ninurta I

Temple of
Anu Adad

Old Palace

Ziggurat

house

houses

royal tombs

Palace of Adad-nirari I

Tabira Gate

gate

Temple of
Ishtar

Temple of Nabu

Temple of Sin and Shamash

◆ house of the
incantation priest

River Tigris

N

city walls

moat

street

private house

building of
Sennacherib

West Gate

inner wall

South Gate

outer wall

Old Assyrian and earlier (before 1600)
Middle Assyrian (1600–100)
Late Assyrian (1000–612)

0   100   200   300m
0   500   1000ft

LEFT   *Plan of Ashur in
northern Mesopotamia. From
the 14th to the 9th century
BC, this important site on the
River Tigris was the capital
and the principal religious city
of the Assyrian empire.*

At Kanesh (near modern Kültepe) in Anatolia, an Assyrian merchant colony was well established by the 19th century BC, and Assyrians based there spent so long away from home that they would start second families, while their wives were left to manage their businesses at Ashur.

Having proclaimed himself king of Ashur and ruler of a kingdom that included the important cities of Mari, Harran and Hit, and that stretched almost as far south as Sippar, Shamshi-Adad applied himself to major works of restoration and building at Ashur, repairing the city walls, and supervising the construction of three ziggurats in honour of the gods Ellil, An and Adad. Subsequent kings added a temple to Sin and Shamash, a palace, a defensive moat, and a great temple to the city's tutelary deity, also called Ashur, who may have been a personification of the city itself.

Ashur was always an important religious and mercantile centre, and throughout its history it was maintained and adorned with loving care, though it was not always the capital. Shamshi-Adad himself established his capital, at least for a time, to the north, at Shubat-Enlil. In any case, his kingdom rapidly disintegrated after his death. The Assyrians did not re-establish a true state until the reign of Ashur-uballit I (1363–1328 BC), of which Ashur became the centre. Ashur-uballit's successors, notably Shalmaneser I (1273–1244 BC) and his son Tulki-Ninurta I (1243–1207 BC), consolidated his work and embellished the city: it was Tulki-Ninurta, a builder-king in the true Mesopotamian tradition, who erected Ashur's temple. He also rebuilt the temple of Ishtar, lavishly decorating it with alabaster, gold and pearls. He rebuilt the city walls, extended the moat, and began work on a new palace. He also implemented an ambitious domestic building programme, and founded a new town a few kilometres to the north.

Ashur would remain the capital of Assyria until 883 BC, when Tulki-Ninurta II (890–884 BC) was deposed by his son, Ashurnasirpal. By that time, much had changed in Mesopotamia.

CHAPTER FIVE

BABYLON AND ASSYRIA

SHAMSHI-ADAD, WHO PROBABLY CAME from minor local royal stock in the north, proved himself as good an administrator as he was a soldier. We know something of him from letters discovered among some 13,000 clay tablets unearthed at the royal palace at Mari, always an important town and often an independent city-state. Situated in the west of the country on the Euphrates, Mari was also a busy trading centre and a crossroads for commerce.

The palace archive is a treasure trove that gives us a detailed view of day-to-day life between 1810 and 1760 BC. Shamshi-Adad's correspondence with his two sons, to whom he delegated much of the running of his kingdom, is vivid. The older son, Ishme-Dagan, was a 'chip off the old block' (though he found it impossible to hold the kingdom together after his father's death); but the younger, Yasmah-Adad, who was put in charge of Mari, left a lot to be desired, being apparently shiftless, idle and much given to the pursuit of pleasure. In one letter, his father upbraids him:

> *Are you a child, don't you have a beard on your chin? Even now, having reached maturity, you haven't established a proper household! ...Who looks after your house? Is it not said that if an administrator doesn't look after his affairs even for two or three days, the administration collapses? Why have you not appointed an administrator? And while your brother has won a great victory over here, you remain there, lolling about among the women. So now, when you go to Kanatum with the army, be a man! As your brother is making a great name for himself, so you, too, make a great name for yourself in your country.*

Shamshi's exasperation continues in another letter: '*How long will it be before you can stand on your own two feet? ... How much longer will you remain incapable of of running your own house? Do you not see your own brother commanding far-flung armies?*' And Ishme-Dagan himself writes: '*Why are you moaning on about this? It's not noble conduct!*' Yasmah-Adad gets into trouble again with his brother for starting to light a series of signal-fire beacons to summon aid for what was no more than a raid: '*It is possible (now) that the whole land will be coming to your assistance,*' writes Ishme-Dagan. '*Have letters written to the whole land ... and send your fastest messengers to deliver them. You should say, "A large number of men raided the land, and because of this two fires were lit. There is no need to come to my assistance".*' The episode is interesting because of the allusion to fast messengers, who would no doubt have been riders, for from about 2000 BC the domesticated horse was coming into use in Mesopotamia, making precise communication over distance far quicker.

Unsurprisingly, it was Ishme-Dagan who inherited the crown from his father after Shamshi's death. Ishme reigned until about 1740 BC, but under him Assyria's

RIGHT *Hammurabi (left) presents his Law Code to a deity identified as either Marduk or the sun god Shamash. The king is holding his right hand up to his mouth in a gesture of reverence. The seated god has many horns, symbolic of his great power. This impressive basalt stele, the rest of which is imprinted with the Code in cuneiform, now resides in the Louvre Museum, Paris.*

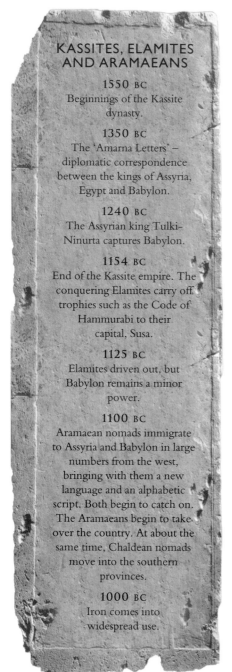

KASSITES, ELAMITES AND ARAMAEANS

1550 BC
Beginnings of the Kassite dynasty.

1350 BC
The 'Amarna Letters' – diplomatic correspondence between the kings of Assyria, Egypt and Babylon.

1240 BC
The Assyrian king Tulki-Ninurta captures Babylon.

1154 BC
End of the Kassite empire. The conquering Elamites carry off trophies such as the Code of Hammurabi to their capital, Susa.

1125 BC
Elamites driven out, but Babylon remains a minor power.

1100 BC
Aramaean nomads immigrate to Assyria and Babylon in large numbers from the west, bringing with them a new language and an alphabetic script. Both begin to catch on. The Aramaeans begin to take over the country. At about the same time, Chaldean nomads move into the southern provinces.

1000 BC
Iron comes into widespread use.

fortunes declined, and before long the great Amorite Babylonian king, Hammurabi, was first requesting and then demanding a troop levy from what he clearly regarded as a vassal kingdom, which was ultimately absorbed into the new Babylonian empire. Meanwhile, at Mari, the unfortunate Yasmah-Adad was usurped by one Zimri-Lin (1782–1758 BC), a descendant of the king of Mari whom Shamshi-Adad had ousted. Zimri-Lin was powerful enough not to be subdued by Hammurabi, and Mari remained independent for the whole of his reign. He maintained diplomatic relations with the Babylonian king, and each of them maintained ambassadors (and spies) in each other's courts. They sought aid from each other from time to time – Zimri-Lin once requiring the loan of 10,000 men, while Hammurabi later made a similar request. Diplomatic language in the letters of the time is of interest: unlike local, internal business correspondence, which is concise, international letters are evasive and circumlocutory. It was considered impolite ever actually to say 'no', and kings who considered themselves as equals addressed each other as 'brother'; dominant kings addressed lesser ones as 'son', and the reciprocal was 'father'.

Another man from Mari, Ishbi-Erra, had established himself at Isin around 2017 BC, and independent rule there lasted until the death of Damiq-ilushu in 1794 BC, but then, and perhaps before, Isin was absorbed into Babylonian territory. The sister-kingdom at Larsa lasted for a very similar period, and maintained its independence a little longer under its last king, Rim-Sin, an apparently cultivated man, whose long reign lasted from 1822 to 1763 BC (the longest recorded, to date, in Mesopotamian history). Rim-Sin remained dominant in the south for the first few years of Hammurabi's reign and indeed (as had the kings of Isin) had been worshipped as a god. This was a practise the much more powerful Hammurabi eschewed, and from his time on the habit fell into desuetude. With Rim-Sin's death, Larsa ceased to be a major power, and it is possible that Hammurabi's diplomatic activity by then had made him powerful enough to annex it.

BABYLON UNDER HAMMURABI

Hammurabi of Babylon (1792–1750 BC) is the next great king of Babylon after Sargon. He was the sixth monarch of his dynasty, which was founded by Sumu-abum in 1894 BC, and when he came to the throne Babylon was still just one of several minor states, all jockeying for power or forming coalitions. He spent his first years concentrating on internal reform, a process that would culminate in his comprehensive legal code.

Hammurabi proceeded slowly, building up both his own strength and diplomatic relationships over the first twenty-nine years of his reign. He then took a more aggressive stance, repelling an Elamite incursion, taking over Babylon's local rival cities, and later, with more difficulty, quelling Assyria and the city of Eshnunna, and defeating his old ally, Zimri-Lin, at Mari. In the end the national state he established did not outlast his dynasty – the Hittites raided Mesopotamia from the north and sacked Babylon itself in 1595 BC – but his achievements ensured that Babylon would remain of central importance for the rest of our period. His reign also saw the beginning of the religious process that would eventually see Marduk, the city's tutelary deity, oust Ellil as the national god.

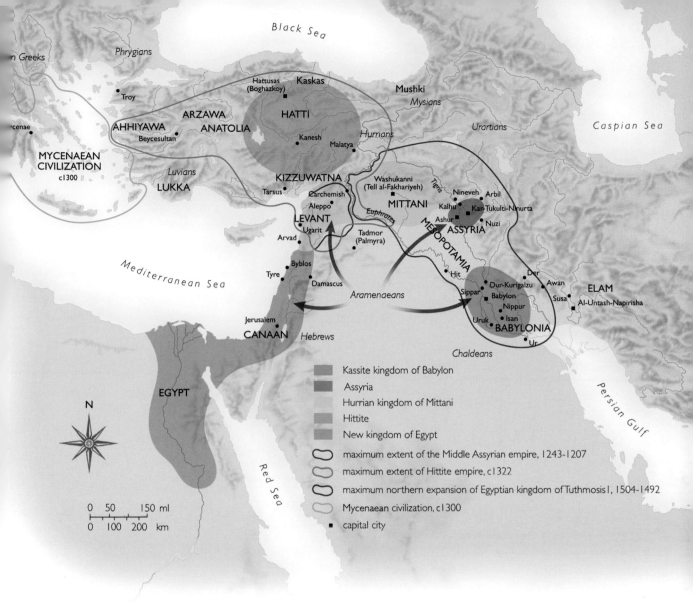

Black Sea

Phrygians

n Greeks

Troy

Hattusas
(Boghazkoy)   Kaskas

Mushki

Mysians

ARZAWA   HATTI
ANATOLIA

AHHIYAWA

Beycesultan

Kanesh

Hurrians

Urartians

Caspian Sea

cenae

MYCENAEAN
CIVILIZATION
c1300

Luvians

Malatya

LUKKA

KIZZUWATNA

Tarsus

Washukanni
(Tell al-Fakhariyeh)

Nineveh   Arbil

Kalhu   Kar-Tukulti-Ninurta

MITTANI   Ashur   ASSYRIA   Nuzi

Carchemish

Aleppo

LEVANT

Ugarit

Arvad

Euphrates

MESOPOTAMIA

Tigris

Tadmor
(Palmyra)

Mediterranean Sea

Tyre   Byblos

Damascus

Aramenaeans

Hit

Der

Dur-Kurigalzu

Babylon

Sippar   Nippur

Awan

Susa

ELAM

Al-Untash-Napirisha

Jerusalem

CANAAN   Hebrews

Uruk   Isan   BABYLONIA

Ur

Chaldeans

Persian Gulf

EGYPT

N

Red Sea

▨ Kassite kingdom of Babylon

▨ Assyria

▨ Hurrian kingdom of Mittani

▨ Hittite

▨ New kingdom of Egypt

◯ maximum extent of the Middle Assyrian empire, 1243–1207

◯ maximum extent of Hittite empire, c1322

◯ maximum northern expansion of Egyptian kingdom of Tuthmosis I, 1504–1492

◯ Mycenaean civilization, c1300

■ capital city

0   50   150 ml

0   100   200 km

Inscriptions and documentation from the reign of Hammurabi provide us with a very profound insight into the workings of society. International decisions, diplomatic tactics and declarations of war were doubtless decided by the king and his councillors. The cities were controlled by assemblies, guided by the heads of the leading families, but open to all, although one proverb warns of the danger of getting one's fingers burned by doing so:

Don't go and stand in the assembly: don't wander into the very place of strife. It is precisely in strife that fate may overtake you, and in any case you may be made a witness for them, and then they'll take you along and get you involved in a law-suit which is nothing to do with you.

Containing a germ of the old democratic processes by which the early communities were ruled, the offices of chairman and mayor were held on a rotating basis. The people were divided into three classes, freemen (*awelu*), serfs or land-bound villeins (*mushkenu*), and slaves (*wardu*). How the law worked for you was dependent

ABOVE *Map showing Babylonia under Kassite control (c. 1531–1154 BC), along with contemporaneous kingdoms in Egypt, the Levant, Anatolia and Greece. By this time, Babylon and Assyria were in decline, while Egypt, the Mitanni and the Hatti were dominant. Meanwhile the Aramaeans spread inexorably into Assyria, Babylon and the eastern Mediterranean.*

HAMMURABI
(r. 1792 – 1750 BC)

The dynasty known as Ur III, founded by Ur-Nammu, had extended its realm as far north as Ashur and Susharra. It had absorbed Elam, and controlled the northern and northeastern shores of the Persian Gulf. However, by about 2035 BC it was already coming under pressure from the Amorites, who gradually infiltrated its territories. But it was the Elamites who dealt Ur its death-blow by sacking it in 2004 BC, leaving it too weak to withstand an eventual Amorite takeover. The Amorites were successful enough to establish a dynasty, basing themselves in Babylon, which now became a major city. Their sixth king was Hammurabi.

When Hammurabi came to the throne Babylon by no means had the ascendancy it had enjoyed during the Sargonid period. It was just one of a number of small, rival states. In his first years, he concentrated on internal reforms, building up defences, repairing and extending irrigation canals, and developing a network of diplomatic alliances. A contemporary account sketches the situation:

ABOVE *The damaged head of a diorite statuette (c. 1750 BC) depicting a king, possibly Hammurabi, found at Susa, Iran.*

> '*There is no king who by himself is strongest. Ten or fifteen kings follow Hammurabi of Babylon, as many follow Rim-Sin of Larsa, Ibalpiel of Eshnunna, and Amutpiel of Katna, while twenty kings follow Yarim-Lim of Yamhad.*'

Hammurabi was a patient man, and his patience paid off, for at the end of three decades of skilful diplomacy he had made himself the strongest king in Mesopotamia. It was now time to concentrate on expansion. He quickly defeated his main rival, Rim-Sin of Larsa, a victory that gave him control of all southern Babylon. Then he turned his attention to the east and north, subduing the Gutians and Eshnunna. He took Mari and eventually, Nineveh. At the end of eight years' campaigning, he held sway over all Mesopotamia. Ultimately, he was to rule over roughly the same area as had the kings of Ur III.

Although Hammurabi's hegemony did not last long – Babylon was sacked by the Hittites in 1595 BC – his lasting achievement was to impart an enduring sense of unity to the cities he had brought under his control. Babylon as a city remained of central importance for nearly 2000 years, while its significance as a religious centre endured until AD 100. The state of Babylon survived, enjoying periods of resurgence – quite glorious under its last rulers in the sixth century – until the Persian invasion of Cyrus the Great in 539 BC. It was around the time of Hammurabi's reign that Marduk, the god of the city of Babylon, supplanted Ellil as the principal deity, a position that remained largely unassailed until the last king, Nabonidus, tried to revive the cult of the moon-god, Sin. Today, Hammurabi is chiefly remembered for the legal code he ordered drawn up.

on your social status. Freemen, for example, carried a lot of responsibility; serfs, on the other hand, enjoyed special protection as dependants of the palace or temple. Slaves had far more extensive rights than they ever did, say, under the Roman empire. Slaves might be prisoners-of-war, military and civil, and these were generally the property of the crown; but most of them were drawn from the local population. Men and women sold themselves or their children into slavery when they couldn't afford to keep themselves, or when they were hopelessly in debt; but that was not necessarily forever, as one of Hammurabi's laws provides:

> If any one fail to meet a claim for debt, and sell himself, his wife, his son, or daughter for money, or give them away to forced labour, they shall work for three years in the house of the man who bought them, or the proprietor, and in the fourth year they shall be set free.

Slaves' well-being and precise status were provided for by law, and they had civil rights. They enjoyed the possibility of becoming freemen, and they were at liberty to marry outside their class, naturally within certain restrictions.

HAMMURABI THE LAW-GIVER

Hammurabi's most famous and probably most important legacy is his legal code. It begins with a pro-forma disquisition on the king's good intentions:

> When An the Sublime, King of the Annunaki, and Bel, the lord of heaven and earth, who decreed the fate of the land, assigned to Marduk, the principal son of Ea, god of righteousness, dominion over earthly man, and made him great among the Igigi, they called Babylon by his illustrious name, made it great on earth, and founded an everlasting kingdom in it, whose foundations are laid so solidly as those of heaven and earth; then An and Bel called me by name, Hammurabi, the exalted prince, who feared god, to bring about the rule of righteousness in the land, to destroy the wicked and the evil-doers; so that the strong should not harm the weak; so that I should rule over the black-haired people like Shamash, and enlighten the land, to further the well-being of mankind.

The laws cover every aspect of life, and pay close attention to the good maintenance of land and irrigation systems, private business deals and contracts between principals and agents, social intercourse, property rights and debt. The system is not free from harsh punishments and a certain belief in 'trial by ordeal', but in many cases what they provide for would not seem unreasonable – would even seem familiar – to a modern eye. The laws governing private enterprise are very detailed, and this reflects an increase in activity in the private sector. Always lacking in the essential raw materials of stone, high quality timber (for house- and ship-building) and precious stones, Babylon had the choice of acquiring them by plunder or trade. In Hammurabi's day, trade was the means chosen. In exchange for the raw materials they needed, Babylonian businessmen exported finished goods, woven cloth, leather ware, ornaments and luxury cylinder seals. They also imported tin from Afghanistan, which they would re-export to such places as Anatolia.

It is hard to make any kind of selection from such a vast document, but a handful of the laws give a flavour of the whole:

> If any one slander a sister of a god or the wife of any one, and can not prove it, this man shall be taken before the judges and his brow shall be marked. (by cutting the skin, or perhaps the hair.)

If a man take a woman to wife, but have no intercourse with her, this woman is no wife to him.

If a man's wife be surprised with another man, both shall be tied and thrown into the water, but the husband may pardon his wife and (if he so chooses) the king may pardon her lover.

If a 'sister of a god' (= ?nun or priestess) or a prostitute (= ?unmarriageable woman), receive a gift from her father, and a deed in which it has been explicitly stated that she may dispose of it as she pleases, and gives her complete disposition thereof: if then her father die, she may leave her property to whomsoever she pleases. Her brothers can raise no claim thereto.

This is not, however, the whole picture. Many laws quite literally prescribe the punishment of an eye for an eye – and a tooth for a tooth, a limb for a limb, and so on; and a set of laws directed at doctors is very severe indeed; for example:

If a physician make a large incision with the operating knife, and kill him, or open a tumour with the operating knife, and cut out the eye, his hands shall be cut off.

One can only hope that such a punishment would only have been implemented in a proven case of criminal negligence. But despite the cruelty of many of the 'laws' enshrined in his code, Hammurabi emerges as a strong and just ruler, who left behind a state which was secure and prosperous, having ushered in his reforms smoothly and without objection. But he had constructed a kingdom out of parts which had strong traditions of independence and self-interest, and held them together by the force of his rule. His successors, as is so often the case, could not maintain the empire, and gradually it unravelled.

AGE OF THE KASSITES

This time the *coup de grâce* was delivered by the Hittites, but their king, Mursilis, did not linger to establish himself permanently in the region. He returned home to face palace intrigues which, in his absence, were threatening to unseat him (in the event, they did). The power vacuum he left behind was filled by a fresh wave of invaders, again from the northwest, the Kassites. Again, the invasion began as a more or less peaceful, but steady infiltration. Once installed, however, the Kassites were to control Babylon and its region, roughly from Sippar in the north to Ur in the south, for nearly 450 years. It was the longest dynasty the country ever knew, though it covered a much smaller area than that which had been controlled by Hammurabi.

The Kassites brought their own gods, but also adopted the indigenous ones, and their own language, though for all the time that they were present we have no text entirely written in it, and we have only a small understanding of what it was like. They used Babylonian-Akkadian – which had become the *lingua franca* of the entire region and was understood even in Egypt – for their official correspondence; they respected the cities they had conquered, rebuilding and renovating Nippur, Larsa, Ur and Uruk; they introduced the skill of horse-breeding, and they brought in the technique, which later Assyrian kings were to develop into a high art form, of carving in low relief. Kurigalzu I (*c.* 1390 BC) built a defensive fortress near the confluence of the Tigris and the River Diyala. It was during their rule that a new calendrical system was adopted, following the number of years in a given king's reign. They also developed a system of small steles known as *kudurru*, which

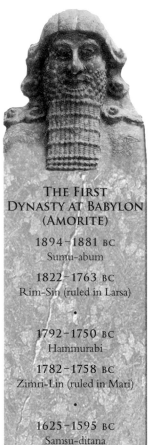

THE FIRST DYNASTY AT BABYLON (AMORITE)

1894–1881 BC
Sumu-abum

1822–1763 BC
Rim-Sin (ruled in Larsa)

•

1792–1750 BC
Hammurabi

1782–1758 BC
Zimri-Lim (ruled in Mari)

•

1625–1595 BC
Samsu-ditana

LAW-MAKING

Although the very first inhabitants of the fertile lands between the Tigris and the Euphrates were nomadic hunters and, soon afterwards, pastoralists, it wasn't long before they began to form settled communities, learning to cultivate and improve the wild wheat and barley, and to domesticate goats and sheep for food and clothing. Once people start living together in any kind of community, some rules are required to keep order. The founder king of the dynasty known as Ur III, Ur-Nammu (r. 2112–2095 BC), is credited with oldest known law code existing today, though now it is thought that it was his son and successor, Shulgi, (r. 2094–2047 BC), who was responsible for it.

This code is the earliest we possess, but it was even then not without precedent. The act of writing laws down was important because it implied that the laws now had a public existence which any literate person could read. Translated as recently as the 1950s and 1960s, the Code already reveals a relatively high level of sophistication, pointing to a well-developed social structure. It provides for a system of fines as punishments for a series of crimes, which makes it less vengeful than later legal systems promulgated in Babylon and Assyria, which were harsher and embraced the so-called *lex talionis,* or 'eye for an eye' approach. Capital punishment was, however, reserved for murder, robbery, adultery and rape. Many of its tenets would strike us as primitive, but it has to been seen in the light of the period of history in which it was written. The Code covers civil as well as criminal law, and emphasises the ideal of the king as the protector of the defenceless.

Society was organized into two classes: the freemen and the slave. Three centuries later, King Hammurabi of Babylon (1792–1750 BC) issued a fuller, more sophisticated, and better-known legal code, which has survived on a large basalt stele now in the Louvre.

By Hammurabi's time, society was further divided – apart from the quasi-aristocratic, ruling class and the priest-administrators – into three basic strata: the freemen, dependent villeins or serfs, and slaves. Legal strictures now, while maintaining the basic pattern of 'if a person should commit such-and-such a crime, then the legal consequence will be...', used by Ur-Nammu/Shulgi, were far more of the *lex talionis* kind, and different levels of punishment were prescribed according to the social standing of the perpetrator and/or the victim. The Code contained 282 laws, as opposed to the 57 of Ur-Nammu/Shulgi.

The structure of the Code provides that each offence receives a specific punishment. Many are harsh, although they arc far more inclusive than those of Ur-Nammu/Shulgi, and thcy contain the idea of presumption of innocence. The Code gives plaintiff and defendant the chance to offer evidence as well, covers civil, mercantile and criminal areas, and gives some provision for the protection of women's rights. It is also notable how in both the codes, trial by ordeal only plays a minor role.

The legal systems must have taken much skill to administer, and testify to the level of development at this still relatively early stage in the history of the Ancient Near East.

approximate to land-deeds. A copy in stone was lodged in the temple, and a clay copy given to the landholder. These are of great use to historians, but scarcely qualify as a major artistic contribution. More significant artistically was the Kassite innovation of placing relief brickwork designs and figures on the façades of the temples they restored, a technique Nebuchadrezzar the Great would employ nearly 1000 years later for the Ishtar Gate. Kassite art is also noted for the delicate realism of its clay figurines, especially in animal sculpture.

Broadly speaking, however, the Kassites became assimilated into the existing culture, and they have left so little evidence of their passing – or at least, so little has yet come to light – that despite the great length of time they were present, we can say little else about them. Their era of ascendancy has been designated a Dark Age by many scholars, though that refers more to our ignorance of the period than to any return to barbarism. It was certainly an age of confusion, but it was also a crucible in which several significant changes occurred, not least, from about 1200, the marked increase in influence of the god Marduk, who would soon replace not only Ellil as national god, but subsume within himself many other individual gods, who now became merely aspects of Marduk. It was a long way from monotheism, nor was it as radical as the actual monotheism propounded by Akhenaten in Egypt (and obliterated at his death) a century and a half earlier, but it was a severe rationalization of the Babylonian pantheon.

THE AMARNA LETTERS

One extremely interesting find relating to this long period came to light at Tell-el-Amarna in Egypt, the site of the ancient city of Akhetaten, the new and very short-lived capital built by Pharaoh Amenhotep IV, better known to us as Akhenaten.

During much of the Kassite period there was diplomatic activity among many of the small states that made up the Ancient Near East at that time. An archive of around 350 letters on clay tablets, written in Akkadian, and directed to the dominant local power, Egypt, was discovered at Tell-el-Amarna around the turn of the 19th and 20th centuries AD. These letters, all diplomatic in nature, and covering a period of about 30 years, were addressed to Akhenaten (1352–1336 BC) and his father, Amenhotep III (1390–1352 BC), from the kings of Babylon, Assyria, Mitanni, the Hatti (the Hittite Empire), Syria, Canaan and Cyprus. The minor kings bicker and complain and jostle each other for attention from Egypt, demanding money, complaining when they don't receive enough, carping when diplomatic precedence seems to have been ignored by the pharaohs (Akhenaten was particularly bad in this respect), and seeking preferment. Polite diplomatic expressions are not at a premium in much of this correspondence.

One of the most successful suitors was the Kassite king, Burnaburiash II (1359–1333 BC), who was powerful enough, apparently, to address Akhenaten on pretty much equal terms – he calls the pharaoh 'brother' – and who married one of his daughters to the Egyptian king. This was as much of a business coup as a diplomatic one, for the list of presents sent to Babylon on the occasion of the marriage runs to over 307 lines of text in over four columns. Not that this prevented Burnaburiash from grumbling from time to time:

The former gold which my brother sent – because my brother did not look to it himself, but an officer of my brother sealed and sent it – the forty minas of gold which they brought, when I put them in the furnace did not come out full weight.

At much the same time the Assyrian king (Assyria having recovered a modest identity following the collapse of neighbouring and dominant Mitanni) Ashur-uballit I (1363–1328 BC) fired off his own salvo to Akhenaten (or possibly his successor, Tutankhamen):

May it be well with you, your family, and your land. When I saw your messengers I was extremely glad. Your messengers are entertained with all due honour in my court. I have dispatched to you as a peace-offering a beautiful royal chariot from among those that I drive myself and two white horses that I likewise drive myself; one chariot without a team of horses and one seal of beautiful lapis lazuli. Are the offerings of great kings like this? Gold is like dust in your land. One simply gathers it up. Why does it appear so valuable to you? I am in the process of building my new palace. Send me enough gold to decorate it properly. When Ashur-nadin-ahi, my ancestor, wrote to Egypt, he was sent twenty talents of gold. When the king of Hanigalbat wrote to Egypt to your father, he sent him twenty talents of gold. I am the equal of the king of Hanigalbat but you send me … (less) … It is not enough to pay my messengers for their trips to and fro! If you are seriously disposed towards friendship, send me much more gold! It is all in the family! Write to me to tell me what you need and I will supply it. We are distant lands – should messengers keep running to and fro like this?

News of this reached Burnaburiash, who was furious. Assyria, he declared, was his vassal, and should only do business with Egypt, if at all, through him. And so it went on. Significantly, though, Ashur-uballit had become sufficiently powerful for Burnaburiash to have considered it politic to take the Assyrian king's daughter as his chief wife.

Assyrian power was on the increase, and by the time of King Tulki-Ninurta I (1243–1207 BC), it was strong enough to attack Babylon, occupy it, and sack its capital. Babylon's king, Kashtiliashu, was taken prisoner to Ashur. Tulki-Ninurta boasted: '*(I) trod with my feet upon his lordly neck as though it were a footstool.*' The Assyrian king now ruled as far south as the Gulf, but his triumph was short-lived; a revolution led by his own son overthrew him, and the Kassites returned, to hang on for another eighty years or so; but their power was waning. Once again, it was an Elamite invasion which put an end to them. The images of Sin and Marduk were carried off to Susa. Sin had to wait 500 years until he was recaptured by the Assyrian king Ashurbanipal; Marduk was redeemed by Nebuchadrezzar I.

The Elamites did not establish themselves but either withdrew or were thrown out by a new dynasty, established in 1157 in Isin, but which moved its power base to Babylon in the wake of the Elamite withdrawal. It lasted until 1026; but of its 11 kings only the fourth, Nebuchadrezzar I (1125–1104 BC) really stands out. It was he who finally saw off the Elamites, and took the war to them, marching in summer: '*It was as if the roads burned like flames; there was no water in the lowlands … Even the best of the great horses faltered; and the legs of the strongest warriors failed …*' Despite these hardships he pressed on successfully, sacked Susa, and brought Marduk back with him in triumph. This moment is significant, for it may well mark the point at which Marduk definitively, and for the remainder of Babylonian history, became chief of the gods.

Yet the so-called Second Dynasty of Isin was not fated to bloom; and Assyrian power continued to grow in the north.

LEFT *Full-height view of the stele containing the Law Code of Hammurabi (c. 1760). The stele is made of basalt and stands a little over 2 metres (6.6 ft) high.*

CHAPTER SIX

THE ASSYRIAN EMPIRE

TOWARDS THE END OF THE SECOND MILLENNIUM, Tiglath-Pileser I (1114–1076 BC) ascended the throne of Assyria. He was a particularly aggressive expansionist, but for a time he concentrated his activities in the north, causing royal annals to be written of his campaigns, and thereby establishing a tradition that would continue throughout the Assyrian ascendancy. However, he largely left Babylon alone.

Unfortunately, Nebuchadrezzar I's younger son, Marduk-nadin-ahi, who succeeded an older brother in 1099 BC, raided the Assyrian town of Ekallate during this period, a foolhardy act that was tantamount to tweaking a lion's tail. Tiglath-Pileser retaliated by attacking northern Babylon, but Marduk-nadin-ahi held on until the end of his 17-year reign, when a dreadful famine struck his country, so severe that the people were reduced to cannibalism. The king simply was not heard of again thereafter, and his successors (about whom we know nothing save their names and dates) limped on until 1026 BC, presiding over a terminal decay.

ENCROACHMENT AND UNREST

Babylon's decline was not solely a result of the Assyrian threat. The end of the second and the beginning of the first millennium BC saw the menace of yet another incursion from outside Mesopotamia, which was to continue stealthily by infiltration over the succeeding centuries, and which affected Assyrians and the Babylonians alike. However, their strategy appears to have been to ignore this development, rather than banding together to face the common danger. The new people, the Aramaeans, were nomads who, descending into Mesopotamia from the north and northwest, gradually took over unpoliced agricultural land and settled in numbers too great to control. Their language, Aramaic, and their alphabet would slowly but surely replace Akkadian and cuneiform, since both, especially the alphabet, were easier to use (cuneiform was a syllabic script). This was a slow but inexorable process.

The Aramaeans were helped by the rivalry between Babylonians and Assyrians. When Marduk-nadin-ahi's successor, Marduk-shapik-zeri, travelled to Ashur on a diplomatic mission to King Ashur-bel-kala, he found on his return to Babylon that his throne had been usurped by an Aramaean, whom the Assyrian king not only promptly recognized, but whose daughter he married. However, this Aramaean king, who took the name Adad-apla-iddina, seems to have honoured his duties to his new country, and for the 20 years of his reign (1068–1047 BC) there seems to have been relative calm. But subsequently raids, incursions and discord typify another 'dark age', which lasted until about 900 BC.

The succeeding period saw an uneasy truce between the northern and the southern rival kingdoms, and though diplomatic relations were sealed by an

RIGHT The archaeologist Austen Henry Layard discovered this black limestone obelisk in 1846 during his excavations of the site of Kalhu, an ancient Assyrian capital. It was erected as a public monument in 825 BC. The relief sculptures on it glorify the achievements of Shalmaneser III and his chief minister, covering 31 years of campaigns, and portray the tribute they exacted from their enemies. This war booty included camels, monkeys, and an elephant; several Assyrian kings were keenly interested in both zoology and botany.

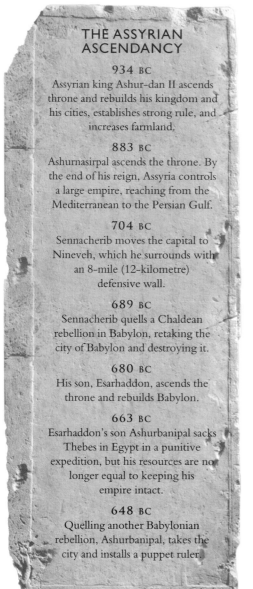

THE ASSYRIAN
ASCENDANCY

934 BC
Assyrian king Ashur-dan II ascends
throne and rebuilds his kingdom and
his cities, establishes strong rule, and
increases farmland.

883 BC
Ashurnasirpal ascends the throne. By
the end of his reign, Assyria controls
a large empire, reaching from the
Mediterranean to the Persian Gulf.

704 BC
Sennacherib moves the capital to
Nineveh, which he surrounds with
an 8-mile (12-kilometre)
defensive wall.

689 BC
Sennacherib quells a Chaldean
rebellion in Babylon, retaking the
city of Babylon and destroying it.

680 BC
His son, Esarhaddon, ascends the
throne and rebuilds Babylon.

663 BC
Esarhaddon's son Ashurbanipal sacks
Thebes in Egypt in a punitive
expedition, but his resources are no
longer equal to keeping his
empire intact.

648 BC
Quelling another Babylonian
rebellion, Ashurbanipal, takes the
city and installs a puppet ruler.

exchange of royal brides, this amounted to little more than papering over cracks. The Assyrians were hitting the stride of aggressive militarism that was to typify their ascendancy, and Babylon grew ever weaker. King Tulki-Ninurta II (890–884) marched his men into northern Babylon, and rattled his sabre at the important north Babylonian cities of Dur-Kurigalzu and Sippar. It was fortunate for Babylon that Tulki-Ninurta's son, Ashurnasirpal II (883–859 BC), concentrated his attentions on the north and west.

Ashurnasirpal was one of the great kings of Assyria. Under him the kingdom expanded vastly, as far as the Mediterranean in the west, and absorbing Mari, and the northern reaches of the Tigris, to its source. He moved the capital to Kalhu (the Biblical Kalah), a city founded about 400 years earlier by Shalmaneser I. Here he laid out a perimeter wall 5 miles (8 km) long, enclosing 360 hectares (889 acres), and within it constructed a new city over 15 years, the centrepiece of which was his magnificent palace, the opening of which he celebrated with a gargantuan feast. Building programmes on a mighty scale had already been established by earlier kings of Ur and Babylon, and the Assyrians followed the tradition. Moving their capital became an almost regular event for them. It was as if they wished to demonstrate and proclaim their existence, their wealth and their triumphs to all the world and to all eternity. In the event, the greatest Assyrian cities were reduced to ruins about 250 years after Ashurnasirpal's death.

Diplomatic and even cordial relations seem to have been maintained between Babylon and Assyria for most of the rest of the ninth century, but towards the end of it a revolution in Assyria brought chaos to the country. Its new king, Shamshi-Aad V (823–811 BC), was aided by his Babylonian counterpart in restoring order, but Babylon demanded terms in exchange for its aid which were too ambitious, and Shamshi-Adad V invaded the country, wholly defeating it and declaring himself king of it. In his decision-making, it should be added, he was assisted and encouraged by his redoubtable consort, Sammuramat, whose name in Greek, Semiramis, has come down to us as that of a legendary queen of Abyssinia, much celebrated in the annals of the first-century historian, Diodorus Siculus. After the death of her husband in 811 BC, Sammuramat ruled as regent on behalf of her young son for five years, making political declarations in her own name, which took precedence over that of the youthful king. So highly was she regarded that a memorial stele was erected to her, which, for a woman in those times, was an extraordinary tribute.

ASSYRIAN MILITARY PROWESS

Assyrian society was pronouncedly militaristic. Ashurnasirpal's son, Shalmaneser III (859–824 BC) spent 31 of his 35-year reign fighting wars. All able-bodied men were subject to the call-up, and the army was the backbone of the nation, giving it its structure and its hierarchy. The king was expected to lead his army into battle personally, and military men also undertook the duties of provincial governors and agents of the law. The legal system itself was severe. At least in the early part of this

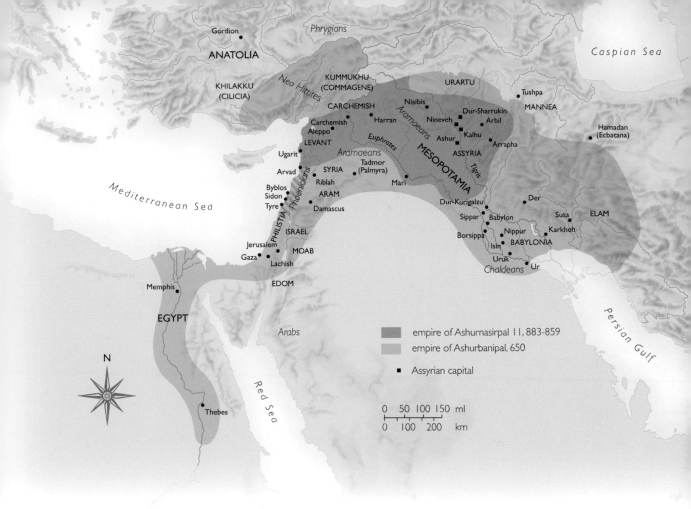

Gordion · ANATOLIA · Phrygians · Caspian Sea

KHILAKKU (CILICIA) · Neo Hittites · KUMMUKHU (COMMAGENE) · URARTU · Tushpa · MANNEA

CARCHEMISH · Nisibis · Dur-Sharrukin · Arbil · Hamadan (Ecbatana)

Carchemish · Harran · Nineveh · Kalhu · Ashur · Arrapha · ASSYRIA · MESOPOTAMIA · Euphrates · Aramaeans · Tigris

Aleppo · LEVANT · Aramaeans

Ugarit · Tadmor (Palmyra) · Mari · Der

Arvad · SYRIA · Riblah · Dur-Kurigalzu · Susa · ELAM

Byblos · ARAM · Sippar · Babylon · Karkheh

Sidon · Damascus · Borsippa · Nippur · BABYLONIA

Tyre · Phoenicians · Isin · Uru · Chaldeans · Ur

ISRAEL

Jerusalem · MOAB · Gaza · Lachish

PHILISTIA

Mediterranean Sea

EDOM

Memphis

EGYPT · Arabs

empire of Ashurnasirpal II, 883–859
empire of Ashurbanipal, 650
■ Assyrian capital

N · Red Sea · Persian Gulf

Thebes

0 50 100 150 ml
0 100 200 km

period, campaigns took place in the summer, after work on the harvest was completed, as standing armies were not created until later on. Even so armies of 50,000 men could be placed in the field, and if Assyrian manpower was not enough, foreigners were conscripted. These were often specialists: charioteers from Samaria, for example, and sailors from Phoenicia.

Military tactics were simple and often brutal, but they were designed to conserve Assyrian forces. Accordingly, a targeted territory would be approached with a massive force. If the ruler did not capitulate, legations might be sent to urge the local population to come over to the Assyrian side; failing that, or alternatively, soft targets such as villages or small cities would be attacked and destroyed, their populations tortured, raped, maimed and burned, their fields sown with salt, and their orchards uprooted. This was usually enough to intimidate the enemy to surrender. If not, local armies (other perhaps than that of Egypt) would be no match for the professional Assyrian military machine. Sieges, which could take a long time and were extremely expensive to maintain, were generally only engaged in a last resort; but the Assyrians left their adversaries in no doubt that once a besieged city had fallen, no mercy would be shown, not even to the last child. Deportation en masse of conquered peoples ensured that no uprisings would follow defeat, and resettled enforced migrants boosted Assyria's manpower and general population. The system of deportation was continued by the Chaldean kings whose major dynasty followed the fall of Assyria, and one of the deportations is well known to us from the Bible as the 'Babylonian Captivity'.

ABOVE *The height of the Assyrian ascendancy, showing the extents of Ashurnasirpal's and Ashurbanipal's great empires. After Ashurbanipal's death, however, the collapse of the empire was swift and complete.*

BELOW *A 19th-century illustration by James Fergusson (from* Layard's Discoveries in the Ruins of Nineveh and Babylon, 1853) *reconstructing the city of Nimrud on the Tigris as it might have looked at its zenith. There is much here, however, that later scholarship has found to be either fanciful or at best highly conjectural.*

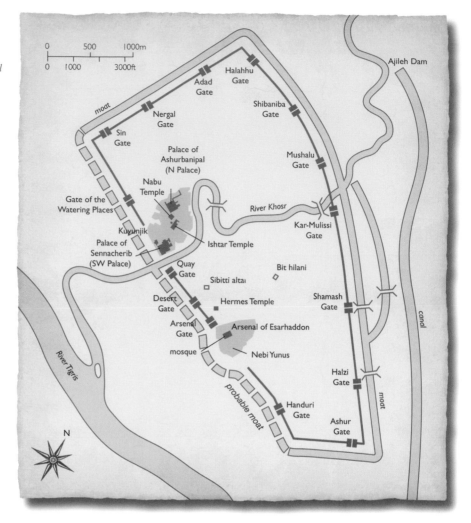

As for the royal succession, when there was a direct line, it fell not necessarily to the oldest son, but to the ablest. Once selected, the crown prince was educated in the House of Succession, learning the arts of war and diplomacy, succumbing to arduous physical and military training, and hunting; but also being schooled in writing and, in cases of exceptional ability, foreign languages. When a king died, regardless of where he had had his capital city, he was buried in the ancestral town of Ashur. According to general Mesopotamian tradition, the king was viewed as the god's (in this case, Ashur's) earthly representative.

A dynasty in Babylon persisted for much of the eighth century, but the kings who sat on the throne following the chaos left by Shamshi-Adad V's incursion, and a temporary decline in Assyrian fortunes which came afterwards, were Chaldeans, a people who now enter the stage. They lived among the marshes and lakes of the lower Tigris and Euphrates, divided into three principal tribes, and were prosperous horse and cattle breeders. Their culture was Babylonian, they spoke and wrote Babylonian-Akkadian and they took Babylonian names. They were an enduring presence during the Assyrian domination of Babylon during the latter half of the eighth and most of the seventh centuries, and then they struck. Here it is sufficient to mention just one of them, Nabonassar (747–734 BC), during whose reign

ASHURNASIRPAL
(r. 883–859 BC)

The Assyrians were great soldiers, and at their height they were also great builders, employing vast workforces and spending huge sums gleaned from their campaigns to create major new cities.

A statue of Ashurnasirpal found at Kalhu (modern Nimrud) and now in the British Museum, shows the face of a man whom it would be fatal to cross. Ambitious, brave, cruel, vain grandiose, but also cultivated, Ashurnasirpal established an extensive northern kingdom which reached the shores of the Mediterranean and laid the foundations of an impressive political and administrative infrastructure.

His military achievements were impressive. As soon as he succeeded to the throne, he started a vigorous and aggressive series of campaigns. He took over the lands formerly controlled by the Hittites, and the Aramaean states in what is now Syria. Any hint of rebellion after conquest was put down so brutally that any further revolts, once the Assyrian army had withdrawn, was rendered unlikely. Rebellious rulers were flayed alive, and their skins nailed to their city walls. Their subjects, regardless of sex or age, could find themselves impaled, maimed or blinded.

Ashurnasirpal replaced local rulers with Assyrian governors (backed by garrisons) to ensure his tenure. The Phoenician cities he left alone, but obliged them to provide him with cedarwood, iron, gold and silver in large quantities as tribute: '*From the inhabitants of Tyre, Sidon, Byblos … I received tribute … gold, silver, tin, copper, linen, large and small monkeys, ebony, boxwood … and they embraced my feet.*'

Nevertheless his real control did not outlive

ABOVE *Statue (ninth century BC) of Ashurnasipal II, renowned for his ruthlessness in extending Assyrian rule.*

him, and his campaigns, viewed objectively, take on the appearance of massive, piratical raids. He also brought Cyprus to heel, showing that, though king of an essentially land-locked country, he could deploy an efficient navy as well. It is possible that Phoenicians and other peoples of the coast managed his navy for him.

Ashurnasirpal started his reign at the traditional Assyrian capital, Ashur, but in 878 BC he had a new capital built for himself at Kalhu, about 60 miles (100 km) to the north. There he indulged in another passion, hunting. Scenes carved in low relief depicting his lion hunts – a sport beloved of Assyrian kings – have survived. He was also interested in botany and zoology, and built up an extensive library, of which he was extremely proud. But first and foremost, he was a builder.

The pride and joy of his new capital was his palace, which was excavated by Max Mallowan (1904–78) in the late 1940s and early 1950s. Its plan is impressive. It covered an area of over six acres, and was divided into three sections, administrative, ceremonial and domestic. The entrance to the ceremonial halls was flanked by vast, massively-carved protective genii – the *lamassus*, creatures with the bodies of winged bulls and the heavily-bearded heads of men. Thousands of people were employed to build it, and only the most expensive materials were used: cedar, cypress, juniper and boxwood, limestone and alabaster, together with silver and gold and iron.

Ashurnasirpal also enjoyed entertaining. A record survives of a banquet he gave that lasted ten days, at which he entertained 69,574 guests.

important advances were made in the field of astronomy, and an accurate calendar was introduced. Nabonassar's rule also saw the commencement of the Babylonian Chronicles, which are an attempt to keep a precise historical record of events, and which continued to be kept until the Parthian period. Indeed, in the much later Greek culture the word 'Chaldean' came to be synonymous with 'astronomer'.

But even Nabonassar's cultivated reign was not without its insurgencies, and the new and able Assyrian monarch, Tiglath-Pileser III, a former general, was called upon to help subdue them. In effect, he and his heir were soon running the country, and his son, Shalmaneser V, was king in Babylon as well as Assyria from 726 to 722 BC. However, on his death a local Chaldean king, recognized by the Assyrians as the ruler of the Sealand, or coastal region around the Gulf, rebelled and seized power in the south. His name was Marduk-apla-iddina II (the Biblical Merodach-Baladan), and he was to remain a thorn in the Assyrians' side, in and out of power, for many years to come.

THE REIGN OF SARGON II

In Assyria itself, Marduk-apla-iddina encountered a worthy opponent in Sargon II (721–705 BC), who marched against him (he seems not to have been able to maintain security along the all-important trade routes) in 710 BC and drove him back to the Sealand. Sargon thereupon became king of both countries. In the 16 years of his reign, the political history of which consists of a constant and generally successful effort to keep his empire in order, he consolidated his father's victories, crushed the Armenian kingdom of Urartu, and expanded into Elam in the east and the Levant in the west, and fully restored the fortunes Assyria had enjoyed under Ashurnasirpal.

Sargon was another major builder-king. He moved the capital from Kalhu to a brand-new city of his own foundation, about 47 miles (75 km) to the north, near modern Khorsabad. This he called Dur-Sharrukin – Sargon's Fortress – and it was modelled on Kalhu. Why he decided on the move is uncertain, but it may have been a way of establishing his individual name. The town was based on a square whose sides were each about 0.8 miles (1.3 km) long, and punctuated with seven ornate gates. Its citadel contained a temple to Nabu, a palace, and the houses of the upper crust. (The *mar banuti*, or 'sons of creation' – the tightly-knit aristocracy who grew rich with the king, and without whose consent and support he could not govern.)

6When Ashurnasirpal, king of Assyria, inaugurated the palace at Kalhu, a palace of joy, erected with great ingenuity, he invited into it Ashur, the great lord, and the gods of his entire country, and he prepared a banquet of 1000 fattened head of cattle, 1000 calves, 10,000 stable sheep, 15,000 lambs – for my lady Ishtar alone, 200 head of cattle and 1000 sihhu sheep; 1000 spring lambs, 500 stags, 500 gazelles, 1000 ducks, 500 geese, 500 kurku geese, 1000 mesuku birds, 1000 qaribu birds, 10,000 doves, 10,000 sukannu doves, 10,000 other assorted small birds, 10,000 assorted fish, 10,000 jerboas, 10,000 assorted eggs ... 10,000 jars of beer, 10,000 skins of wine ... 1000 crates of vegetable, 300 containers of oil ... 100 jars of fine mixed beer ... 100 pistachio cones. When I inaugurated the palace at Kalhu I treated for ten days with food and drink 47,074 people, men and women, invited from across my entire country, as well as 5000 VIPs ... and 16,000 citizens of Kalhu from all walks of life, 1500 officials from my palaces ... in all, 69,574 invited guests. I provided them with the means to clean and anoint themselves. I did them due honour and sent them home happy and healthy. 9

FROM A STELE DESCRIBING ASHURNASIRPAL'S BANQUET CELEBRATING THE INAUGURATION OF HIS NEW PALACE AT KALHU

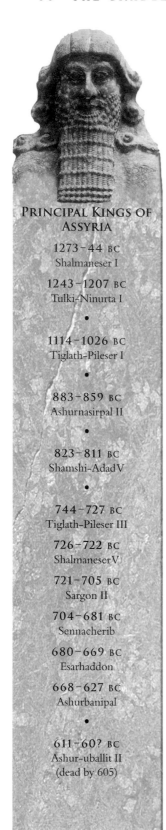

An intriguing note in Sargon's annals of the use to which he intended to put Dur-Sharrukin clearly refers to uprooted, conquered peoples brought to Assyria: *'Peoples of the four corners of the world, who speak foreign languages and different dialects, inhabitants of the plains and of the mountains … I unified them and settled them in the city.'* Nor was Sargon a patient man. He wrote to the governor of Kalhu: *'700 bales of straw and 700 bundles of reed, each bundle more than a donkey can carry, must arrive in Dur-Sharrukin by the first of the month of Kislev. Should one day pass by [this deadline], you will die.'*

The building of Dur-Sharrukin involved tens of thousands of workers and took 10–15 years, but it was never completed, and probably never even occupied for long. Sargon's ambitions were cut short when he fell in battle in Anatolia in 705 BC.

RELOCATION TO NINEVEH

He was succeeded by his son Sennacherib (704–681 BC), who moved the capital from Sargon's only partially completed new city to the ancient town of Nineveh, whose roots went back to before 3000. The choice of Nineveh enabled Sennacherib to distance himself from his father, whose death in battle was, as usual, interpreted as a bad omen, but it may also have been a political move: Nineveh was of symbolic importance to the army. From here Ashurnasirpal had started his campaigns, and it was to Nineveh that tribute from conquered lands was delivered.

The Assyrians' successful warmongering had paid huge dividends along with the problems attendant on keeping a large empire together, and Sennacherib had plenty of money to lavish on his own personal building programme. He built a new palace at Nineveh, called the Palace Without A Rival:

> *Beams of cedar, the product of Mount Amanus, which they dragged with
> difficulty out of the distant mountains, I stretched across the roofs. Great
> door-leaves of cypress, whose odour is pleasant as they are opened and closed,
> I bound with a band of shining copper, and set them up in their places.*

Silver, copper and white limestone *lamassu* – the human-headed winged bulls that protected the thresholds – were set up; the walls were lined with vast scenes of Sennacherib's triumphs, carved in low-relief on stone and painted; the main façade of the palace was 500 metres (1640 ft) long. Beside it, a park was laid out, comprising a botanical garden (botany was one of Sennacherib's passions), and probably stocked with (non-aggressive) wild animals.

REBELLIONS AND WARS

Sennacherib was also involved with rebellions in the Levant and Judea, so for a time Babylon fell back into political instability, during which Marduk-apla-iddinia attempted a comeback. This was too much for Sennacherib, who in the course of two punitive expeditions around 700 BC, drove him out for good, and installed his eldest son on the throne of Babylon. Crown Prince Ashur-naddin-shumi ruled in relative peace for six years, but the Elamites, former allies of Marduk-apla-iddina, continued to menace the eastern frontiers. In response, Sennacherib had a fleet built by Phoenicians at Nineveh, which he sailed downriver to the coast and there attacked and routed his enemy. But it was not enough. While Sennacherib was occupied in dealing with the Elamites in the south, his son in Babylon was assassinated and replaced by an Elamite puppet monarch, who in turned was ousted after only a few months by an Aramaean-sponsored king. He lasted three years before the exasperated Sennacherib abandoned any sense of goodwill towards Babylon. He marched on the city, and in 689 BC stormed and razed it:

SENNACHERIB
(r. 704–671 BC)

By Sennacherib's reign, Babylon was under Assyria's sway, but it was not necessarily docile. Sennacherib inherited an unruly southern province, though not all its cities were rebellious. Enough of them were, however, to cause him trouble. There was trouble, too, in the west of his empire, in the Mediterranean districts. As a chastiser of Judah, Sennacherib earns a place in the Bible second only to Nebuchadrezzar. However, Isaiah's hopeful description – the inspiration for Byron's famous poem – of the angel of the Lord slaying 185,000 in the camp of the Assyrians is wishful thinking. No Assyrian records support this, although the army, en route to Egypt after extracting a punitive tribute from King Ezekiah in exchange for sparing his city, may have been stricken by some disaster or other – a plague of rats, according to Herodotus, or a pestilential sickness, according to Berossus – which persuaded the Assyrians to abandon their planned invasion of that country.

ABOVE *Limestone bas-relief (seventh century BC) of Sennacherib. In his campaign against Judah, his armies captured forty-six of of King Ezekiah's cities, but failed to take Jerusalem.*

With the death of Marduk-apla-iddina, the Garibaldi of Babylonian independence, rebellion in the region died – at least for the time being. In the meantime, there were the Elamites to deal with. Sennacherib had a fleet built at Nineveh by Syrian shipwrights, then had it sailed down the Tigris to Opis, dragged on rollers overland some 25 or 30 miles (40–50 km) to the Euphrates, then on to the sea. The Elamites had meanwhile managed to put a king of their own choosing on the throne of Babylon, and Sennacherib's navy had to confront a joint force. The ensuing slaughter resulted in a victory for the Assyrians, who claimed to have killed 150,000 of their enemy; but Babylon held out, only falling, after a long siege, in 689 BC. Sennacherib's patience was at an end. Despite its standing as a religious and cultural centre, he had the city sacked and flooded. The great statue of Marduk was carried off in triumph to Nineveh, where it was to remain for 20 years.

In the midst of all this, Sennacherib had had time to move the Assyrian capital from Dur-Sharrukin (modern Khorsabad) to Nineveh, which he developed lavishly, and built himself a new palace of great magnificence (carved scenes celebrating his victory against Ezekiah at Lachish decorated this palace, and are now in the British Museum). The previous capital had been built by Sennacherib's father, Sargon II, who had in turn abandoned Kalhu. But Sargon II had died in battle, and that was always considered a bad omen for a king in Mesopotamia. Sennacherib himself was careful to let most of his own wars be handled by his generals.

*Like a hurricane, I attacked the city, like a storm, I overthrew it. ... Its
citizens, young and old, I did not spare, and with their corpses I filled the
streets ... The town itself and its houses, from their foundations to their roofs I
devastated, I destroyed; by fire I overthrew ... So that in the future even the soil
of its temples should be forgotten, by water I ravaged it, I turned it into pastures.*

After this, Sennacherib assumed the kingly title himself, but handed over day-to-day administration of the country to his son, Esarhaddon.

Sennacherib was assassinated in 681 BC and was duly succeeded, after a power-struggle with his male siblings, by Esarhaddon, Sennacherib's choice as heir. Esarhaddon retained the kingship of Babylon, and restored the city, whose sacking had been seen as a great sacrilege, to its former glory. Esarhaddon had married a Babylonian and his eight years as the country's governor had left him sympathetic to its traditions, but he was also motivated in his programme of reconciliation and renovation by omens which spelt out a grim fate if he did not follow such a policy. Once Babylon was secure, Esarhaddon embarked on a campaign of military expansion against Egypt, by this time a far less potent force than it had been in its glory days. He was probably not the first king to use camels alongside horses in his campaigns, but they certainly facilitated fast crossing of desert tracts. He was in any case successful in this extension of his dominions; but he fell ill and died in 669 BC, on his way back to Egypt with his army to drive the pharaoh Taharqa from Memphis, which the latter, driven back to the far south in earlier wars with the Assyrians, had by then retaken.

Mindful of the difficulties that had attended his own succession (Sennacherib had been killed by two of his other sons) Esarhaddon had, in consultation with his mother, Sennacherib's widow Naqia-Zakutu appointed his own younger son, Ashurbanipal, king of Assyria, while Ashurbanipal's older brother, Shamash-shuma-ukin, got Babylon. For 20 years the brothers ruled their neighbouring kingdoms in apparent harmony, but in about 650 BC Shamash-shuma-ukin, perhaps envious of his brother's greater power, perhaps influenced by Babylonian nationalists under whose sway during his long spell in their country he had fallen, raised a rebellion. Two years' fierce fighting ensued, culminating in extended sieges by the Assyrians of Babylon and Borsippa. By 648 BC Babylon stood alone, plagued by famine and, no doubt, disease. Cannibalism was again reported, while the dead lay piled high in the streets. Shortly afterwards it capitulated, but not before Shamash-shuma-ukin had thrown himself into the flames of his burning palace.

Ashurbanipal took the customarily harsh Assyrian revenge on the rebels and allowed his men to loot the palace, but he spared the city, causing it to be cleaned up and purged of the effects of the long siege, repairing and restoring as necessary, and resettling the surviving citizens there. He installed a regent by the name of Kandalanu, who reigned in his name for the next twenty years until his death in 627 BC, the same year that Ashurbanipal himself died, a fact which has led some scholars to think that the two were one and the same man, Kandalanu being a throne-name taken by the Assyrian king for his rule in Babylon.

By 627 BC, the Assyrians had the largest empire yet achieved by the Mesopotamians, or indeed by anyone. It stretched from Egypt to Elam, from the Gulf to the Mediterranean, whose eastern coastline they controlled from the Taurus Mountains to the Nile. But it was fated to last for only another 20 years.

RIGHT *Reconstruction of the interior of an Assyrian palace (from Layard's*
Discoveries in the Ruins of Nineveh and Babylon, *1853).*

'SARDANAPALUS'

Immortalized in the monumental painting *The Death of Sardanapalus* by the French Romantic artist Eugène Delacroix (1798–1863) this king of Babylon never existed in reality. Delacroix's huge canvas was inspired by Lord Byron's play Sardanapalus, written in 1821, and Byron himself got his idea from Diodorus, an entertaining but unreliable historian writing in about the middle of the first century BC.

> *Now Sardanapalus was the thirtieth king following Ninos, the founder of the empire. He was the last monarch of the Assyrians and surpassed all his predecessors in luxury and sloth. For besides keeping hidden away from everyone outside the palace, he lived the life of a woman. Consorting with his concubines, and also spinning purple thread of the softest wool, he wore the dress of a woman, and, by means of white lead and the other wiles of the courtesans, he rendered his face and his entire body more delicate than any girl's; he even took pains to have a voice like a woman. In his revels, he not only indulged in those foods and drinks most capable of stimulating continual lust, but he also partook of the carnal delights of a woman as well as those of a man; for he practised sexual promiscuity toward either gender without restraint, caring not a bit for the disgrace attending this behaviour. Such being his character, not only did he bring his own life to a shameful end, but he utterly ruined the empire of the Assyrians, which had existed longer than any other known to man.*

Diodorus got his information, most likely, from Ctesias, a fifth-century BC physician and historian, whose own original work had since been lost. Neverthelsess, it is possible that Sardanapalus was based on a historical figure.

When the Assyrian king Esarhaddon died unexpectedly of a fever while on campaign, his empire was divided between his two sons. Ashurbanipal, the younger, ruled Assyria, from 668 to 627 BC. His older brother, Shamash-shuma-ukin, took control of Babylon from 667 to 648 BC. On the surface this was an equal division of power, but in fact Ashurbanipal had the controlling share.

The two brothers seem to have lived in amity for some time, but Shamash-shuma-ukin must have known that there was a garrison at Nippur loyal to his brother alone; and that, moreover, several of the Assyrian-manned garrisons in Babylon itself felt their ultimate duty to be to Ashurbanipal. Letters survive from a governor of Ur, in the king of Babylon's province, which show that he, too, was chiefly concerned with paying homage to the Assyrian king, and Ashurbanipal was clearly involved in restoration work in Babylon, the honour of which should have fallen to his elder brother. Inscriptions on restored temples and monuments carry polite references to Shamash-shuma-ukin, but in time the king of Babylon must have become irked by his younger brother's evidently proprietorial attitude; either that, or he was genuinely won over by those locals who sought real independence from Assyria. He formed an alliance with the Elamites, always ready to make trouble in Mesopotamia, with a coalition of other tribes and peoples, and with diehard Chaldean tribes who had never ceased in their desire to throw off the Assyrian yoke. In about 650 BC an open revolt began.

Two years later, after fierce fighting, Assyria had gained the upper hand, and laid siege to both Babylon and Borsippa. Shamash-shuma-ukin's allies had been neutralized, and the Elamites were by now involved in a civil war of their own. By 648 BC, Babylon, in the grip of horrible famine (its citizens were reduced to cannibalism) and probably disease, capitulated, and Assyrian troops entered the city. But before the gates were opened, Shamash-shuma-ukin locked himself into his palace with his immediate entourage and had it set alight, turning it into one vast funeral pyre. This scene is the inspiration for Delacroix's painting, with his calm, resigned and yet somehow indulged king reclining on a massive bed while his soldiers slaughter his wives and his best horses around him. It well sets off, indeed

surpasses, the grandiose closing speech which
Byron gives his Sardanapalus.

Some commentators remark that it is more
likely that Shamash-shuma-ukin committed
suicide by throwing himself into the flames of his
already burning palace. He may simply have been
unable to escape. Either way, it was probably a
better fate than might have befallen him at the
hands of his furious brother: 'As for those men …
who plotted evil against me, I tore out their
tongues and defeated them completely. The
others, alive, I smashed with the very same statues
of protective deities with which they had

smashed my own grandfather, Sennacherib – now
finally as a burial sacrifice for his soul. I fed their
corpses, cut into small pieces, to the dogs, pigs,
zibu-birds, vultures, to the birds of the sky and to
the fish of the ocean.'

Ashurbanipal's grandfather had in fact been
murdered by a couple of his own sons in a palace
coup, but propaganda is nothing new, either.

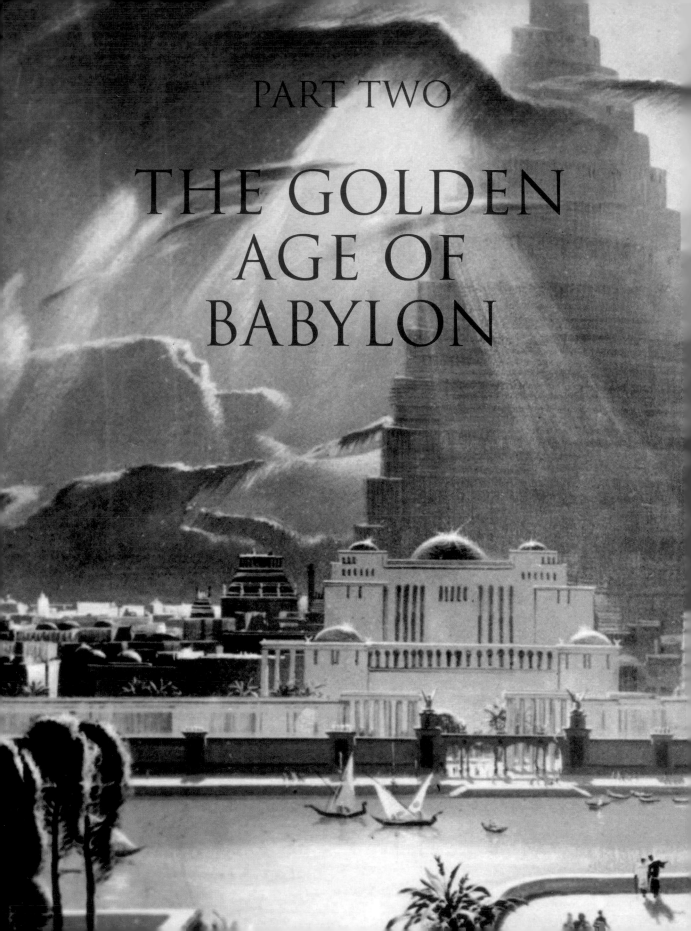

PART TWO

THE GOLDEN AGE OF BABYLON

CHAPTER SEVEN

THE BABYLONIAN REVOLUTION

T HE SILENCE INTO WHICH THE ANNALS OF ASHURBANIPAL lapse after 639 BC points to a period of serious instability. After Ashurbanipal's death there was once again internal discord, and certainly the kings who succeeded him in Assyria were unable to hold on to power in Babylon, as a result of troubles elsewhere in an empire that was already starting to crumble. In any case, during the last 20 years of Ashurbanipal's reign, the city had become politically unimportant.

PREVIOUS PAGES *A wildly fanciful reconstruction (c. 1950) by the Italian illustrator Mario Larrinaga of the city of Babylon in around 625 BC. The 'Tower of Babel' can be seen in the distance, while the Hanging Gardens of Nebuchadrezzar II are in the right foreground.*

RIGHT *A limestone relief of Nabu-apla-iddina, a ninth-century king of Babylon, discovered in Sippar and now in the British Museum. The god Shamash, seated on his throne, receives the homage of two of the faithful, led by a minor deity, identifiable by his fringed robe. On the altar is the sun-disk, the symbol of Shamash.*

The Chaldeans, however, had hung on in the Sealand, and now, in 625 BC, a new leader, Nabopolassar, took advantage of the situation to proclaim himself king of Babylonia. That is not to say that he yet controlled the city of Babylon itself. We know little of Nabopolassar's qualities as a military leader, since his inscriptions concentrate on his building programmes, but he must have been a gifted general. From the inscriptions we learn that he was 'the son of a nobody', and thus not of any royal house. He may not even have been a Chaldean, though he must have held high office in the Sealand region, and he himself claims (perhaps for political reasons) Babylonian nationality. The historian Berossus, writing in about 260 BC, almost 400 years after the events, states that Nabopolassar '*had been appointed a general by Sin-shar-ishkun*'. This muddies the water a little. Sin-shar-ishkun was the penulitmate, and last effective, king of Assyria, who reigned from 623 to 612 BC. Might Nabopolassar have been an Assyrian appointee, sent to southern Babylon to maintain order; but who, seeing a chance of power, organized a rebellion there instead?

Nothing was clear-cut. Through the four much-weakened kings who succeeded Ashurbanipal, Assyria still clung on to the throne of Babylon; and it kept control of its garrison at Nippur, well to the south, during the early years of Nabopolassar's reign. By 620 BC, however, the citizens of that city had become so desperate that they were reduced to selling their children into slavery in exchange for food. History was repeating itself, as the region fragmented into petty rival statelets. Two Assyrians, one a general and the other the crumbling empire's penultimate king, were briefly recognized as rulers in Babylon; archive sources mention several sieges, including ones at Uruk and Nippur, but contemporary reports conflict, and had it not been for Nabopolassar, the whole country might have slid into quasi-anarchy.

THE REDOUBTABLE NABOPOLASSAR

Nabopolassar was clearly a strong-minded and strong-willed individual, a fine general and a good organizer, who could command and depend on the absolute loyalty of his Chaldean followers. He was perhaps aided in this by tribal affiliation. Other circumstances aided him. Elam, for so long the one country to take quick

advantage of any dip in Babylon's fortunes, had been neutralized for good. Already riven by internal strife, the country had been attacked, invaded and devastated by Ashurbanipal's troops in 640 BC. The Assyrian king reported:

> *Susa, the great holy city, abode of their gods, seat of their mysteries, I conquered. I entered its palaces, I opened their treasuries where silver and gold, goods and wealth were amassed … I destroyed the ziggurat of Susa. I smashed its shining copper horns. I reduced the temples of Elam to naught; their gods and goddesses I scattered to the winds. The tombs of their ancient and recent kings I devastated, I exposed to the sun, and I carried away their bones to the land of Ashur. I devastated the provinces of Elam and on their lands I sowed salt.*

Elam only made a partial recovery from this, and its ruin was a double-edged sword, for it would in a very short time be unable to withstand pressure from the southeast, from the rapidly-growing kingdom of Persia which, less than 200 years later, would control an empire which reached from Macedonia to Sind.

Through patience, military skill, determination and diplomacy, Nabopolassar had gained ascendancy over all of southern Mesopotamia by 616 BC, and was ready to march north. So real was the threat that even the pharaoh, Psamtek I (despite the fact that it was less than half a century since Ashurbanipal had sacked Thebes) joined forces with Sin-shar-ishkun of Assyria to face what both kings clearly regarded as a very dangerous new enemy.

Undaunted, in 615 BC Nabopolassar marched on Ashur. He was repulsed, but did not lose all the ground he had gained, falling back as far as Takrit. At this point unsought help came from the Median king, Huvakshatra (624–585 BC), better known to us by his Greek name, Cyaxares, who was pursuing his own territorial ambitions. The Assyrians had besieged Nabopolassar in Takrit, but, getting wind of Cyaxares' troop deployment on their eastern frontier, withdrew to face this new threat.

The Medes were an ancient Iranian people who had migrated westwards in around 1000 BC and settled in what is now northwestern Iran. They were in the process of establishing their own extensive empire, and it was in the common interest of Cyaxares and Nabopolassar to crush what remained of Assyria. In 614 BC the Medes crossed into Assyria from the east. They took the fortress of Tarbisu, only a few miles from Nineveh, sacked Kalhu, and finally took Ashur itself:

> *The Medes made an attack on the town … They destroyed the city wall. They inflicted a terrible massacre on the greater part of the people, plundering the city and carrying off prisoners.*

When we read this, however, we should bear in mind what the Assyrians did to the cities they conquered. The Medes had an ancestral fellow-feeling for the Elamites, whose destruction was fresh in people's memories. It is not unusual even in modern warfare for revenge destruction to be carried out.

Nabopolassar was already marching north again to join his new allies, but arrived too late to take part in the battle for Ashur. Nevertheless, he met Cyaxares on equal terms outside the devastated city and drew up and ratified a formal treaty with him, sealed, so later sources tell us, by the marriage of Nabopolassar's oldest son, Crown Prince Nebuchadrezzar, with Cyaxares' daughter (possibly granddaughter), Amyitis.

THE BABYLONIAN ASCENDANCY

612 BC
Twelve years into his reign, the Chaldean king Nabopolassar of Babylon, together with his allies, the Medes, storms Nineveh and sacks it, bringing the already tottering Assyrian empire to an end forever.

605 BC
The Battle of Carchemish sees Babylonian Crown Prince Nebuchadrezzar rout the remaining Assyrian forces and their Egyptian allies.

597 BC
Nebuchadrezzar crushes first rebellion in Judah. First Babylonian Capitivity.

587 BC
Nebuchadrezzar crushes second rebellion in Judah. Second Babylonian Captivity.

585–572 BC
The siege of Tyre.

555 BC
Nabonidus acquires the throne of Babylon through a palace coup.

552–545 BC
Nabonidus removes the court to Taima in Arabia. His son Belshazzar remains in Babylon as regent.

539 BC
Cyrus II 'The Great' of Persia invades Mesopotamia and takes Babylon. Belshazzar is killed, Nabonidus dies in captivity.

> In the tenth year, in the month of Iyyar, Nabopolassar called out the Babylonian army and marched up the bank of the river Euphrates. The men of Suhu and Hindanu made no attack against him, their tribute they placed before him. In the month of Ab they reported that the Assyrian army was in the city of Qablinu; so Nabopolassar went upstream against them and on the twelfth day of the month of Ab made an attack on the Assyrian army, the Assyrian army then broke off contact from him and he inflicted a great defeat on Assyria.

FROM THE CHRONICLES OF THE CHALDEAN KINGS: NABOPOLASSAR DEFEATS THE ASSYRIANS

BELOW *A reconstructed section of the city walls of Nineveh.*

Clearly Cyaxares regarded Nabopolassar as already too strong to crush. A deal was much the better course of action.

Another setback followed. Nabopolassar had to withdraw to deal with a local uprising in his own territory, possibly fomented by the Assyrians, who sent an army in its support. The Medes were experiencing their own problems to their rear, in the form of a potential threat from the Scythians, formerly allies of Assyria. The Assyrians, who still had a powerful army, counterattacked. In 613 BC they marched on Babylon, as well as recapturing Kalhu, whose shattered defences they repaired. In the event, however, the Scythian menace proved a chimera – they were to join the Median-Babylonian alliance, as each of the three emergent nations sought to help themselves and each other to a share of the empire that was slipping from Assyria's hands. In Babylon, Nabopolassar had no difficulty in crushing the revolt.

THE TIDE TURNS

The tide of war turned in the following year, when a coalition of Babylonian, Median and Scythian forces marched on Nineveh and destroyed it after a siege of only three months. King Sin-shar-ishkun died in the burning city (another possible candidate for the original of Sardanapalus) in 612 BC, and his successor, Ashur-uballit II, now king of virtually nothing, withdrew to the city of Harran. Nabopolassar pursued him there and took the city in 610 BC, establishing a garrison, while Ashur-uballit fled westwards to await Egyptian backup. An inscription of Nabopolassar reads:

> *The Assyrian, who since distant days had ruled over all the peoples, and with his heavy yoke had brought injury to the people of the Land; his feet from Akkad I turned back; his yoke I threw off.*

In the meantime, the Medes would take control of Anatolia, the Scythians spread as far as modern eastern Balkans, as well as the tracts between the Danube and the lower Don rivers; and Babylon got central Assyria and the whole of the region between Babylon itself and Ashur – effectively, all Mesopotamia. At this point it should be stressed that, very possibly, Ashur-uballit met his end at Harran, or even earlier. There is no mention of the Assyrians in that part of *The Chronicles of the*

6In the twenty-first year the king of Akkad (Nabopolassar) stayed in his own land. Nebuchadrezzar his eldest son, the crown prince, mustered the Babylonian army and took command of his troops; he marched to Carchemish which is on the bank of the Euphrates, and crossed the river to go against the Egyptian army which lay in Carchemish … He accomplished their defeat and beat them into non-existence. As for the rest of the Egyptian army which had escaped from the defeat so quickly that no weapon had reached them, in the district of Hamath the Babylonian troops overtook and defeated them so that not a single man escaped to his own country. At that time Nebuchadrezzar conquered the whole of the Hatti country. For twenty-one years Nabopolassar had been king of Babylon. On the eighth of the month of Ab he died; in the month of Elul Nebuchadrezzar returned to Babylon, and on the first day of the month of Elul he sat on the royal throne in Babylon.9

FROM THE CHRONICLES OF THE CHALDEAN KINGS: NEBUCHADREZZAR DEFEATS
THE EGYPTIANS AT CARCHEMISH

ASHURBANIPAL
(r. 668 – 627 BC)

Well-known on account of the exquisite low-relief scenes of his lion hunt in the British Museum, Ashurbanipal was the last major Assyrian king. The empire he presided over from Nineveh stretched from the Zagros Mountains in the east, to Urartu and Anatolia in the north, and from the Taurus Mountains in the west down the whole of the eastern Mediterranean coast, along the Nile in Egypt down as far south as Thebes.

He was the younger son of his predecessor, Esarhaddon. Esarhaddon had unexpectedly fallen ill and died while on his way westwards with his army to quell the forces of Egypt, which had just retaken Memphis. It was Esarhaddon's mother, Naqia-Zakutu, the widow of Sennacherib, who arranged the succession and enforced loyalty to it. Ashurbanipal got Assyria; his older brother got Babylon (which their father had restored). In theory these were equal parts of the empire. In practice, Ashurbanipal's was the controlling power.

He did not base his reputation on military prowess. Though a formidable hunter and campaigner, he emphasized a gentler, more scholarly side of his personality. He was an excellent scribe, proficient in both Akkadian and Sumerian, a mathematician and an astronomer. His library was the greatest collection in the world. Additionally, he managed to hold together his huge empire throughout his reign, definitively crushing

ABOVE *Ashurbanipal, shown in a detail from the alabaster low-relief portraying the king on a lion-hunt.*

Elam, and ultimately Babylon too. But forces were gathering all round the fringes of the empire which his successors would be powerless to resist, and within his borders his own brother would rebel against him at last. Ashurbanipal defeated him in 648 BC, and replaced him with a regent called Kandalanu, who is worth mentioning since he died in the same year as Ashurbanipal, and may have in fact been one and the same man, Kandalanu being possibly a Babylonian name under which Ashurbanipal took the throne. On other fronts, he forced the Egyptian king, the Nubian Taharqa, back down the Nile as far as Thebes, but it was an untenable position: his army was 1242 miles (2000 km) from home, in a hostile and unfamiliar country whose language, customs and religion were completely strange to them. He reinstalled local appointees of his father's, who had fled before Taharqa, as his regents and governors, and withdrew. The Egyptians were soon in rebellion again.

The same thing happened in other parts of the empire, which had grown frankly too large to police. Only in Elam were the locals effectively and totally crushed. But this in itself was a double-edged sword, for the power-vacuum left there would gradually be filled by a new force from the east, the Persians. Their ascendancy spelt the end of the 3000-year history of Mesopotamian independence and even identity.

ABOVE *The king as heroic hunter. Ashurbanipal skewers a lion in a typical regal show of prowess. This moment is the culmination of the hunt shown on the famous relief panel now in the British Museum.*

Chaldean Kings which deals with the final conflict, which appears to have been a straight fight between the Egyptians and the Babylonians.

Psamtek I does not appear to have been a very effective ally to the Assyrians, but his son and successor, Neko II, sent an army, either to support what was left of 'Assyria', or, more likely, simply to block Nabopolassar's westward expansion. It finally linked up with the rump of the Assyrian forces at Carchemish in 605 BC. Neko's army had had a hard time getting there, since Nabopolassar, knowing that Egypt would not welcome a major power once again controlling the Mediterranean coastline so close to its own doorstep, had established diplomatic links with Judea and Gaza, both of which resisted Neko's progress.

By this time, Nabopolassar had been in power for 20 years, and was an ageing man. Moreover, although he had most of Assyria and Babylon under control by that time, there were still pockets of resistance, and it was not considered politic for both the king and the crown prince to be out of Babylon at one and the same time. In 605 BC, Nabopolassar was back in Babylon, and almost certainly dangerously ill. It was his son, Nebuchadrezzar, still in the field in the west, who met the combined Egyptian and Assyrian forces at Carchemish, about 47 miles (75 km) west of Harran. A bloody battle ensued between Egypt and Babylon for the control of the Levant and Syria, since the Assyrian empire was already finished. There were heavy losses on both sides, but the Babylonian troops emerged victorious, finally routing the enemy. The Egyptian army retreated in disorder, and Nebuchadrezzar pursued them southwestwards, down into the Levant. *The Chronicles of the Chaldean Kings* tell us that the Egyptians ran away so fast that '*no weapon had reached them*', and furthermore, that when the Babylonian force caught up with them they were so soundly defeated that '*not a single man escaped to his own country*'.

In this confrontation between Babylon and Egypt, Babylon was the clear victor, and, according to the Roman–Jewish historian Josephus, writing in around AD 80, now controlled the eastern Mediterranean coast and inland of it as far south as the borders of Judea. As for Assyria, it was no more. There were not even survivors to write dirges.

The crown prince only pulled up in his southbound pursuit when news reached him of his father's death. It was imperative for him to return to Babylon immediately to secure the succession, and he did so, leaving the heavy infantry and his captives and booty to follow. According to Berossus:

> … he went in haste, having but few with him, over the desert to Babylon; whither once he was come, he found the public affairs had been managed by the Chaldeans, and that the principal person among them had preserved the kingdom for him. Accordingly he now entirely obtained all his father's dominions.

Nebuchadrezzar got home in 23 days, and was crowned sometime in September 605 BC. In Babylonian terms, the day that he arrived back in what was now his capital was the first day of the month of Elul.

> 'The shield of his mighty men is red, his soldiers are clothed in scarlet; the chariots flash like a flame when mustered in array; the chargers prance.
> The chariots rage in the streets, they rush to and fro through the squares; they gleam like torches, they dart like lightning.
> The officers are summoned, they stumble as they go, they hasten up to the wall, the mantelet is set up.
> The river gates are opened, the palace is in dismay; its mistress is stripped, she is carried off, her maidens lamenting, moaning like doves, and beating their breasts.
> Nineveh is like a pool whose waters run away …'
>
> NAHUM 2; 3–8: ON THE DESTRUCTION OF NINEVEH BY THE BABYLONIANS AND THE MEDES

CHAPTER EIGHT

THE GREAT KING OF THE CHALDEANS

NEBUCHADREZZAR II, 'THE GREAT', whose name literally means 'O Nabu, Defend My Firstborn Son', was the third and last of the kings of Babylon who are familiar to posterity. He is better known to us than Sargon the Great or Hammurabi because scholars, notably the German archaeologist Robert Koldewey, have been able to unearth more of his monuments and other architectural achievements than those of any of his predecessors. Yet the main reason his name is so well-known is due to his appearances in the Hebrew Bible, the *Tanakh*, notably in the Book of Daniel.

Thanks to the eccentric way he is presented in the Book of Daniel, we have a distorted image of the man, about whom, personally, little is known. We do not even have an exact idea of what he looked like, though an engraving of a clean-shaven, helmeted young man in profile may depict the monarch. There are no statues or reliefs of him; indeed very few artefacts have come down to us from his period. His reputation rests almost exclusively on his inscriptions and on his buildings.

True to the long-standing traditions of his forebears, Nebuchadrezzar was prouder of his merits as a builder than of his military triumphs, yet under him the Babylonians expanded their empire once again to the size it had enjoyed in Sargon's day, and indeed exceeded it. But that was not all: during his long reign, which lasted from 604 (his official accession year) to 562 BC, all the disciplines that had been developing over the preceding two millennia were to come to full flower. Babylonian influence in the fields of architecture, astronomy and mathematics were to have an influence that would extend far beyond the frontiers of the

> *How lonely sits the city that was full of people!*
> *How like a widow she has become, she that was great among the nations!*
> *She that was a princess among the cities has become a vassal.*
>
> LAMENTATIONS, 1; 1: JEREMIAH LAMENTS THE FATE OF JERUSALEM AFTER ZEDEKIAH'S ABORTIVE REBELLION

RIGHT Slaughter of the Sons of Zedekiah before their Father, *by the French artist Gustave Doré (1823–83). This brutal act – related in the Old Testament Book of II Kings 25:7 – took place after Zedekiah, king of Judea, rose up against his overlord, the Babylonian ruler Nebuchadrezzar.*

empire, and continue to be influential long after the empire had been swallowed up. His energy, his resilience and his consistency brought a hard-won stability to Mesopotamia that it had seldom enjoyed since it first began to grow into a nation 3000 years earlier. Without detracting from Nebuchadrezzar's military achievements, in which he seems to have followed a broadly Assyrian *modus operandi*, it is true to say that we know so much about them largely because they are unusually well documented. Unlike the Assyrian kings, it was not the habit of Babylonian rulers to devote long sections of their annals to their military achievements. The two most significant of Nebuchadrezzar's successors, Neriglissar and Nabonidus, made important conquests, but of these we know little other than the fact that they took place.

THE HANGING GARDENS OF BABYLON

The Hanging Gardens of Babylon were one of the Seven Wonders of the Ancient World. They were reputedly built by Nebuchadrezzar II to please his wife, Amytis of Media, who was homesick for the lush foliage of her native land. The gardens were apparently destroyed by earthquakes sometime after the second century.

They did not 'hang' in any literal sense; the name derives from an incorrect translation of the Greek word *kremastos* or the Latin *pensilis*, whose sense was closer to 'overhanging'.

They were described by Greek historians such as Strabo and Diodorus Siculus. Strabo wrote that the Gardens consisted of '*vaulted terraces raised one above another, and resting upon cube-shaped pillars. These are hollow and filled with earth to allow trees of the largest size to be planted.*' But Herodotus, arguably a more reliable source, does not mention them, nor do they appear in any contemporary Babylonian documents. This is a telling omission, as Nebuchadrezzar was very proud of his architectural achievements.

The German archaeologist Robert Koldewey thought he had unearthed their foundations, but these were too far from the Euphrates to make irrigation practicable; the remains he found are now thought to be those of vaulted storerooms.

If the Gardens did exist, it is possible that they were in another location. Several Assyrian kings were keen horticulturalists, and the Babylonian location may have been confused with other terraced gardens at Nineveh, which are attested by contemporary clay tablets.

BELOW The Hanging Gardens of Babylon, *by Ferdinand Knab (1834–1902), from a German children's book of 1886.*

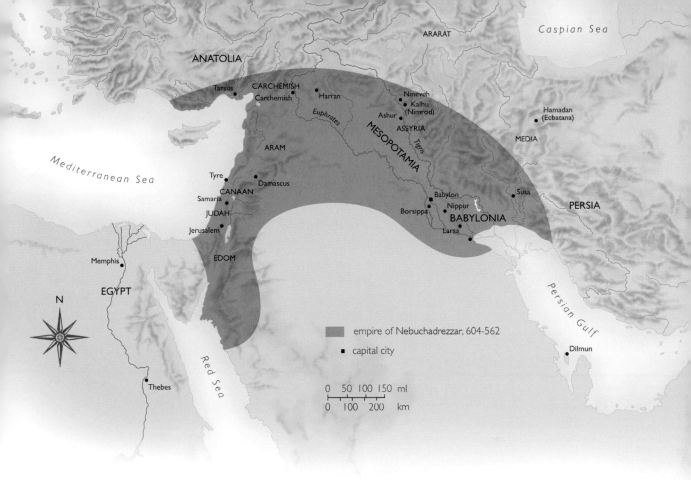

Within 35 years, Nebuchadrezzar had established an empire larger than the one lost by the Assyrians. Across it he established Babylonian law and order, and a mixture of severity and fairness ensured acceptance by most of his vassals, most of the time. Any move towards independence, however, was swiftly slapped down.

It is not easy to say when the Babylonians began to have a true sense of their place in history, or a consciousness that they were responsible for pioneering not only what we would call modern statehood, but also a wealth of institutions and bureaucracies, from government and the development of the professional army, to private and public financial management, private ownership, and the class system. By Nebuchadrezzar's time such matters were fully organized, and the literate élite were well aware of their legacy. Despite the vicissitudes visited on society by imperial ambition down the ages, it had worked in society's favour that religious traditions had very largely remained constant. That we have as great an understanding of their society as we do is due to the fortunate fact that when he took over the Babylonian empire in 539 BC, the Persian overlord Cyrus the Great did so without mass destruction, and not only left the existing infrastructure wholly alone, but respected it. In the course of his invasion, even the Babylonian banks did not close. (Cyrus, unlike the invaders who had gone before him, was taking over a going concern.)

For all that he brought new blood to the throne, then, Nebuchadrezzar was heir to a grand tradition. His father's exploits had, by the time of his son's accession, brought peace and stability to his core region, and the last pockets of dissent were quelled soon after Nebuchadrezzar's arrival (although there was a local uprising as late as 595 BC, which was only suppressed with difficulty). From the moment he ascended the throne, he was able to concentrate on the business of conquest and consolidation abroad.

ABOVE *The empire of Nebuchadrezzar at its height. He spent his entire reign consolidating his empire, and rebuilding the city of Babylon in imperial splendour.*

THE BABYLONIAN CAPTIVITY

When Zedekiah king of Judah and all the soldiers saw them, they fled, going out of the city at night by way of the king's garden through the gate between the two walls; and they went towards the Arabah. But the army of the Chaldeans pursued them, and overtook Zedekiah in the plains of Jericho; and when they had taken him, they brought him up to Nebuchadrezzar king of Babylon, at Riblah, in the land of Hamath; and he passed sentence upon him. The king of Babylon slew the sons of Zedekiah at Riblah before his eyes; and the king of Babylon slew all the nobles of Judah. he put out the eyes of Zedekiah and bound him in fetters to take him to Babylon.

JEREMIAH 39; 4-7

RIGHT *An illumination showing the siege of Jerusalem by Nebuchadrezzar, from* Antiquités Judaiques, *c.1470–76, by the French chronicler Jean Fouquet (c.1420–80).*

After waging a successful war against a rival or an unruly vassal, it was not unusual for the victorious side to carry off with it the gods from the temples of the losers, along with other trophies. Prisoners–of–war became slaves, but although kings boasted of reducing rivals' cities to rubble, this was frequently an exaggeration. Complex though it is, Mesopotamian history can be reduced to a repetition of waves of invaders – more primitive than the occupants but hungry for a better place to live – who then took over the customs and language of those they had defeated, the majority of whom carried on much as before. Especially if the defeated kingdom or city-state had been a rebellious vassal, large numbers of its population were often shifted to places within the dominant country, a puppet ruler or governor set up, and members of the aristocracy or other élites taken to the capital of the dominant country to be brought up and trained in its manners and methods. The Biblical prophet Daniel (who took the Babylonian name Belshazzar) and his companions, who took the names Shadrach, Meshach and Abednego, were among such deportees.

When Nebuchadrezzar put down rebellions in Judah and Israel – actions that have earned him such a bad press in the Bible – he was merely doing to the Judaeans what he would have done to any other rebellious people under his rule. The Babylonian Captivity made famous by the Old Testament was one of several such deportations. In terms of historical accuracy, we should also remember that the Biblical accounts were written in the post-exilic period, that is, after the Persians had sent the Judaeans home. At the time of the Exile and the Captivity, formal modern Judaism had not yet fully evolved. At the time of the Exile, in Nebuchadrezzar's day, attitudes to the gods and to monotheism were more fluid. In Judah itself, Yahweh and his wife Aserah were the principal deities; in Israel, which was more open to foreign (especially Canaanite), influence, other cults, such as those of Bel and Ellil, were perfectly acceptable.

CONTROL OF THE EASTERN MEDITERRANEAN

Since the Medes, who remained allies at least until towards the end of Nebuchadrezzar's reign, held the lands to the north and the east, and the nomadic Arabs in the deserts to the south presented no threat (or inducement to conquer), the challenge came from the east. Nebuchadrezzar had occupied Aram (roughly, modern Syria and Jordan), the Levant and the countries bordering the Mediterranean, Phoenicia, Philistia (from which Palestine derives its name), Moab, Ammon and Israel. The rulers of Damascus, Tyre and Sidon paid him homage. Subsequently, Tyre was to rebel, and when besieged apparently held out for 13 years, after which a compromise peace was reached.

Nebuchadrezzar now inaugurated what was to become an annual tradition of marching through these newly-acquired regions, partly as a show of strength, to remind the inhabitants of who was boss, partly to collect taxes and other tributes, and partly, when necessary – and, following effective Assyrian policy – to crush the slightest hint of dissent wherever it occurred. For example, the *Chronicles* recount the suppression of a rebellion in Ashkelon, after which numerous citizens – including sailors, whose skills were highly sought-after – were forcibly taken back to Babylon. Characteristically, the images of local gods were confiscated; removing a city's protective deities had always been an effective way of ensuring future compliance.

Early on, hitherto unoccupied Judea, under King Jehoiakim, volunteered its allegiance and vassalage, and at this time a number of prominent Judaeans, including Daniel and the three companions who were to endure the ordeal of the 'burning fiery furnace', were taken to Babylon as surety. Daniel was probably not unusual in rising to high rank in his forcibly adopted country, and although in the Bible he is put to many trials both by Nebuchadrezzar and his Persian successors, he overcame them all, and probably ended his days in Babylon, though his triumphant conversions in the name of the Hebrew god Yahweh are Biblical propaganda, written well after the event, after the period of Jewish exile, and in the early years of the emergence of formal Judaism as we know it.

But harsh Assyrian domination was still within living memory and unrest was bound to arise. Not only that, but Necho, the pharaoh of Egypt, had not forgotten his humiliation at Carchemish and needed to nip any possible threat of Babylonian expansion into his rich kingdom in the bud. There was a short and bloody war between the two countries, near the Egyptian frontier, in 601 BC, whose outcome appears to have been inconclusive, and after which both sides withdrew to their own countries to lick their wounds. Nebuchadrezzar's *Chronicles* refer to a major refit of horses and chariots, indicating that what might have been a victory had been thwarted by shortcomings within the mounted division of the Babylonian army.

This setback for Babylon encouraged Egypt's closest neighbour in the region, Judea, to attempt to throw off the Babylonian yoke. Despite the warnings of his advisor Jeremiah, an influential and pro-Babylonian member of the priestly caste, King Jehoiakim stopped paying taxes to Nebuchadrezzar and allied himself to Neko instead. Nebuchadrezzar's response to this was to lead an expeditionary force to Jerusalem, the capital of Judea, and besiege it in 597 BC. Egypt offered no military

> 'I dug out that town gate, I grounded its foundations facing the water strong with bitumen and baked bricks, and caused it to be finely set forth with baked bricks of blue enamel, on which wild oxen and dragons were pictured. I caused mighty cedars to be laid lengthways for its ceiling. Door leaves of cedar covered with copper, thresholds and hinges of bronze I fitted into its gates. Lusty wild oxen and raging dragons I placed at the thresholds. The same town gateways I caused to be made glorious for the amazement of all peoples.'

NEBUCHADREZZAR ON THE ISHTAR GATE

support, and by the time the Babylonian troops arrived, or certainly soon afterwards, Jehoiakim died.

MASS DEPORTATION OF THE JEWS

After a short campaign lasting little more than three months, Nebuchadrezzar's army emerged victorious, and Jehoiakim's young son and heir, Jehoiachin, together with his army, his family, most of the principal civil and military leaders (and all those whose loyalty was in the remotest question) and useful craftsmen were deported to Babylon and resettled there. Jehoiachin was to spend most of his life there, mostly under a form of house arrest. Hebrew records maintain that 10,000 of their nation were uprooted in this exercise. Deportation on a large scale was not uncommon as a way of drawing the teeth of an adversary, while at the same time being an effective means of injecting Babylon with new blood and talent. Apart from the inconvenience – and no doubt, in many cases, heartache – of being uprooted, as Psalm 137 attests, the enforced immigrants were not badly treated, in the main. Nevertheless, the *Tanakh* naturally makes propaganda capital out of Nebuchadrezzar's act (as indeed it does with Sennacherib, the other important Mesopotamian to figure significantly in the Hebrew Bible). Cities such as Lachish and Gaza were left deserted; on the other hand, useful local industries such as wine production were kept in place, supplying wine to Babylon as they formerly had to the royal household in Jerusalem.

The city of Jerusalem, which surrendered, was not razed or even damaged, but a heavy financial tribute was exacted, and – again in accordance with Babylonian custom and practise – treasure from the temple and the palace was confiscated. Nebuchadrezzar returned home in renewed triumph, leaving behind a representative, Mattaniah, who took the official name Zedekiah, to rule Judea.

But the Babylonian king's problems in the region were by no means over. The Egyptians, while they didn't intervene during the operation against Jehoiakim and Jehoiachin, certainly worked on Zedekiah in Nebuchadrezzar's absence. This led to another Judean revolt a decade after the first. Nebuchadrezzar reacted swiftly and severely. He led a large army to Judea, causing the Egyptian ruler Apries (r. 589–570 BC; second successor to Necho II, who had died in 595) to drop his protégé like a hot brick. The Babylonians invaded the country, quickly taking Lachish, which had in the interval been repopulated, and a number of other significant towns before laying siege to Jerusalem. The town held out for eighteen months, at the end of which famine had reduced its ability to resist. The Babylonians breached the walls in 586 BC. Zedekiah and his entourage fled to Jericho but were captured before they could reach it, and they were brought before Nebuchadrezzar at his headquarters on the river Orontes in Syria. Zedekiah, regarded as a traitor, was treated very differently from Jehoiachin; and Nebuchadrezzar, closely following the example set by his Assyrian predecessors, meant to send a clear message to his other client states. First, Zedekiah was forced to witness the execution of his sons. Then he was blinded, and taken to Babylon in chains, where he ended his days in a dungeon. Jerusalem was sacked, its walls torn down, and the temple and palace razed. All Zedekiah's co-conspirators were executed, and another large section of the population carried off captive to Babylon.

Certain radical Islamists have recently chosen to make a hero out of Nebuchadrezzar for his harsh treatment of the people we now call Jews. Yet it should be borne in mind that Nebuchadrezzar's behaviour towards the inhabitants of Israel and Judea was no different from that towards any other vassal or client state, nor did it diverge from that of his Assyrian predecessors. Nebuchadrezzar lived about 150

THE CHALDEAN
DYNASTY AT
BABYLON

625–605 BC
Nabopolassar

604–562 BC
Nebuchadrezzar II
(the Great)

561–560 BC
Amel-Marduk

559–556 BC
Neriglissar

556 BC
Labashi-Marduk

555–539 BC
Nabonidus

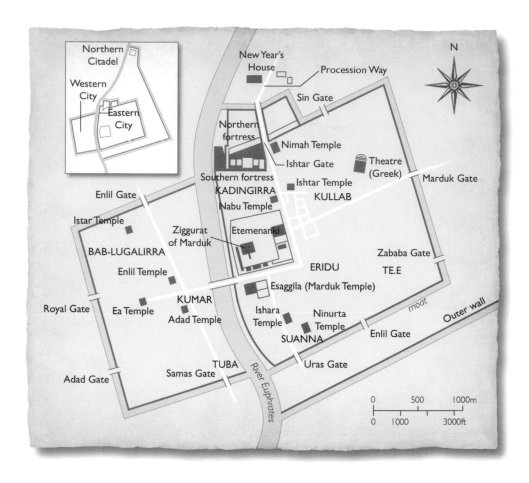

ABOVE *Plan of the city of
Babylon, as rebuilt during the
reign of Nebuchadrezzar II.
Excavations begun here in
1899 by the Deutsche
Orientgesellschaft unearthed
many architectural treasures,
including the magnificent
Ishtar Gate.*

years before the beginning of what we would recognize as formal modern Judaism,
and about 1200 years before the advent of Islam.

STORM CLOUDS IN THE EAST

The two major deportations of Hebrews that constituted the Babylonian Captivity
were brought to an end with the Persian takeover of Mesopotamia. When Cyrus the
Great granted the Hebrews permission to return to their native land, 40,000 of them
accepted the amnesty and left. The lands they returned to had suffered much through
depopulation, especially at the hands of the Assyrians, under whom Israel had lost
almost its entire population. A considerable number elected to remain in Babylon,
where indeed many of them had been born, others stayed because they had married
Babylonians; but for those who did go back it was a time of regeneration and of
reformulation and refounding of their religion. This was a period of great significance for the Hebrews, but Nebuchadrezzar's conquests, impressive though they
were, were only of relative importance in the general scheme of eastern politics at
the time. He might profitably have paid more attention to the storm clouds gathering
on his eastern frontiers. However, even if he had been able to act on any information
his spies brought him from there, it is doubtful that even he would have been able
to stem the tide that would engulf his empire just over 20 years after his death.

NEBUCHADREZZAR'S BUILDING PROGRAMME

Perhaps he had no inkling of what was coming; in any event, the latter years of his reign are shrouded in mystery for us. What we do know is that during the active, documented years, he concentrated his energy at home on a vast programme of building and reconstruction, as if he were creating the foundation of a dynasty he imagined would last for centuries. What we know of the city of Babylon as a structure is his city, built, as was the general habit, on top of what had gone before.

Today, more than 2,500 years later, all that greets the eye at the site are piles of bricks and heaps of sand. The city's state of dereliction has been brought about by the sheer passage of time, long neglect, and the recent barbarism of yet another invader in the region. Even so, it is still possible to imagine the incredible impression that Babylon – then the foremost city in the world – must have made when it was in its heyday.

Nebuchadrezzar was justly proud of his work as a builder, reconstructed examples of which can at least be seen in the Vorderasiastisches Museum in Berlin, in the form of a reconstruction of the Ishtar Gate. Stamped on many thousands of the millions and millions of bricks he had made for his construction programme – bricks so well made that not only in Persian but well into the Hellenistic period and even recent times they have been continually pilfered for use in other structures – he set various forms of proclamation, including:

> 'The word of the Lord came to me: "Son of man, you dwell in the midst of a rebellious house, who have eyes to see, but see not, who have ears to hear, but hear not; for they are a rebellious house. Therefore, son of man, prepare yourself an exile's baggage and go into exile by day in their sight; you shall go like an exile from your place to another place in their sight. Perhaps they will understand, though they are a rebellious house'
>
> EZEKIEL 12; 1–3: THE PROPHET WARNS OF THE BABYLONIAN CAPTIVITY

> *Nebuchadrezzar, King of Babylon, the fosterer of Esagila (the temple of Marduk in Babylon) and Ezida (the temple of Nabu in Kalhu), son of Nabopolassar, King of Babylon, am I. The palace, the dwelling-place of my majesty, I built on the place of Babil. I grounded its foundations firm on the bosom of the Underworld, and with asphalt and baked bricks I raised it mountain high. By thy behest, Marduk, wise one of the gods, may I be satisfied with the fullness of the house that I have built, along with my posterity. May my posterity bear rule in it forever over the black-haired people.*

Inscriptions also appeared on flagstones and thresholds, but those on the bricks were hidden as they were laid. As such, they have been preserved for posterity, as Nebuchadrezzar intended.

The practice of brick-stamping was continued by Nebuchadrezzar's successors, Neriglissar and Nabonidus. The possibility of marking bricks in this way in such numbers suggests that the Babylonians had invented typesetting, and this has been confirmed by cuneiform experts, who have discovered on a fragment of a clay tablet one line which has been 'printed' in error upside-down. In additon, certain individual touches are also apparent on some of the bricks; for example, sometimes the workmen would add to the formal Akkadian inscription their own signature in Aramaic, which had become the language of the common people by Nebuchadrezzar's day.

Despite the fact that they are battered and heavily weathered, Nebuchadrezzar's temples and palaces are still *in situ*; and remain his greatest and most enduring monument.

NEBUCHADREZZAR II
('THE GREAT' r. 605–562 BC)

Nebuchadrezzar, son of Nabopolassar, who in alliance with the Medes had conquered and routed the Assyrians and their Egyptian allies, was campaigning in the west, mopping up the last pockets of Assyrian resistance and an Egyptian expeditionary force sent by Pharaoh Necho II (r. 610–595 BC) when news came to him of his father's death in Babylon. It had been impolitic for both father and son to be away from the capital together, and to forestall any possible power vacuum, Nebuchadrezzar hastened back to his capital, where he was crowned on 6 or 7 September, 605 BC.

A tough, energetic man, and a tireless campaigner, once Nebuchadrezzar had brought order and stability to his empire, which covered most of the old Assyrian empire plus swathes of northern Arabia and the northeastern coast of the Red Sea, he set about the task of rebuilding and restoring his capital. What has been excavated indicates that in his day it must have been the most magnificent city in the world. Here, he constructed a splendid palace, a great ziggurat, a vast temple to Marduk, and, possibly, the famous Hanging Gardens. These last, legend has it, were built for his wife, a granddaughter of the Median king Cyaxares.

According to his own records, he was prouder of his work as a builder than his work as a general. A tunnel and a bridge linked the two sides of the city separated by the Euphrates, and a triple line of defensive walls was constructed to defend his capital. Built to last forever, his edifices were a mark of his greatness, and were designed to proclaim for all eternity: I was here. A sense of one's place in time, and of history, was already well-implanted in the Babylonian psyche. In Nebuchadrezzar's day, there was already a national museum in Babylon.

Nebuchadrezzar is most familiar to us through several books of the Old Testament, notably in the books of Jeremiah, and Daniel (where his name is given in its incorrect but well-known form of 'Nebuchadnezzar'). Jeremiah led a pro-Babylonian faction in Judah, while Daniel was a well-treated captive in Babylon (the lions' den episode is supposed to have occurred after the Persians had taken over). Daniel evidently elected to stay behind in Babylon after his fellow-countrymen had been allowed to go home, and had a job as a senior satrap, taking the Babylonian name Belshazzar ('Belteshazzar' as the Bible spells it). In the Book of Daniel, Nebuchadrezzar emerges as an intemperate and credulous character, but the emphasis on the importance of the interpretation of dreams, at which Daniel is a past master, has its basis in fact. One of the most interesting episodes is that in which the king is punished for hubris by being condemned to live in the wild: '*He was driven from among men, and ate grass like an ox; and his body was wet with the dew of heaven till his hair grew as long as eagles' feathers, and his nails were like birds' claws.*' Various interpretations have been placed on this: that Nebuchadrezzar went temporarily mad; or that this is a confusion with a later Babylonian king, Nabonidus (r. 556–539 BC), who left Babylon for the desert station of Taima for ten years for reasons not yet definitively explained; but it should also be borne in mind that letting one's hair and nails grow was

ABOVE *The English mystical poet and painter William Blake (1757–1827) worked on this vision of the madness of Nebuchadrezzar between 1795 and 1805. It graphically shows the Babylonian king's madness during his banishment in the wilderness.*

often an indication of mourning. No explanation detracts from the beauty of the poetry of the writer of the Book of Daniel, nor from William Blake's powerful etching.

The Bible's interest in Nebuchadrezzar derives from his activities in Israel and especially Judah, where he was obliged to put down two rebellions, resulting in the deportation of tens of thousands of Judaeans, who were settled, in accordance with custom, within the frontiers of the Babylonian empire, in an area south of the city of Babylon, along the banks of the Euphrates. Encompassing the city of Borsippa, the settled area reached almost as far as Uruk. It is highly likely that the rank-and-file of the Judaeans were used as labourers on Nebuchadrezzar's enormous projects.

His last years, and the manner of his death, are obscure. Together with Sargon and Hammurabi, Nebuchadrezzar had been one of the greatest of the Babylonian kings. After him, night drew in swiftly on the Babylonian empire.

CHAPTER NINE

BUILDING AND REBUILDING

S INCE SARGON'S DAY KINGS HAD BEEN BUILDERS. The importance of building to the Mesopotamian imperial psyche is attested by figurines showing the king carrying a bricklayer's basket on his head, which existed from the earliest times through to the reign of Ashurbanipal. What is more, copper figures of gods holding pegs used in the building process, and often covered with votive inscriptions, were ritually buried in the foundations of buildings to protect them.

The basic building material in Mesopotamia was the brick, made of mud, either sun-dried or hard-baked (the best quality) in furnaces, while the mortar used was clay or bitumen, with reed matting dispersed along the courses. Gypsum, which has a high tolerance to water, was used for gutters and drainage systems. So effective was it that on one occasion, after archaeologists had unearthed such a system that had lain buried for thousands of years, a sudden downpour demonstrated to them that it was still effective.

What we know of Babylon is limited to the late period – namely, the building programmes of Nabopolassar, Nebuchadrezzar and their principal successor, Nabonidus. Sargon's city was obliterated by the shifting course of the Euphrates, while later constructions were swept away at the destruction of Babylon by Sennacherib; and Esarhaddon's reconstruction was absorbed into the work of the later Babylonian kings.

MONUMENTAL STRUCTURES

Palaces and temples were built on a monumental scale. Few or no windows pierced their high uncompromising walls, which rose above the streets and the poorer parts of the town. In humbler dwellings, too, no windows were to be found, although open frontages indicated the presence of shops. Houses were built along narrow streets (some so narrow that a donkey and a person could not pass) and were contiguous with one another. Rubbish of all sorts was simply thrown into these streets, so that the ground level of cities rose over time, with new buildings simply erected on top of the debris. An interim measure was to build steps down from one's front door into the house, as the street level rose above the level of the interior. This habit of filling the public thoroughfare with detritus, extraordinary in a climate that did not promote hygiene, persisted over millennia.

Inside the houses, behind thick walls, it was dark and cool. Most people lived their daily lives in the open or on the roofs of houses. The interiors of palaces were sometimes illuminated with light from above, and the walls were decorated with murals or painted low-relief sculpture celebrating in narrative form – a kind of strip

RIGHT *A deliberately antique-style stele depicting Ashurbanipal as a hod-carrier, a pose that builder-kings had affected in their public image for two millennia. This artefact was found in the Sumerian city of Borsippa.*

cartoon – the king's achievements on the field of battle and as a sportsman. From a very early date, lion-hunting became a royal prerogative.

'Babylon lies in a wide plain, a vast city in the form of a square with sides nearly fourteen miles long and a circuit of some fifty-six miles, and in addition to its enormous size it surpasses in splendour any city of the known world. It is surrounded by a broad deep moat full of water, and within the moat there is a wall fifty royal cubits wide and two hundred high ... On the top of the wall they constructed, along each edge, a row of one-roomed buildings facing inwards with enough space between for a four-horse chariot to turn. There are a hundred gates in the circuit of the wall, all of bronze with bronze uprights and lintels.'

HERODOTUS: *THE HISTORIES* (c. 450 BC)

BUILDING FOR DEFENCE, PIETY AND PLEASURE

Nebuchadrezzar was not just interested in building palaces and renovating temples, however, though the latter work was of enormous theological importance. He was especially preoccupied with strengthening the defensive walls of his capital. Babylon was built on either side of the Euphrates, the greater, older part, which contained the palace and the temple complexes, on the east bank, and a smaller, newer section on the west. These were encircled by two walls, an inner and an outer, separated by a distance of 7 metres (23 ft). The outer wall was about 3.5 metres (12.5 ft) thick, but the inner was a massive 6.5 metres (22 ft), wide enough for chariots to be driven along the road that surmounted it. This facilitated fast communication between the towers and a central command post.

The walls were punctuated by guard-towers every 18 metres (60 ft), and in all probability pierced by a total of eight gates, each named after a god. To complete the defences, Nabopolassar had breached the Euphrates to create a moat, which his son completed by increasing the height of its embankments. In addition, he added a third defensive wall beyond the moat for the eastern sector; serious trouble had always come from the east. This was also protected by a second moat. The Euphrates itself was crossed by a toll-bridge, with limestone piers and brick pontoons facing upstream, connecting the two sides of the city, although the two sides would also have been linked by ferries. The Achilles heel of the defences, the points at which the river entered and left it, were protected by heavy iron grilles across the water.

The sheer size of the city was also impressive. It covered an area of about 200 hectares (c. 500 acres), had a population of 100,000 – though it was large enough to hold 250,000 – and contained some 1200 temples. Its ground-plan was roughly square, within the two original defensive walls, but the third wall, about 9 miles (14 km) long, built in the east by Nebuchadrezzar, added '*four thousand cubits of land to each side of the city*' (the Nippur cubit measured c.0.5 metre), and encompassed a sprawling suburb of mud houses and reed huts amidst palm groves and allotments.

Within the city of Babylon, Nebuchadrezzar restored and embellished the great temple of Marduk, the Esagila, as well as its ziggurat, the Etemenanki. Despite the fact that they had been badly damaged by Sennacherib, neither of these buildings required extensive renovation, since much had been done in the interim by Esarhaddon and Ashurbanipal. Nevertheless, both as a public gesture of piety and as a politically expedient measure, Nebuchadrezzar needed to put his own stamp on them. The Esagila, for example, was furnished with new cedarwood fittings, and decorated with gold, silver and precious stones. Some modern writers maintain that Nebuchadrezzar's building works occupied the greater part of his reign. Even towards the end, he was constructing a defensive wall in the neighbourhood of

Sippar, which suggests that the Median alliance was wearing thin. (This 'Median Wall' was erected at the 'waist' of the Tigris and the Euphrates, close to the site of Ibbi-Sin's earlier defensive structure. It immediately calls to mind the historical parallel of the walls of the Roman emperors Hadrian and Antoninus in northern Britain.) But Nebuchadrezzar's work outside Babylon did not stop there: his men were busy restoring and rebuilding in Ur and in most of the other ancestral cities of the region.

He had at least three palaces. The original palace of Babylon, the Southern Palace, was expanded to five courtyards, with room in the complex to house the garrison, the administrators' offices and quarters, a ceremonial wing containing the formal throne-room, and another for his own private residence. It was here, on the north side, that Robert Koldewey thought he may have discovered the remains of the foundations of the fabled Hanging Gardens, though that supposition has now been discounted. What he had actually found is now believed to be vaulted store rooms – the vaults acting as supports for the Processional Way, part of which ran above them. But if this was not the site of the Hanging Gardens (if, indeed, the Hanging Gardens were ever here; the *Chronicles* contain no reference to them) there would certainly have been other, more conventional gardens, and splendid ones at that, for the king, his consort, and the city's élite to enjoy.

ABOVE *An Assyrian building site: workmen are seen carrying implements and ropes for moving a Winged Bull in plate 17 from* Nineveh and its Remains *(1849) by Austen Henry Layard. Layard's sketch is of an original relief sculpture depicting the scene.*

There was also a 'summer palace', north of the main complex and situated between the outermost and middle city walls, which housed a private museum, containing, among other treasures, artefacts from Ur III. A third palace abutted the outermost wall on the northern edge of the city.

ARCHITECTURAL JEWELS IN BABYLON'S CROWN

What remains most vivid in our conception of Babylon, however, thanks to the painstaking excavation and reconstruction by Koldewey, is the ceremonial Ishtar Gate and its Processional Way, built in the northwest quarter of the city, near the Southern Palace and the citadel. The image of the god Marduk passed through the Gate and along the Way on his annual journey to the *bit-akitu*, or New Year Festival House, every spring, on the occasion of the festival. The *bit-akitu* was set in a fastidiously well-planted park just to the north of the city, probably within the confines of the third wall. The Processional Way, which was also used for the ceremonial departure on campaign of the army and its triumphant return, was 21 metres (69 ft) wide, and flanked on each side by walls covered with coloured glazed decorative bricks and a motif of walking lions, all in relief. Its Akkadian name was *ai-ibur-sabu*,

NEBUCHADREZZAR THE BUILDER KING

The German archaeologist Robert Koldewey (1855–1925), who conducted major digs in Babylon between the closing years of the 19th century and the opening years of the 20th, was responsible for revealing to us for the first time the magnificence of Nebuchadrezzar's building programme. Among the jewels, now to be seen (in reconstruction) in the Vorderasiatisches Museum in Berlin, were the Ishtar Gate and the Processional Way that led to it.

The Ishtar Gate is one of the most beautiful buildings of the ancient world, and we are fortunate that it survived. Its ceremonial purpose (and that of its contiguous Processional Way) was to allow the ceremonial passage of the image of the city-god, Marduk, from his temple out of the city to the *bit akitu* (House of the Spring Festival) in commemoration of his victory over the forces of chaos, as part of the Akitu, the most important festival in the Babylonian year. It stands 14 metres (46 ft) high and is 30 metres (98 ft) wide. Clad in the most expensive, coloured and glazed brick, it was originally decorated with nine alternating rows of beasts, all in relief on brick: each brick depicting an animal had to be designed and then placed so that the animal's form would emerge precisely when in position. The background is blue, and the beasts are yellow. They are the bull, associated with the storm-god, Adad, and the *mushushu*, a mythical creature associated with Marduk, although some scholars have tried to link it to the *mkolo-mbembe*, a giant lizard or sauropod of the Congo; however, the existence of that animal is disputed. The *mushushu* has all the attributes of a mythical beast, combining the strongest features of several: the head of a horned viper, the body of a lizard, the forelegs of a lion, the hindlegs of an eagle, and a scorpion's tail.

The Processional Way, 21 metres (69 ft) wide, is adorned with lions, the beast of Ishtar, who prowl along under an ornate pattern of columns or stylized trees embellished with a floral motif, all similarly in painted and glazed low-relief brick.

Nebuchadrezzar was also responsible for the Hanging Gardens of Babylon, of which no trace remains. Certainly hanging (terraced) gardens of the type described by early historians such as Herodotus and Diodorus did exist, but have only been attested at Nineveh. The legend claims that Nebuchadrezzar had them built for his wife, Amytis of Media (the nation most closely allied to Babylon) who was homesick for the trees and fragrant plants of her homeland. Scientists and archaeologists have pondered long and hard about the engineering problems associated with creating such gardens and keeping them irrigated. It has been calculated that they would have required 300 cubic tonnes of water a day to be lifted to the upper terraces, possibly by Archimedean screw. Although there were lavish royal parks, furnished with wild animals, close to the city, no

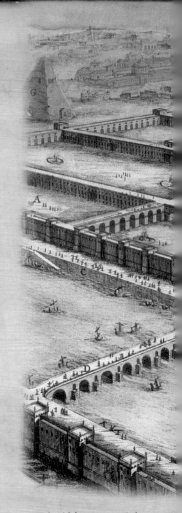

ABOVE *An 18th-century artist's impression of Nebuchadrezzar's Babylon, looking approximately northeast, and showing the Euphrates Bridge, the ziggurat, and the Royal City, from* Entwurf einer historischen Architektur, *1721, by the Austrian architect Johann Fischer von Erlach (1656–1723).*

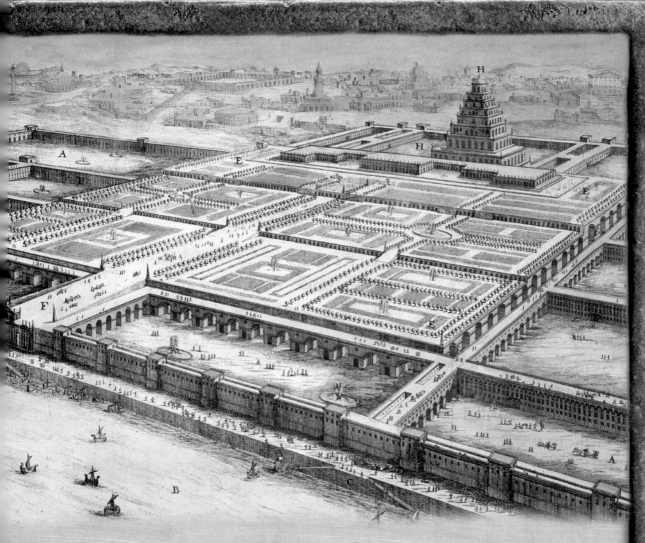

mention of the gardens has ever been found in any extant text from the period.

In addition, Nebuchadrezzar renovated and expanded the royal palace (the 'Shining Residence'), the Esagila, or Great Temple, of Marduk, and the mighty ziggurat, *Etemenanki* – a Sumerian word meaning 'House of the Foundation of Heaven on Earth'. The *Etemenanki* is a strong candidate for being the original of the Tower of Babel.

Nebuchadrezzar also organized the building of a system of massive fortified walls. For these projects he is reputed to have had baked 15 million bricks in his furnaces, many thousands of them stamped with his name.

He also undertook some restoration work at Ur, continued by his later successor, Nabonidus. It is no wonder he considered his work as a builder more important than his achievements as a general (though these were also considerable).

variously translated as: '*may the proud not flourish*', or '*may the enemy not cross it*'. The Gate, covered in blue glazed brick, displayed reliefs of bulls and the dragon-like beast associated with Marduk. So great was this building's votive importance that the rows of relief animals were continued, though not in glazed brick, right down into the foundations. The estimated total number of animal images is 575.

The Ishtar Gate gives us a fleeting impression of what at least the imperial quarter of the city would have looked like at the height of its power. Everything would have been lavishly decorated with the most expensive materials available, as an inscription indicates: '*Silver, gold, costly precious stones, bronze, wood from Magan* [a region variously identified with Nubia, Oman and the Indus Valley], *everything that is expensive, glittering abundance, the products of the mountains, the treasures of the seas, large quantities of goods, sumptuous gifts, I brought to my city of Babylon before Marduk.*'

A MAGNIFICENT CITY BUILT TO LAST

The impression that Nebuchadrezzar thereby wished to convey – of wealth and might beyond imagination – would thus not simply have been sent but positively hammered home. In his passages on the splendour of the city, Herodotus mentions gates of bronze; it is certainly attested from archaeology that lintels and thresholds were cast in that metal, while heavy wooden gate-doors were clad in copper or bronze. The effect of the sun shining on them would have been dazzling. One curiosity is worthy of note: although, unlike the Egyptians, the Babylonians mastered the vault and the arch, they never adopted the hinge. Doors swung on a pivot-and-socket principle. Sometimes votive figurines were buried beneath these.

Above all, Nebuchadrezzar had his buildings designed to last. His kilns produced the finest-quality bricks ever made. More than any of his predecessors, he took precautions against the vagaries of the shifting course of the Euphrates, and paid particular attention to refurbishing and maintaining his canal systems. Nor did he neglect the suburbs on the west bank. In addition, all citizens of Babylon enjoyed special tax privileges and other concessions.

Prior to Nebuchadrezzar's reign, even the greatest Mesopotamian cities had been victims of sand, rain and river. Mud-brick can never be as durable as stone, and the incentive, money and technical means to produce fire-baked bricks in great quantities had not hitherto been strong enough. Nebuchadrezzar regarded himself as the scion of a new dynasty that would establish Babylon once and for all as the centre of the world, and from his point of view he controlled most of it, and had the means to buy what he could not produce at home. Also, lurking at the back of his mind was the spectral memory of the Assyrian empire, which after 300 years had crumbled to nothing in thirty. He was determined that such a fate was not going to befall his realm; and accordingly he would build a city so strong that no-one could destroy it.

FAR LEFT *A reconstruction of the Ishtar Gate in situ at Babylon. Clearly visible are the alternating rows of glazed-brick reliefs showing aurochs and the mythical dragon-like beast known as the* sirrush.

BELOW *One of the many thousands of bricks carrying the identifying stamp of Nebuchadrezzar. Inscriptions varied according to where and for what purpose the bricks were used.*

CHAPTER TEN
LITERACY AND LANGUAGE

AT ROOT, LANGUAGE IS A MEANS OF COMMUNICATION, while literacy is a means of keeping records, and of fixing that communication. The need to keep records began very early in ancient Mesopotamia. By Nebuchadrezzar's time, Akkadian, which had been the dominant language of speech and writing since the days of Sargon, had largely – except for official records and formal discourse – been supplanted by Aramaic, a far more flexible language.

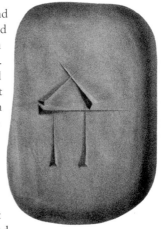

Since it had an alphabet, Aramaic was much easier to read and write than cuneiform, which required specialized knowledge, and time and patience to master (and which also evolved over the millennia in which it was in use). In consequence, Aramaic inexorably gained widespread acceptance among the country's population. The advent of Aramaic marks the true democratization in Mesopotamia of the written word, which had hitherto been the preserve of the priestly and administrative classes. Creative writers, whose identities (apart from that of Sargon's daughter Enheduanna) we do not know, would have come from one of those two classes, or from an educated élite. From Sumerian times there is evidence of the existence of the *edubba*, the Tablet House. The *edubba* was the scribal school, usually attached to a temple, and here it was that scholars learned to become scribes, a highly-regarded and highly specialized profession. Even after the introduction and development of cuneiform the art of writing could take years to master, since countless different combinations of forms had to be learned by heart in order to create words.

NEAR RIGHT *A cuneiform sign on a bulla, a clay token used for tallying goods. Cuneiform script was devised by the Sumerians no later than c.3100 BC and spread to other language groups in Mesopotamia.*

THE DISCOVERY OF AKKADIAN AND SUMERIAN

Akkadian had itself supplanted Sumerian, the first language of Mesopotamia so far discovered that scholars can confidently identify and read. Sumerian was spoken in southern Mesopotamia from at least the fourth millennium and lasted until the beginning of the second, although it continued to be used in a rarefied, classical form for another two thousand years thereafter. During the whole time it was in use, it continued to evolve, and experts divide it into several different periods. It is a language isolate (that is, no other languages relate to it), and its origins are obscure to us. Akkadian, a more accessible language which is part of the Semitic linguistic group, provided scholars with the key to understanding it, since many bilingual Akkadian–Sumerian documents have survived.

FAR RIGHT *A fine example of deeply incised cuneiform script from Nimrud. By around 100 BC, cuneiform had been largely superseded by the North Semitic script used to represent the increasingly dominant Aramaic language.*

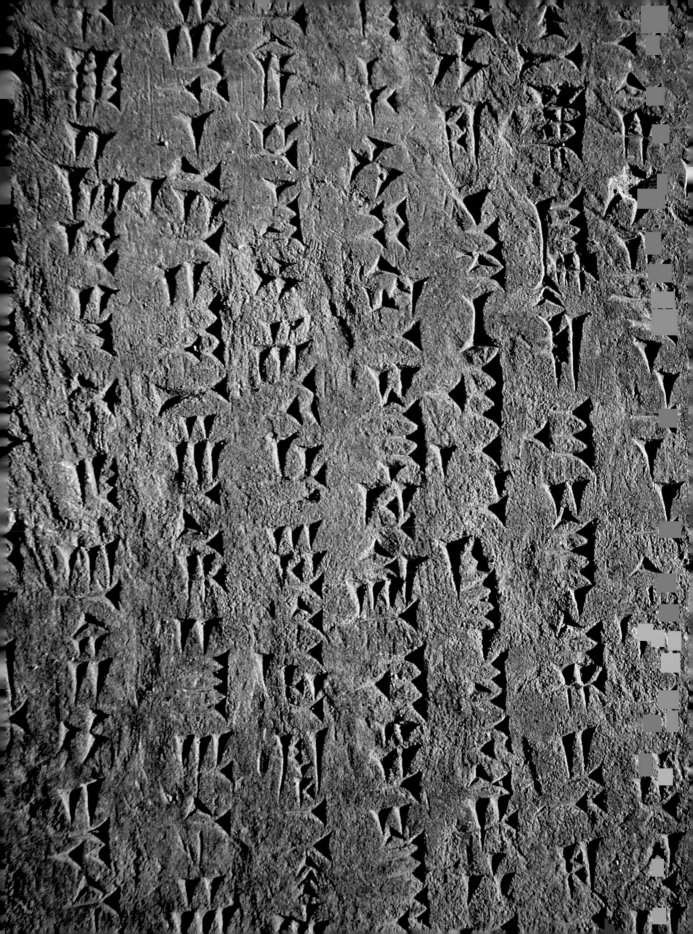

In the 1830s, Sir Henry Rawlinson (1810–95), a young English baronet and Oriental linguist working for the Persian army, copied an inscription carved high on Mount Bisitun, situated in what had been ancient Elam. The inscription was in three different types of cuneiform, one of which Rawlinson recognized as Old Persian, and a second, from previous experience, as Old Elamite. Starting with the Persian, and inspired by the French scholar Jean-François Champollion's deciphering a few years earlier of Egyptian hieroglyphs on the Rosetta Stone, Rawlinson worked his way towards a similar decipherment of Akkadian. The first door was opened. Yet cuneiform is not an alphabet, but a syllabary, which means that it binds consonants to certain vowels, and these series of combinations have to be learned.

Not long after Rawlinson's breakthrough, it was noticed that certain words, both in the Bisitun inscriptions and ones discovered subsequently, were not Akkadian. In addition, as several archaeological expeditions towards the end of the 19th century, notably that of the University of Pennsylvania to Nippur in 1888, began to discover Sumerian sites, it became apparent that an earlier language than Akkadian had also been written in cuneiform. Sumerian is the first written language we know of,

THE DEVELOPMENT OF WRITING

No society with any degree of complexity, however rudimentary, can do without administration. Administration means bureaucracy and bureaucracy means records. The invention of writing was inevitable, and it was the Mesopotamians who first developed it.

There was a need, first of all, to identify ownership of or responsibility for goods – goods, for example, that were being traded or handled on behalf of another person. There was also the need to keep accounts, which had been done in the very early Ubaid period by the use of tokens as counters, which were then sealed in clay 'envelopes', the number they contained being stamped on the outside, so that numbers in all likelihood preceded 'words'. But there was then the need to describe what precise commodity the number referred to – sheep, measures of barley, numbers of bricks, for example. To do this the thing referred to had to be identified in some way or another – by a seal attached to the 'envelope' which would establish ownership, or by a pictogram, or basic drawing, of the object, with the number placed by its side. These original texts, the earliest of which so far discovered were found at Uruk, date from around 3400 BC, roughly a century or so after the foundation of the first real cities, and concurrent with the rise of the priest-administrator, for in the beginning the temples were also the centres

ABOVE *Early Sumerian stone document showing ideograms, the precursor of true writing, from Uruk (late fourth to early third millennium).*

of food distribution and general social regulation. The original 'texts' are very terse indeed.

There were technical difficulties too. The cylinder seal, which, rotated over the damp clay, could carry more information than the stamp seal, was one solution; but it remained hard to 'draw' pictures with a reed in damp clay. The Ancient Egyptians had available to them papyrus, pens and ink, and their language and written records developed exponentially from the middle of the third millennium. The Mesopotamians had to seek another solution. By 2500 BC, the Sumerians had developed arrangements of wedge-shaped symbols (called cuneiform, from the Latin *cuneus*, 'wedge') which replaced the pictograms and could easily be stamped into soft clay with an appropriately shaped tool. This improvement opened the doors to true writing, and liberated its use from mere record-keeping. Gradually, the means was found to write real words. Before the last quarter of the third millennium, literature was being created.

Many of the clay tablets dealing with everyday life seen in museums today are about the size of a modern BlackBerry smartphone. Like the BlackBerry, they were deliberatley sized so that they could conveniently be held in one hand, while the other worked on the surface.

although cuneiform may be said to derive from the pictograms employed by recording scribes in the Uruk period which predated Sumer.

Sumerian presents several challenges: it is not only an isolate, but also agglutinative; this means that any given word might consist of a number of prefixes and suffixes and other recognizably separable word-forming units. Hungarian and Finnish (the Finno–Ugric language group) are modern examples of agglutinative languages; anyone used to other, more common modern languages, which are not agglutinative, finds them difficult to learn. Many Sumerian words persisted long after the language's demise, and recur frequently in any study of ancient Mesopotamia, for example, *lugal*, king (which is composed of the elements *lu-gal*, literally 'man-big').

BELOW *A heavily inscribed cuneiform stone tablet, known as the Saturn Ephemeris (c. 500 BC), from the British Museum collection.*

A great king or an emperor would be: *lugal-gal-gal*. Similarly the word for a palace, *egal*, is *e-gal*: 'house-big'. The basic term for a woman, *nin*, is apparent in the Sumerian names of several goddesses, such as Ninhursag or Ninlil. However, there were also many gods whose names are prefixed '*Nin-*'. Experts are still not agreed upon the precise nature of the Sumerian language and its grammar.

Akkadian was introduced when the Amorites, whose language it was, took over control of southern Mesopotamia from the rulers of Ur who had hitherto held sway there. It is generally agreed that as a common language, Sumerian did not survive the Ur III period, and although Ur-Nammu had a Sumerian name, it is likely that Akkadian was already being spoken during his dynasty. In the *edubbas*, and in scholastic centres like Nippur, Sumerian may have clung on a little while longer, just as Latin survived in universities, the Church, and among scholars, throughout the medieval and post-medieval periods, and into the modern day.

Akkadian survived in Mesopotamia from around 2400 BC to AD 100. The Akkadians adopted cuneiform to write their language, although it had to be adapted, since cuneiform was incapable of reproducing certain Akkadian linguistic forms. Akkadian had three genders – masculine, feminine and the rare common or neuter – and three cases, the nominative, accusative and genitive. Adjectives and nouns were declined in the same way. The bulk of the literature, records and correspondence that has come down to us is in Akkadian. Even after the advent of Aramaic, it remained the language of record-keeping.

> ‘If the young son of the *edubba* [tablet-house, or scribal school] Has not recited his tasks correctly The elder brother and his father will beat him.’

> ‘This is the roster of the days I spent at school: I had three days off a month, There were three holidays a month, That makes twenty-four days a month That I spent at school, oh, no, that wasn't so long!’

> AKKADIAN DICTA ON THE IMPORTANCE OF LEARNING

THE RISE OF ARAMAIC

Aramaic has a long history, dating back 3000 years, and is still spoken today, though only in an extremely limited way as a liturgical language among certain groups such as Syriac Christians. It is a Semitic language, and at its height was so widespread that it embraced several different forms, which over time evolved into an entire group of related languages and dialects.

The Aramaeans began to settle in Mesopotamia during the 12th century BC and their numbers grew fast. Their language spread with them, and the use of their alphabet, which was much easier to use and more adaptable than Akkadian, also became widespread. The alphabet was based on Phoenician script, and forms of Aramaic were spoken in the eastern Mediterranean lands conquered by the Assyrians and thereafter the Babylonians. As Aramaic spread eastwards and southwards, different dialects developed in, for example, Babylon and Egypt, but it was the form used in Babylon, which in turn had been influenced by Akkadian, that became predominant. So successful was it that its spread continued long after the end of the last Babylonian empire, surviving the Persian invasion, and only being supplanted by Greek in Egypt and Syria in the third century BC. To the east of those countries, and in Palestine, it continued to flourish, and was still in common use there in Roman and early Christian times.

CHAPTER ELEVEN
THE ARTS

THE LEISURE CREATED BY GROWING PROSPERITY IN MESOPOTAMIA stimulated the growth of a specialized class of people who could support themselves through their skills – artists. Four forms of art were especially prevalent: music, dance, literature and sculpture. There was as yet no drama as we would understand it, nor any painting other than decoration on pottery and figurines.

RIGHT *Seventh-century* BC *limestone stele from the palace of Ashurbanipal in Nineveh showing a group of musicians – probably eunuchs, to judge from their long hair and beardless faces – with dulcimers and harps.*

Hundreds of Sumerian and Akkadian documents give evidence of a longstanding musical tradition in ancient Mesopotamia. Musical accomplishment was highly regarded, as attested by the fact that several kings boast of their own ability in both playing and singing. Many relief sculptures show musicians and dancers performing, and archaeologists have found numerous fine examples of harps and lyres, especially, buried in the tombs of the high-born, such as those discovered by Leonard Woolley at Ur. They were not the only instruments played, however.

Many surviving examples of sculpture also depict flutes, cymbals and drums. Flutes were made of bone, wood or metal, while lyres and harps came in various designs, the most sophisticated of which had soundboxes and supports made of wood, inlaid with scenes in pearl or lapis lazuli and abstract designs. Some of the scenes are humorous, depicting animals cavorting like humans. The best lyres were further decorated with a golden bull's head at the front of the sound box.

Both music and dance probably had their roots in ancient religious rituals, and the scenes acted out through them constitute the earliest form of drama. Some of the earliest instruments found come from the royal cemetery at Ur, in the form of flutes and lyres. It is highly likely that terracotta ocarinas and horns (which take their name from the animals' horns from which they were originally made) were also among the earliest instruments. Harpists are shown in Assyrian reliefs of the first millennium, and on clay plaques from the 19th century BC. There is a scene of dancers with performing monkeys on a small circular clay tablet, now in the National Museum of Iraq, which dates from around the 18th century BC. An alabaster image in the British Museum which originated in seventh-century Nineveh shows a quartet of portly, clean-shaven musicians – possibly eunuchs – entertaining Ashurbanipal at a banquet, and a similar character is shown elsewhere playing a flute or pipe. We have

'Gilgamesh, where are you hurrying to? You will never find that life for which you are looking. When the gods created Man they allotted to him death, but life they retained in their own keeping. As for you, Gilgamesh, fill your belly with good things; day and night, night and day, dance and be merry, feast and rejoice. Let your clothes be fresh, bathe yourself in water, cherish the little child that holds your hand, and make your wife happy in your embrace; for this too is the lot of man.'

FROM *THE EPIC OF GILGAMESH: THE GODDESS SIDURI WARNS GILGAMESH OF THE FUTILITY OF SEEKING IMMORTALITY*

An early stone relief (c.1830–1600 BC) of a musician playing a stringed instrument with a sound-box attached. Music played an important part in religious and other liturgical ceremonies and possibly had its origins in such functions. Such images recur frequently on Mesopotamian stone carvings.

no idea what the music sounded like, or what steps were danced; but we do know that these two art forms are among the earliest known to Man.

Literature also had its origins in religion. Most works we have are intimately bound up with religion, either in the form of hymns, or in epics that attempt to explain the workings of the gods, cosmic forces, and humankind's relation to them (though many can also be read as allegories of conquest and discovery). Other forms of literature include paeans of praise to the kings, biographical and autobiographical works relating either to them and their achievements in architecture and war; or to prominent members of Mesopotamian society. In addition, there are the annals and the chronicles of the kings, which are important historical records. To these we should add the many letters that have come down to us, which are clear indications of the development of free, individual thought and which indicate that, whatever else has changed, human nature has not. Letters cover every aspect of life, from love to personal grievance; from theft, divorce, debt and adultery to business transactions. All these various sources demonstrate that the people of ancient Mesopotamia enquired into the movement of the planets and the stars, and explored new modes of agriculture, magic, astrology, philosophy, medicine and mathematics. It can come as a shock to realize that they had proved Pythagoras' theorem 1000 years before he did.

THE EPIC OF GILGAMESH

One of the central themes of the literature proper is the questioning and acceptance of the inevitability of death. Fear of it was sharpened by a stoical conception of the afterlife as a kind of conscious non-being, in which everything effectively returns to mud.

The best-known piece of Mesopotamian literature, *The Epic of Gilgamesh*, has the questioning and acceptance of death as its central theme, and the fact that it exists in more than one version – and that the one most familiar to us has roots that go back centuries – shows how important this preoccupation was to the people of Babylon. Gilgamesh is a powerful king and hero, two-thirds divine, without a peer in the world. For this reason he becomes arrogant and overweening, irritating his subjects, the people of Uruk. '*No son is left with his father, for Gilgamesh takes them all; yet the king should be a shepherd to his people. His lust leaves no virgin to her lover, neither the warrior's daughter nor the wife of the noble ...*' The gods in their wisdom create Enkidu, a wild and innocent man who lives in the hills and has only wild beasts for company, but who is nevertheless the equal of Gilgamesh. Hearing of him, Gilgamesh sends a whore to seduce him, and after six days and seven nights of lovemaking, Enkidu is tamed. The wild animals now shun him, and he accepts the whore's invitation to return with her to Uruk, where he fights Gilgamesh, who finally defeats him after a fierce struggle. The two become close friends, and set off

‘There is the house whose people sit in darkness; dust is their food and clay their meat. They are clothed like birds in wings for covering, they see no light, they sit in darkness. I entered the house of dust and I saw the kings of the earth, their crowns put away forever; rulers and princes, all those who once wore kingly crowns and ruled the world in the days of old ... and there was Ereshkigal the Queen of the Underworld; and belit-sheri squatted in front of her, she who is the recorder of the gods and keeps the book of death. She held a tablet from which she read. She raised her head and saw me and spoke: "Who has brought this one here?"’

FROM *THE EPIC OF GILGAMESH: A VISION OF THE AFTERLIFE*

LEFT *Shell inlay decoration on the sound-box of a Sumerian lyre found in King Abargi's tomb at the Royal Cemetery in Ur. Animals and mythical beasts cavort, while, at the bottom, an anthropomorphic goat seems to have invited a scorpion-man round for drinks.*

ABOVE *A clay tablet, found at Nineveh, inscribed with text recounting* The Epic of Gilgamesh. *The fragments shown relate the legend of the Great Flood.*

for the forest in the mountains, where they defeat its demon guardian, Humbaba, and carry off timber. Following their success, the goddess Ishtar proposes marriage to Gilgamesh, but, aware of her fickleness, he brusquely rejects her. Meanwhile, in dreams – always of central importance in the Babylonian psyche – Enkidu has intimations of his mortality, and duly dies. Gilgamesh is over come by grief:

> *Let the great ones of strong-walled Uruk*
> *Weep for you,*
> *Let the finger of blessing*
> *be stretched out in mourning.*
> *O Enkidu, my brother,*
> *You were the axe at my side,*
> *My hand's strength, the sword in my belt,*
> *The shield before me,*
> *A glorious robe, my fairest ornament.*

When his mourning is at an end, he sets forth on an epic journey to Dilmun, the land of Utnapishtim, the only survivor, along with his family, of the Flood, and the only man to whom the gods had granted everlasting life. Utnapishtim tries to persuade Gilgamesh to accept philosophically the fate that awaits all men, but in the end tells him of a plant that will bestow immortality. He finds it, but before he can eat it, a serpent steals it; this incident explains why snakes can slough their skin and be 'reborn'. Gilgamesh, resigned at last, goes back to Uruk, taking sad pride in what he has achieved there: *'Did not the seven wise men lay these foundations? One third of the whole is city, one third is garden, and one third is field, with the precinct of the goddess Ishtar.'*

THE INEVITABILITY OF FATE

The theme of fatalism runs through many of the Babylonian sagas. The story of Adapa tells of a man who unwittingly offends the gods, but who manages with the help of Ea, who is always mankind's friend and intercessor, to redeem himself so successfully that the great god An offers him the bread and water of eternal life. Yet Adapa has been warned by Ea, who has no idea how successful his protégé has been, to accept nothing from the gods in case it is poisoned, and so he refuses, and misses his chance. In another, Etana flies up to heaven on a eagle's back to seek a cure for his infertility, but at the last moment, terrified by the great height to which he has flown, tells the eagle to return to Earth, and so fails in his mission. Other sagas have to do with the gods' control over man's fate. In the story of Anzu, the demon of that name steals the Tablet of Destinies, without which the gods cannot command anything. Ninurta, god of war and the plough, volunteers to get it back, and succeeds. What is interesting here is that Anzu, whose Sumerian name is Imdugud, usually portrayed as a lion-headed eagle, is usually a benevolent creature. A copper relief of 2300 BC, from the lintel of the temple door of Ninhursag at Tell el Ubaid, shows the demon with his wings protectively stretched over two stags. Many other stories attempt to explain the forces of nature, the mystery of the seasons, and the origins of the stars. *The Epic of Creation* has a political slant, in that it is designed to place Marduk at the centre of the pantheon, casting him in a role originally taken by Ea, and ending by according him the power of fifty major gods, who are subsumed within him.

Much of the extant 'creative' literature of Mesopotamia is thanks to the collection Ashurbanipal made for his massive library in Nineveh. It is a measure of the degree

'She was not ashamed to take him, she made herself naked and welcomed his eagerness, she incited the savage to love and taught him the woman's art. For six days and seven nights they lay together, for Enkidu had forgotten his home in the hills; but when he was satisfied he went back to the wild beasts. Then, when the gazelle saw him, they bolted away; when the wild creatures saw him, they fled. Enkidu would have followed, but his body was bound as though with a cord, his knees gave way when he started to run, his swiftness was gone ... Enkidu had grown weak, for wisdom was in him, and the thoughts of a man were in his heart.'

FROM *THE EPIC OF GILGAMESH: ENKIDU THE WILD MAN IS TAMED BY THE WHORE SENT BY GILGAMESH*

of interest Mesopotamians took in the written word that, although his was the largest, Ashurbanipal's was far from the only library in the country. Moreover the nature of his collection is a pointer to the preoccupations and tastes of the time. No fewer than three hundred tablets are concerned with omens and portents; 200 with lexical lists – effectively, dictionaries, and lists of words – all copies of mainly lost originals; 100 assorted bilingual texts in Sumerian and Akkadian, largely dealing with incantations and prayers; 60 medical dissertations, and around 40 epic poems and sagas. Ashurbanipal had several copies of a version of *The Epic of Gilgamesh*, whose authorship was attributed to one Sin-leke-unnini.

In ancient Mesopotamia there was a thriving oral tradition of reciting the epics. Some of them are surprisingly terse, suggesting that they may well have been written down as a skeleton text for a performer to extemporize upon and embellish. Others, such as the Creation Epic, contain interminable lists. The one naming the various gods whose attributes were subsumed within the person of Marduk might have been very tedious to sit through.

SCULPTURE

In the Louvre in Paris there is a massive statue, sometimes supposed to be of Gilgamesh, carved in high relief, standing, grasping a lion in his left hand and a weapon in his right. Carving in stone was a luxury that the Assyrian kings indulged in to a great extent, especially from the reign of Ashurnasirpal on. It is less apparent in Babylonian culture, perhaps because traditionally large blocks of stone were not readily available in the south. Babylon concentrated its aesthetic sense into its monumental architecture. The 'Gilgamesh' statue, from Dur-Sharrukin and dating from the reign of Sargon II (722–705 BC) shows the hero in sandals, dressed in an ankle-length, short-sleeved robe over a kilt. He wears simple ornaments – a bracelet on each wrist – and his hair is thick, heavy, and worn long. His thick beard is elaborately plaited and curled. The whole work gives us a good impression of what a well-born person might have worn.

Little of the sculpture shows us the life of common people, though battle scenes depict footsoldiers in action, and people who are clearly from ordinary walks of life being led away captive, and scenes of banquets, feasting and rituals give us an impression, in the humbler attendants, of what everyday inhabitants of the land might have looked like. In one vignette, for example, Ashurbanipal's plump consort sits on a high carver, her feet on a footstool, and drinks wine from a shallow bowl

'Last night I dreamed again, my friend. The heavens moaned and the earth replied; I stood alone before an awful being; his face was sombre like the black bird of the storm. He fell upon me and he held me fast, pinioned with his claw, till I smothered; then he transformed me so that my arms became wings covered with feathers. He turned his stare towards me, and he led me away to the palace of Irkalla, the Queen of Darkness, to the house from which none who enters ever returns, down the road from which there is no coming back.'

FROM *THE EPIC OF GILGAMESH: ENKIDU FORESEES HIS DEATH IN A DREAM*

LEFT *This massive statue (height 4.45 m/14 ft) in high relief has generally been thought to be of Gilgamesh. It certainly depicts a hero, in a typical pose, subduing a small lion with his left arm, while his right holds a sickle-like weapon or a club. The sculpture dates from the period of Sargon II (c. 705 BC). The beard and hairstyle are neo-Assyrian in style; note, too, the detail of the sumptuous clothing the figure wears.*

before a table whose legs have clawed feet. Behind her a pair of stout eunuchs keep her cool with fans. There are perhaps fewer depictions of day-to-day life in Mesopotamian art than in its Egyptian counterpart, but there is still plenty to go on.

Mural painting, and small wooden sculpted scenes and models, which have survived from Egyptian culture, often from tombs, have not come down to us from Mesopotamia; but we do have bitumen models of gondola-like riverboats, and occasional models of houses, one of which shows a ram with a very heavy fleece lying on the corner of a roof – both these examples come from the late third millennium. There are also occasional scenes of ploughing and farm activity, including canal-work. One scene shows a watercourse being diverted so that a huge sculpture can be transported without getting bogged down. There are scenes of scribes at work, of fishermen in their coracles, of quarry-workers armed with saws, picks and shovels extracting a block of partially-prepared limestone destined to be sculpted into a *lammasu*, and of grooms tending horses. All of these also impart information about the vegetation that existed – orchards of dates, figs, pines and pomegranate; about animal life, domestic and wild; and about the fish and crustaceans

BELOW *Gilgamesh is aided in his quest by two fantastic creatures – bull-men, who hold over him the winged disk of the sun-god, Shamash. This relief was found at Tell-halaf in Syria.*

ABOVE *Inlaid bust of an unidentified woman (eighth century BC), unearthed in Babylon and now in the National Museum of Iraq.*

that teemed in the rivers. Scenes showing palace interiors, or war booty being itemized, give us a clear idea of the kind of furniture and furnishings which went into an Assyrian dwelling. Depictions of battles give us details of armour and weaponry, siege engines and the counter-measures of the besieged. Some of the scenes from daily life also give us clues about the timing of technical developments. For example, in the depiction of a pair of scribes, dating from about 730 BC, which was found at Kalhu, one is shown taking notes on a traditional clay tablet, while the other holds a scroll of papyrus. Given the date, and the fact that these are official records, the scribe would not yet be writing in Aramaic, but it is evidently late enough for paper to have made its way into the country. From the context of the scene, created late in the reign of the belligerent Tiglath-Pileser III (745–727 BC), it is likely that the man portrayed is a war artist. Both men, to judge from their long hair but shaven chins, are probably eunuchs.

But the bulk of plastic art, from monumental statuary to the miniaturist art of cylinder seals, is concerned with gods, kings and monsters. In early times, gods were shown sitting in glory on their thrones, often accepting homage from a king who is introduced by a lesser, intermediary god. A popular image was that of a god holding a round vase from which twin streams of water endlessly flow, perhaps a reference to the Tigris and the Euphrates. But as time passes, the gods are reduced to their emblems, and the king-hero takes centre stage. A stele of Ashurnasirpal, again from Kalhu, shows the king standing, his arms held in a ritual gesture of respect as he seems to point to five gods, who simply occur as their symbols: the horned helmet of Ashur, the winged disc of Shamash, the crescent of Sin, the twin-pronged fork of Adad, and the star of Ishtar. There are many superb cast-bronze and copper statues, statuettes and busts, especially from the early periods, and all employing the sophisticated lost-wax process; plus many fine terracotta figures. However, the large pieces that the Mesopotamians sculpted in stone never quite emerged fully into the round, except for small figurines, and for stiff, columnar statues. Plasticity and fluidity in art were possibly not aesthetic values they aspired to. The great *lammasus*, the human-headed winged bulls that guarded the portals of palaces and temples, never broke free from their stone blocks. Thus it is that the earlier examples have five legs: viewed head on, the front legs are together; from the side, one is drawn back; this gives an aesthetic impression of balance from face on and side on, but in a three-quarter view all naturalism disappears. In any case, the *lammasus'* bodies are too massive ever to have been supported by free-standing legs.

> 'If I take you in marriage, what gifts can I give in return? What ointments and clothing for your body, what bread for your eating? How can I give food to a god and drink to the Queen of Heaven? Moreover, if I take you in marriage how will it go with me? Your lovers have found you like a brazier which smoulders in the cold, a back-door which keeps out neither squall of wind nor storm, a fortress which crushes the garrison, pitch that blackens the bearer, a leaky waterskin that wets the carrier, a stone which falls from the parapet, a sandal that trips the wearer, a mangonel set up in the enemy's land. '
>
> FROM *THE EPIC OF GILGAMESH: GILGAMESH REJECTS ISHTAR'S OFFER OF MARRIAGE*

THE LION-HUNT RELIEF

The Kassite period witnessed a high degree of naturalism in sculpture, especially in the portrayal of animals. Yet the true high point of Mesopotamian sculpture was reached by the anonymous craftsmen who carved the stone low-relief (the style in which Assyrian art found its fullest expression) depicting Ashurbanipal's lion-hunt. This artefact decorated his palace at Nineveh and now resides in the British Museum. By Ashurbanipal's time, the lion-hunt had become an almost ritual occurrence, and here the animals are shown being released from cages in order to be killed, perhaps in a park, in an orgy of slaughter. The Middle Eastern lion, smaller than its sub-Saharan cousin, along with other species of wild animal, such as the onager and the gazelle, survived until the 20th century AD, but from these hunting scenes we may well imagine that if Ashurbanipal had had our technology the lions would not have outlasted the the seventh century! Putting aside modern squeamishness at the subject matter, the extraordinary skill with which the lions have been portrayed, and their pathos, is breathtaking. It is hard to suppress the thought that the sculptors' sympathies were with the animals rather than with the much more stiffly-drawn king and his retinue.

As with the Egyptians, perspective was never explored by Mesopotamian artists. This is remarkable, since their mathematical knowledge certainly equipped them with the theoretical ability to portray depth in space. Perhaps it was a matter of aesthetic choice (though when they attempt to show, say, four horses one behind the other, it is striking how stiff the attempt is).

Yet even in the absence of perspective, the drama and the immediacy of the British Museum relief is electric. The lions have a vigour and a courage that emerges from every rippling muscle. Dying and dead, appallingly shot through with arrows, they have a heartrending sadness. Blood pours from the mouth of one beast, still on

his feet but tottering, and from the wounds made by the five arrows or spears that pierce him. A lioness, down on her rear legs but still raised on her front, gives a last defiant roar before succumbing to death. Elsewhere, keepers in protective cages on top of the lions' cages release them for the hunt. The lions are kept from escaping from the killing field by a ring of soldiers, and gamekeepers with huge, savage mastiffs. To one side, men and women clamber up the slope of a hill to get a good view. The king, wearing his crown and many ornaments, his long hair and beard plaited and curled, and dressed magnificently, is flanked by attendants with spears and wields his bow and arrow from his chariot. In another scene, he shoots heavy-bodied gazelle, perhaps a species of eland, from a hidden pit, towards which the animals are driven by beaters. In another, in a classic pose also used by his ancestors, he stands face to face with a rearing lion. He seizes the beast's throat with his left hand and plunges his sword through it with his right. But, even here, it is still the lion that steals the show.

ABOVE *A lion leaps at Ashurnasirpal's chariot. The king, just visible at top right, seems to be shooting at his bodyguard rather than at the lion, which, though well conceived, lacks the finesse of the beasts in Ashurbanipal's hunting scenes of about 200 years later. This relief (c. 865 BC) is from Nimrud.*

CHAPTER TWELVE
THE SCIENCES

THE BABYLONIANS WERE GREAT BELIEVERS IN ASTROLOGY and omens – subjects they invested much time and effort in, but that we would now deem pseudosciences. Nevertheless, they must at the same time have been possessed of extremely analytical and deductive minds, since they made unprecedented strides in astronomy and mathematics. Several of the discoveries we usually attribute to the ancient Greeks, such as Pythagoras' theorem and the Archimedes screw, were in fact of Babylonian origin. They also invented the Zodiac and the calendar, and were well practiced in medicine.

The greatest of the Babylonian astronomers, Kidinnu, who was active in the second half of the fourth century BC was able to calculate the duration of the solar year with an error of only 4 minutes and 32.65 seconds. This calculation was fractionally more accurate than that of the Czech astronomer Theodor von Oppolzer (1841–86) in a posthumously published work of 1887. The fact that Kidinnu reached such a result at all is impressive, but his achievement should be measured against a scientific tradition that dates back to Sumerian times.

Having only rudimentary instruments with which to work, and no telescopes, the Babylonians depended on their knowledge of mathematics, coupled with patient and constant observation of the movement of the planets and stars, to reach their conclusions. But astronomy, in turn, derived from their study of astrology. It was an accepted part of their thinking that the movement of the stars and planets was linked to the gods' intentions regarding the future of mankind. If they could be understood and interpreted, any evil in the future could arguably be avoided or at least prepared for. Consequently, phenomena such as eclipses, seen from the earliest times as terrifying portents, became, after long and consistent study, predictable, and therefore far less mystifying. Early on, the paths of the sun and the known planets were tracked, and their 'roads' divided into 12 stations, each in turn split into 30 degrees. This provided the basis for our own Zodiacal system.

CALENDRICAL CALCULATIONS

Astrology played a subordinate role during the period when mathematics flourished, but it gained in significance towards the end of the second millennium, and this called for a more precise observation of the stars than previously. This in turn led to the identification of a larger number of constellations. They divided 36 of these among the three circles of the gods An, Ellil and Ea. The sun, moon, planets, and fixed stars were even more carefully observed in the first millennium. During the period of Assyrian domination, Kalhu was the centre of astronomical observations, followed

RIGHT *A kudurru (boundary marker) of Nazi-Maruttash, King of Babylon, c. 1328–1296 BC. Nazi-Maruttash was one of the long dynasty of Kassite kings, who introduced* kudurru *to Mesopotamia. A god, perhaps Marduk or Shamash, sits enthroned, with a scorpion and the sun-disc above him.*

THE BABYLONIAN YEAR

The Babylonian year began in the spring and consisted of 12 lunar months, each of which began when the first crescent of the moon was seen on the western horizon at sunset. To keep time balanced, an intercalary month was inserted roughly every three years – as the lunar year is just under 11 days shorter than the solar one. The calendar was not fully regulated until relatively late, around 600 BC. The names of the Babylonian months and their approximate correspondence with ours (there is some overlap) are as follows:

Arax Nisanu – March
Arax Aru – April
Arax Simanu – May
Arax Du'uzu – June
Abu – July
Ululu – August
Tis-ri-tum – September
Arax-samna – October
Arax Kislimu – November
Arax Tebetum – December
Arax Sabatu – January
Addaru – February

The Babylonians were also the first to name the days of the week after the sun, moon and planets. Their naming scheme is still followed today:

Monday - *Moon* (**Sin**)
Tuesday – *Mars* (**Nergal**)
Wednesday – *Mercury* (**Nabu**)
Thursday – *Jupiter* (**Marduk**)
Friday – *Venus* (**Ishtar**)
Saturday – *Saturn* (**Ninurta**)
Sunday – *Sun* (**Shamash**)

RIGHT *A famous white marble bust, dating back to perhaps 3000 BC, and popularly known as the 'Lady of Warka', is thought to be an image of the moon goddess Inanna. This exquisite artefact was looted during the US-led invasion of Iraq in 2003, but was subsequently recovered.*

by Dur-Sharrukin and Nineveh; and drawings of special phenomena in the heavens were already being made from very early on. Lists of eclipses, for example, were kept with absolute precision from the year 747 BC, at the beginning of the reign of Nabonassar (747–734 BC), a king of the obscure Babylonian 'Dynasty of F'. But however obscure his dynasty and even his reign, it was during his time on the throne that Babylonian science took an enormous leap forward, and calendrical accuracy, freed of the vagueness of associating years with kings' or officials' names (limmu lists), or with significant events, was assured. The process was neither tidy nor swift, but it was consistent; and the later Greek astronomers, notably Ptolemy (c. AD 85–165), acknowledged Nabonassar's brief reign as a turning-point in astronomy. The reason that it happened then may perhaps be ascribed to an unusually spectacular conjunction of the moon and planets that occurred in his first year on the throne. Over the course of time the term 'Chaldean' came to signify 'astronomer'.

An initial result of painstaking observation was that lunar eclipses could be reckoned with approximate accuracy after the year 700 BC; previously such eclipses had been taken as portents of the wrath of the gods. The same was true of the much rarer solar eclipses. In this way, superstition gave way to scientific understanding, and other benefits followed, almost as a by-product of astrology. Acting on the advice of his scientists, Nabonassar decreed the intercalation of seven months in the course of 19 lunar years, to regularize the calendar.

Babylonian astronomy resonated far beyond ancient Mesopotamia, as Greek and Babylonian astronomers began to collaborate. It was developed still further in the Seleucid and Parthian periods. The co-operation of Babylonian astronomers with their Greek counterparts was hugely important, not least in the fixing of the modern calendar. Somewhere between 388 and 367 BC, Nabonassar's system was refined, with the establishment of a 19-year period with eight leap years. For the sake of simplifying calculations, astronomers worked on a basis of 12 months, each of 30 days' duration. The names of the months used in Nebuchadrezzar's day were first adopted by the Judeans and the Syrians.

MATHEMATICS

What we know of Babylonian mathematics come from two types of documentation – firstly, lists of numbers arranged in various sequences, such as increasing and decreasing series, tables of multiplication and division, and so on; and secondly, sets of problems. It is entirely reasonable to suppose that mathematics evolved from certain practical needs, such as knowing how to calculate the dimensions of buildings and their stress factors, dividing up the year the better to organize agriculture, and weighing and measuring goods. But those mathematical problems that have come down to us from Babylon indicate that the Babylonians were also interested in mathematics for its own sake.

ABOVE *A clay tablet impressed with cuneiform script and a rectangular diagram details an algebraic-geometrical problem.*

Two examples illustrate this. The first is couched in terms of a problem for a pupil to solve, whereas the second is fully argued through.

1) *I found a stone but did not weigh it; then I added one-seventh and one-eleventh. I weighed it: one mana. What was the original weight of the stone?*

2) *If somebody asks you thus: as much as the side of the square which I made I dug deep, and I extracted a volume of one* musaru *and a half. My base ground I made a square. How deep did I go?*

You, in your procedure, operate with 12. Take the reciprocal of 12 and multiply by 1,30,0,0 which is your volume. 7,30,0 you will see. 30 is the cube root. Multiply 30 by 1, and 30 will you see. Multiply 30 by 12, and 6,0 (360) you will see. 30 is the side of your square, and 6,0 (360) is your depth.

BABYLONIAN MEDICINE

Medicine is a far less exact science than mathematics, but the Babylonians assiduously documented their researches into it. They did not always operate from what we would see as a scientific standpoint, but they were more investigative and less conservative than their Egyptian contemporaries in this field. However, they believed that illness resulted from sin, and should therefore be viewed as a punishment. They also believed that it could be the result of demonic possession – something that was believed of epilepsy in our own society until relatively recently.

That did not mean that no attempt should be made to cure illnesses, but since they were initially regarded as visitations by evil spirits, a special priest was called in first to divine the causes of the affliction. Another specialized priest would then perform any act of exorcism that was deemed necessary. However, there also existed two other kinds of specialist, who gradually gained precedence, and whose methods were more scientifically based. Terms are still disputed, and Babylonian medical science was still bound up with priestly ritual, yet broadly speaking the *asipu* may be likened to a professional doctor. He was trained for many years in the known scientific disciplines, and taught to recognize causes other than divine retribution for illness and disease. He would take dirt, contaminated food or drink, and contagion into account as contributory factors, and his job was to find remedies to combat them. He was able to advise on ways of avoiding the causes of illnesses, for example, greater hygiene or a better diet, and he had the means of effecting cures. The *asipu* was aided in his work by another specialist, the *asu*, whom we might equate to a pharmacist.

Hammurabi's legal code provided for punishments in cases of malpractice, but the medical profession was held in high regard and its members came from the élite, educated classes. There were almost certainly quack practitioners, as there have been in all ages, but generally medicine in ancient Mesopotamia was a more exact science than it was in, say, medieval or even Tudor England. For instance, Babylonian doctors were dispatched to attend Amenhotep III of Egypt (r. 1390–1352 BC) and the Hittite

ABOVE *This is perhaps the earliest known map of the world, and the only one found in Babylon. The circle is the Salt Sea. Beyond it is a region 'where the sun is not seen'. Through the middle of the map runs the Euphrates. Babylon is shown as a rectangular box. To the north (top of the circle) are the mountains of the river's source; to the south, the marshes of the Gulf. This small artefact (12.2 cm / 4.8 ins high) was made in the first millennium* BC *to illustrate the exploits of the third-millennium* BC *hero-king, Sargon the Great.*

ASTRONOMY AND ASTROLOGY

The Mesopotamians were well versed in mathematics, and its application to astronomy enabled them to reach a degree of exactitude scarcely rivalled in the ancient world. Their interest in the movements of the stars was both metaphysical and chronological. In the first case, astronomy blurred into astrology, as the Mesopotamians believed that what happened in the heavens could be reflected on Earth.

They knew five planets – Jupiter, Venus, Saturn, Mercury and Mars. These were identified with the principal gods of the Babylonian pantheon, as follows: Jupiter with Marduk, Venus with Ishtar, Saturn with Ninurta, Mercury with Nabu, and Mars with Nergal. The movements of the sun, moon and five planets were seen as representing the activity of the five gods, together with the moon-god Sin and the sun-god Shamash, in preparing occurrences on Earth. If the planets, the sun, the moon and the constellations were related to gods, kings and cities on Earth, and if the relationships between them could be predicted, then it should also be possible to predict the future. Observational records enabled Babylonian scholars to construct planetary theories by which to predict celestial phenomena, such as the phases of the moon. The Babylonians made

such great strides in astronomy that some earlier commentators believed that the ziggurats were constructed as observatories.

However, the night sky in the Near East is not always clear – it can often be obscured by dust, sandstorms or simply clouds. How, then, did the Mesopotamians make their calculations? They certainly had no sophisticated instruments, so it must all have been achieved by the application of mathematics to precise and continuous observation, as in the Mayan calendrical system of ancient Mesoamerica.

BELOW *An astronomical tablet from Kish, recording the rising and settings of Venus from the first six years of the reign of the King of Babylon (seventh century* BC*).*

> 'The Chaldeans say that the nature of the universe is eternal, and that it had neither an original beginning, nor will it come to an end in the future, but that the order and regulation of the entire cosmos came about through a certain divine intent, and that every phenomenon now occurring in the heavens is caused neither by chance, nor yet spontaneously, but by a predetermined and immutable decree of the gods. The Chaldeans have observed the stars since ancient times; and discerning more keenly than all other men the movements and powers of each, they foretell to mankind many things which are destined to take place. '
>
> DIODORUS SICULUS: LIBRARY OF HISTORY (C. 35 BC)

king Hattusilis (r. 1275–1250 BC) – proof that their expertise was held not only in local but in international regard.

Surviving medical documents include lists of symptoms and their cures and medical correspondence. These data show a fairly comprehensive understanding of most of the illnesses and diseases that physicians of this period would have had to deal with. One simple example of identification and cure comes from Ashurbanipal's personal physician, Arad-Nanna, on the subject of severe nosebleed (epistaxis):

As regards the nose-bleeding … the dressings are not properly applied. They have been placed on the side of the nose, so that they interfere with the respiration and the blood flows into the mouth. The nose should be plugged up to its end so that the air entry will be blocked, and the bleeding will cease.

It is also apparent, from a letter written around 1000 years before the reign of Ashurbanipal, from Zimri-Lim of Mari to his wife Shibtu, that the Mesopotamians had a clear understanding of contagion:

I have heard that the Lady Nanna-Me has been taken ill. She has many contacts with the people of her palace. She meets many ladies in her house. Now then, give strict orders that no-one should drink in the cup where she drinks, no-one should sit on the seat where she sits, no-one should sleep in the bed where she sleeps. She should no longer meet many ladies in her house. This disease is catching.

Although progress in the science was slow, certain afflictions were found by experience to respond positively to certain cures, and already by the Ur III period we find extensive pharmacological lists and recipes for the preparation of lotions and ointments, poultices, enemas and suppositories. Medicine was administered in every way short of injection. Some of the herbal cures would still be effective today. Opium was used medicinally. Here, for example, is one recipe to counter urinary retention: *Crush poppy seeds in beer and make the patient drink it. Grind some myrrh, mix it with oil, and blow it into his urethra with a tube of bronze. Give the patient anemone crushed in alappanu-beer.*

Mesopotamian medicine and to a certain extent anatomy (for surgery was successfully practised alongside the clinical branch) may have continued to develop alongside superstitious and religious belief in cause of illness, but it paved the way to the breakthrough made by Hippocrates of Cos in the fifth century BC, and made a significant contribution to the development of the discipline in Europe.

RIGHT *A stone tablet inscribed with fourteen lines of a mathematical text in cuneiform script and decorated with a geometric design.*

CHAPTER THIRTEEN

BUSINESS AND TRADE

NO SOONER HAD MESOPOTAMIA BEGUN TO DEVELOP A SENSE OF nationhood than it began to trade with other countries, especially in the south, where basic raw materials such as building timber and stone were unavailable. As time passed it became apparent that such raw materials could also be obtained by conquest, but over the 3000 years and more of Mesopotamia's ascendancy trade was the more consistent manner of acquiring such commodities. Conquest was an expensive business, as was the maintenance of garrisons in unruly vassal states.

Fortunately for them, the Mesopotamians had plenty to trade with. Their innovations in agricultural technology (for example, highly efficient irrigation, the seeder plough, cultivation of the best strains of wild wheats and barleys, sensible land distribution and management) meant that they obtained such a successful yield on their crops that they were not only able to feed their own burgeoning population but also had plenty of corn to pay for imported goods. From the time they started breeding sheep, they also developed a thriving wool and textile industry. Over time, a thriving export trade developed in cloth and other finished goods such as pottery, and luxury items like jewellery made by specialized Babylonian craftsmen. And, long before they became aware of what wealth lay beneath their soil in the form of oil, they were exploiting its parent substance, bitumen, which they obtained from naturally-occurring seepages in the central Euphrates region, north of the city of Hit. It was used as mortar, and as waterproof lining for drains and bathrooms, as well as a material for sculpture, inlay-work, caulking, fuel, and even as a drug. They also exported it.

By Hammurabi's time, trade was highly organized and controlled, as this selection of laws from his legal code attests:

> If a merchant gave silver to an agent for buying and selling, and sent him on a journey … and he has seen a profit where he went, he shall calculate the interest on as much silver as he took and they shall count up the period which has elapsed, and he shall pay the merchant accordingly.

> If he has seen no profit where he went, the agent shall double the silver he received and give it to the merchant.

> If there are no mercantile arrangements in the place whither he went, he shall leave the entire amount of money which he received with the broker to give to the merchant.

> If a merchant entrust money to an agent (broker) for some investment, and

RIGHT *A ninth-century BC Assyrian relief showing porters laden with goods. The sheer number of legal provisions relating to trade in the Law Code of Hammurabi attests to the importance of trade in ancient Mesopotamia.*

the broker suffer a loss in the place to which he goes, he shall make good the capital to the merchant.

If, while on the journey, an enemy take away from him anything that he had, the broker shall swear by god and be free of obligation.

If a merchant give an agent corn, wool, oil, or any other goods to transport, the agent shall give a receipt for the amount, and compensate the merchant therefor. Then he shall obtain a receipt from the merchant for the money that he gives the merchant.

If the agent is careless, and does not take a receipt for the money which he gave the merchant, he cannot consider the unreceipted money as his own.

From these laws (which form just part of a huge body of legislation relating to trade), it is clear that haulage agents and hauliers were already specialized occupations, expert in the arduous and often dangerous business of managing caravans. Transport was available in the form of the four-wheeled cart or waggon, and the sledge (for heavy loads that would otherwise become bogged down in the soft alluvial soil), but these were slow and unsuitable for uneven terrain. Roads at this time were really just well-established tracks, not formal thoroughfares of any kind. Accordingly, the preferred mode of carrying goods was the donkey caravan. Donkeys were hardy, could carry heavy loads, were easy to breed, and resellable at the end of a journey, particularly if one was trading bulky goods, such as sacks of grain, for copper ingots or bushels of pearls. In such a case any surplus donkeys could be sold off at the merchant's destination, to add a little cream to his profit. Later on, the introduction of the camel to Mesopotamia meant that long trans-desert journeys became possible.

BELOW *Stone tablet with cuneiform script detailing a contract for selling a field and a house, from Shuruppak, c.2600 BC. The circles and crescent-like depressions are probably numerical values.*

THE GROWTH OF TRADE

As the earliest city-states were established close to, or on the shores of the Lower Sea (the Persian Gulf) whose northern shores lay further inland than they do today, transport by ship down the northeastern coast of what is now Saudi Arabia offered tempting possibilities, and ships would voyage right down the Gulf and across the Arabian Sea to trade along the southern littorals of what are now Iran and Pakistan, as far as the northwestern shores of India, and from outpost ports along those shores, inland expeditions could be organized. From Meluhha in the Indus Valley came carnelian, ivory, steatite and timber; from Tepe Yahya in southern Persia came chlorite. More carnelian and the ultimate status symbol, lapis lazuli, were obtained from Afghanistan. To the northwest of that country, towards the coast of the Caspian Sea, copper, tin and turquoise were found. More tin, and silver, came from from the region near Hanaslu just to the south of Lake Urmia. Obsidian and copper were traded from the areas northwest of Lake Van. Pearls and shells were fetched from Dilmun (Bahrain), an island stopping-off point on the Indian route. Copper also came from northern Sinai, and from Cyprus. The Nile delta was a source of alabaster, diorite and gold, while highly prized cedarwood was imported from the region on the northern banks of the Orontes river in the Levant (Lebanon). Nearby

'You wrote and said, keep the bracelets and rings, you'll need them to buy food. It's true that you sent me half-a-pound of gold through Ili-bani, but where are the bracelets you say you left behind? When you left, you didn't leave me one shekel of silver; you cleaned out the house and took everything with you. Since then, a dreadful famine has hit the city, and you didn't leave me as much as a litre of barley. I need to keep buying barley for our food … Where is the extravagance you keep on about? We have nothing to eat! Do you think we can afford to indulge ourselves? Everything I had available I scraped together and sent you. Now, I live in an empty house and the seasons are changing. Make sure you send me the value of my textiles in silver, so that I can at least buy ten measures of barley … Ashur-immiti has caused a lot of trouble to the business and has seized some slaves as security. It seems your representatives have settled the affair, but I've had to pay out two-thirds of a pound of silver to stop him lodging a complaint before your return. Why do you keep on listening to slander, and write me irritating letters?'

A WIFE WRITES FROM ASHUR TO HER HUSBAND, ABSENT ON BUSINESS IN ANATOLIA, C. 1200 BC

Ugarit provided shells. More silver came from the eastern ranges of the Taurus Mountains, while to the north, in Anatolia, lay a further source of copper. Some trading in slaves and livestock also took place.

Tin was also re-exported to Anatolia for the production of bronze. The Hittite-controlled area of what is now Turkey was a major metallurgical centre and from the days of Sargon the Great there had been Mesopotamian trading colonies there. One colony certainly existed at the Hatti/Hittite capital, Hattusas (modern Boghazköy), and a more important one at Kanesh (near modern Kültepe). In excavations between 1948 and 2005, the Turkish archaeologist Tahsin Özguç unearthed traders' houses and hundreds of letters on clay tablets, some still in their clay 'envelopes', written in an Akkadian dialect known as Old Assyrian. These letters cover at least six generations of traders, and from them we learn that they exported home precious stones, iron, silver and gold, and imported tin and textiles. Cash payments were made in silver. The colonizers effectively controlled the local economy, but were on good terms with their Hittite hosts. Many individuals stayed for years, some permanently in all likelihood. Despite having families at home, many also married locally and established second households.

THE PERILS AND RISKS OF COMMERCE

The network of routes required careful management and policing. In the periods of centrally-controlled empires there was less of a problem, because roadhouses could be established along the land routes, at least within the empire, and vassal states and trading partners, to whom the trade was as important as it was for the Mesopotamians, could be depended

BELOW *Plaster copy of a Mesopotamian letter in its 'envelope' (Musée de la Poste, Paris).*

WEIGHTS, MEASURES AND CURRENCY

Mesopotamia developed a system of weights in which units were divided into sixtieths. Thus a talent weighed about 30 kilograms (66 lb), a mina about 500 grams (1.1 lb); a shekel, about 8.4 grams (0.3 oz), and there were smaller weights usually one-sixtieth of the value of the last. Weights were often made of expensive stone, basalt or diorite, and were either egg-shaped with a flattened base, or in the form of a duck. Larger weights, especially popular in Assyria, were made in the shape of lions, the tail arcing forward to rest on the animal's back, forming a handle by which to lift it. Weights could also be made of precious and semi-precious metal. Some merchants travelling abroad might carry up to nine different sets.

The length of any given object was similarly divided: to give some examples, the beru, nearly 7 miles (11 km), was equal to 30 ush, and each ush (about 360 metres) was equivalent to 60 nindan. One nindan (or gar) was thus 6 metres. A kush was half a metre, and there were other subdivisions. The basic unit of area was the sar, or 'garden plot', worth one square nindan, or 36 square metres. The sixtieth part of a sar was called a gin, and the iku was worth 100 sar.

Volume, important for the measurement of beer, oil, grain and bricks, was based on the sila (one litre), of which a sixtieth part was called a gin. 60 sila made one bariga.

The division of the day into hours, minutes and seconds is thought have been a Babylonian invention. The day, sunrise to sunset, was split into 12 parts, and the night

ABOVE *A weight in the form of a resting duck with its neck bent over its back. It is made from basalt and comes from the second millenium* BC.

into 12 more. Each of these 24 subdivisions was then split into sixty equal parts. Babylonian astronomers had no clocks, but they did have sundials, and so could map the hours of night by observation of the stars (when the skies were not overcast). Distances to be covered were often expressed not in terms of their physical length, but in terms of how long they would take to travel. Using the same system of sixtieths, mathematicians also split the circle into 360 equal divisions, and each of these into 60 equal parts.

Money developed from weights, which were used as currency (as was barley), as early as the third millennium BC. In time, the talent, the shekel and the mina gave their names to coins. Barley was only useful for local transactions, as its food value was lost over long periods of distance or time. Likewise, many weights proved impractical to transport. But precious and semi-precious metals did not have either problem. Gold and copper were used, but silver was the most common currency during the Bronze Age (*c*.3000–1200 BC) and Iron Age (from *c*.1200 BC). Values depended on availability, so copper and lead were worth less than silver and gold.

The first recognizable coinage did not appear until about 650 BC, in Lydia (in modern Turkey). Weighed coils and standard small weights of gold, silver, copper and bronze were used from *c*.2110 to 1590 BC, gold gaining on silver from *c*.1500 BC as more of it flowed into Mesopotamia from Egypt. During the Assyrian ascendancy (*c*.880–625 BC), copper predominated, then silver again.

LEFT *Four carnelian-stone seals, dating from 3000–1500 BC and depicting (clockwise from top left) a bull, a rhinoceros, a tiger and an elephant, together with pictographic symbols. Made in the ancient city of Harappa in the Indus Valley, Pakistan, three of the seals were found there, whereas the elephant seal was discovered in Mesopotamia. Nor is it the sole evidence of early trade relations across Asia. Indian businessmen may well have settled in Babylon.*

on to protect traders' interests. But the routes often led through inhospitable countryside, occupied by independent tribes and bandit gangs, which caravans were obliged either to buy off or to fight. Merchants were pretty well indemnified from loss by the laws of Hammurabi, and there is no reason to suppose that his provisions changed much as long as there was a strong central government; but agents and hauliers carried a great risk. Their fees must have been high, but they would also have had to arrange guards to 'ride shotgun', as it were, for their caravans. These must have been supplied through either state or private sources, but unless a caravan was the direct concern of palace or temple, the latter seems more likely. Journeys were often long, usually taking months, and the people who staffed and ran the outlying trading posts might be away from home for years. Seaborne trade was vulnerable to predation by coastal pirates. Nevertheless profit, and the sheer necessity of trading, outweighed any risks the businessmen involved took.

Merchants had to pay state taxes on their transactions. As a result, they (in company with landowners and tenant farmers) sometimes needed to raise capital by taking out loans. These were available from palace and temple, but also, as time passed, from private banks, which no doubt evolved from companies run by professional moneylenders. It is uncertain when this took place, but certainly by Nebuchadrezzar's reign private banks were well established, notably that of the Egibi family, which made fortunes by charging huge interest rates of around 20 to 30 percent. They thus hedged themselves comfortably against such vicissitudes as inflation caused by war, flood or famine, invested in property and trade, and became colossally rich – richer than the temples, and richer than some states. When the Persian ruler Cyrus the Great invaded, ending forever the Babylonian empire, and Mesopotamian hegemony, the Egibi family business did not even miss a beat in continuing its acitivities.

CHAPTER FOURTEEN

FESTIVALS AND RITUAL

THE WATER TABLE IN THE TIGRIS AND EUPHRATES BASIN was usually very high, and it was topped up annually by winter rainfall in the mountains of eastern Turkey where the two rivers had their sources, and from melting snows in the spring. Before Sargon's day, salination of the soil, brought about by poor irrigation, affected wheat crops and led to an increase in production of barley, which is more salt-tolerant.

Despite floods and the occasional drought, however, arable farming and sensible storage against times of shortage meant that during the Akkadian period Mesopotamia, especially the south, had a fast-growing population, which gave it both its military advantage and the manpower for its building programmes.

Repairs to irrigation systems were carried out by organized companies of labourers, raised by corvée to work for the common good, during August, September and October, the period following harvest, and the time when Ishtar descended to the Underworld in search of her lost lover (see page 55). Prior to seizing power, Sargon himself may have been the official organizer of these corvées under the king of Kish.

Crops were harvested in the late spring and early summer. Nomadic pastoralists would then come down from their winter pastures and graze their flocks in the stubble fields, watering them at the canals and rivers. For this privilege they paid taxes in kind – meat, fleece, milk and cheese – to the palace and temple.

> 6I have not sinned, Oh Lord of the Land,
> I have not been negligent to your divinity,
> I have not done harm in Babylon ...
> I have not interfered with the temple,
> I have not been heedless of its rites,
> I have not afflicted the people under
> your protection. 9
>
> THE KING'S RITUAL PRAYER TO MARDUK AT THE SPRING FESTIVAL

THE SPRING FESTIVAL

There were many festivals throughout the year involving rituals in homage to the gods, including regular sacrifices and other oblations; but by far the most important public festival was the one that began the agricultural year in the spring. Called the *akitu*, it took place in March, beginning on the first day of spring, and lasted for 12 days – effectively a holiday before work began, like the period in medieval England, that linked Christmas Day with Plough Monday.

Babylon was traditionally the great centre for this festival, and all those who were able would travel from far and wide to the city in order to attend it. In an age which, despite its growing commitment to rationality, remained superstitious and retained a profound belief in the gods, this was regarded as a moment of renewal, a time in which, by paying homage to the king and the national god, the people could put the woes of the past behind them and look forward to a period of resurrection.

RIGHT *Three alabaster and gold votive figures, possibly priests, in ritual kilts, from the religious centre and university city of Nippur, c.2800 BC.*

Ishtar would return from Kur, and, after seed-time, the crops would push up green shoots and grow again.

Before any of that could be assured, however, the gods in general had to be fully propitiated through a series of spells and rituals, in order to avert any malign fate that might await the crop and the country. We have seen the importance placed on astrology. Society was shot through with a belief in omens and portents, a belief that was not unique to Mesopotamia; and the peoples of the Ancient Near East were constantly seeking ways to curry the favour of the gods in order to avert bad events, which they always saw as far more likely than good ones.

The bulk of the texts in Ashurbanipal's library were concerned with omens and the occult, dealing with how to interpret everything from the pattern of flight of a flock of birds, to the birth of a deformed animal, such as a calf with six legs. Recognized, highly trained and highly respected specialists knew how to read the future in animals' guts, livers or hearts (a practice known as haruspicy). A well-known sculpture of the head of Humbaba depicts the demon with a face composed of artfully-coiled intestines. Clay tablets representing the heart and liver of sheep exist, which were used as training aids, showing special points to look out for, and their significance. The only hope – and the purpose of divination – was that if the future was known to be bad, then something might be done to change the gods' minds about it.

ABOVE *Small (15 cm/6 in-high) bronze figure of the dog-headed demon Pazuzu, from the sixth century BC. These figurines were popular in the neo-Babylonian period. Pazuzu was king of the wind demons and controlled the southwest wind, known for bringing droughts and famine during dry seasons, and locusts during rainy seasons. Pazuzu amulets protected the owners against the malicious goddess Lamashtu, who was believed to cause harm to mother and child during childbirth. Although Pazuzu is himself an evil spirit, he drives away others, thus protecting humans against plagues and misfortunes. His four wings emphasize his power. He also often sports a huge penis.*

'The temple is a square building, two furlongs each way, with bronze gates, and was still in existence in my time; it has a solid central tower, one furlong square, with a second erected on top of it and then a third, and so on up to eight. All eight towers can be climbed by a spiral way running round the outside, and about half-way up there are seats for those who make the ascent to rest on. On the summit of the topmost tower stands a great temple with a fine large couch in it, richly covered, and a golden table beside it. The shrine contains no image, and no-one spends the night there except (if we may believe the Chaldeans who are the priests of Bel) one Assyrian woman, all alone, whoever it may be that the god has chosen. The Chaldeans also say – though I do not believe them – that the god enters the temple in person and takes his rest upon the bed.'

HERODOTUS: *THE HISTORIES* (c. 450 BC)

By the reign of Nebuchadrezzar the Spring, or New Year, Festival had become a fusion of two earlier traditions. One derived from an ancient fertility cult going back to pre-dynastic times and beyond, while the other came from the pantheon developed by the Sumerians and adopted and adapted by their successors.

The fertility cult ritual, called *zagmuk* by the Sumerians, was based not only on a mystical coupling of Ishtar and her consort, the chthonic god Tammuz, but also on the assumption that the power of procreation (or the embodiment of it) was not confined to just one pair of deities. This had to do with the intimate relationship a god or goddess had with his or her city. Ishtar and Tammuz (Inanna and Dumuzi in Sumerian) were originally linked with Uruk, but other gods –

ABOVE *Votive tablet (2600 or 2500 BC), from the region of Dyala or Ur, showing priests paying homage to a seated god (top row) and engaged in other ritual activities.*

despite not having the direct connection those two had with propagation and reproduction – would certainly perform that function for their city at the Spring Festival. Thus in the early days each city-state jealously ensured the well-being of its own fields and flocks through a mystical marriage.

This was enacted by ritual sexual intercourse between the high priestess of the temple, and the king or governor of the city, who stood in for the god. It was almost certainly a memory of this practise that led Herodotus to his mistaken assertion that all Babylonian women had, once in their lives, ritually to prostitute themselves, and his equally erroneous conclusion that the priestesses of Ishtar were religiously-sanctioned whores.

By Nebuchadrezzar's time, this sacred coupling had been synthesized with the Creation Myth, thereby linking the reaffirmation of the Earth's fruitfulness with an idea of the comforting restoration of divine order.

HOMAGE TO MARDUK

Marduk, tutelary deity of the city of Babylon, had by now long since completed the journey begun around 1000 years earlier from local to national god. He now embodied 50 of the major deities, and was in the unassailable position of being virtually the sole god. Certainly he overshadowed the rest, and now, in and by himself, he was both the procreative force and the divine defender of mankind. Even so, the Spring Festival still incorporated a ritual coupling of Marduk with Ishtar, the principal and long-enduring female deity. Marduk was even credited with the creation of man from *adamah* (clay). We come from clay and we return to it; everything is clay to be wrought in Marduk's hands.

The Spring Festival began with three days of mournful prayers and dirges led by the priests of the Esagila, Marduk's great temple in Babylon. The prayers expressed the people's fear of the unknown, and doubts about the future. The high priest would utter a special prayer daily to the still absent Marduk, imploring him to protect Babylon and its people, and to forgive them their sins.

On the fourth day the same rituals were repeated, but in the evening a more hopeful note would be struck by the recital of the Enuma Elish, the Creation Epic, in a version dating perhaps from sometime in the middle of the second millennium,

ABOVE *A rare wall painting showing a priest leading a bull to sacrifice, from the Palace of Zimri-Lim, Mari on the Middle Euphrates. Created in the 18th century* BC, *it is now in the National Museum of Syria at Aleppo.*

in which Marduk is established as the heroic champion of the gods, the creator of mankind, and the vanquisher of the forces of chaos, embodied in the shadowy Ur-goddess, Tiamat. The same night the king would prepare to submit himself to the judgement of Marduk the following day.

The fifth day was in many ways the most dramatic, and in its central ritual a very fundamental symbolism exists. The fifth day also marks the beginning of the 'drama' delineated as the Festival runs its course. In the morning, in his full regalia, the king entered the Esagila, with an escort of priests. They walked in procession to the high altar, where the high priest awaited them. For this ceremony, the high priest embodied Marduk, and in that role he formally stripped the king of all his regalia, his jewellery, sceptre and crown.

The king would then utter a prayer. Intriguingly, this was of the 'negative-confession' kind encountered in Ancient Egyptian funereal rites: '*I have not sinned, oh Lord of the Universe; I have not neglected your Might ...*' while the high priest proceeded to slap him hard, the harder the better, for if he managed to bring tears to the king's eyes, the better pleased would be the god. Then the priest would customarily say a prayer of absolution: '*Fear not. Marduk hears your prayers … increases your power, and the greatness of your reign … he blesses you forever. He will destroy your enemy, fell your adversary*', before restoring to the king his finery; but once dressed again, the king was subjected to a final slap in the face.

RITUAL ABASEMENT

In Nebuchadrezzar's time, the Babylonian king was the most powerful in the world, since Egypt was by then launched on its long period of decline. The ceremony reducing the monarch to mere manhood – in effect to a common member of his own people, sharing their pain – symbolized both the decline of the state and its subsequent rebirth, when the regalia of office were restored to the king. Once the ceremony was over, Marduk 'left' the high priest and retreated into the ziggurat, where he had to do battle with the Ekimmu, the evil gods of the Underworld. Taken prisoner by them, he then had to await rescue by his son Nabu, god of writing, who arrived by river on the sixth day amid rejoicing, accompanied by a retinue of tutelary deities from the other major cities of Babylon. Nabu frees his father on the seventh day of the Festival. On the eighth, the gods would hold a council and 're-elect' Marduk as their leader (and the embodiment of most of them). This ritual was a reaffirmation of the cosmic order.

The ninth day saw the procession of the god from his temple to the *bit-akitu*, the Festival House, along the Processional Way and through the Ishtar Gate, cheered by a population rejoicing at his liberation and reinstatement, as well as his triumph over the Ekimmu. On the tenth day, Marduk holds a feast for the gods (their images were arranged around a laden table for this ceremony). The god returned to the city that night for his union with Ishtar – enacted on the deities' behalf by the king – and the high priestess of Ishtar. These two would be enthroned before the people in triumph, and the product of their union would be the Spring.

On the eleventh day the gods met again in council to decide the fate of mankind for the coming year, reaching the conclusion that as long as mankind continues to serve them well, it has nothing to fear. The twelfth and final day of the festival saw the gods, represented by their images, return to their temples. Reassured, and armed against any possible vicissitudes during the next twelve months, the people returned to work.

ABOVE *Copper and silver vase dedicated by King Entemena to the god Nigirsu, from Telloh (ancient Girsu) c.2400 BC.*

'There is one custom amongst these people which is wholly shameful: every woman who is a native of the country must once in her life go and sit in the temple of Aphrodite and there give herself to a strange man … Most … sit in the precinct of the temple with a band of plaited string round their heads – and a great crowd they are, what with some sitting there, others arriving, others going away – and through them all gangways are marked off running in every direction for the men to pass along and make their choice. Once a woman has taken her seat she is not allowed to go home until a man has thrown a silver coin in her lap and taken her outside to lie with her …'

HERODOTUS: *THE HISTORIES* (c. 450 BC)

CHAPTER FIFTEEN

DAILY LIFE

MOST OF WHAT WE KNOW ABOUT ANCIENT MESOPOTAMIA necessarily concerns the major events and players, since they were what was written about. Likewise, their buildings and monuments have survived better than most. Even so, excavation at Ur and Babylon in particular has given us a hint of what daily life was like for the common people. Personal letters, and business and legal correspondence provide us with further clues, as do certain traces left behind by artisans and craftsmen.

As a result of the wealth accumulated by Babylon and Assyria through trade and conquest at different stages in their history, cities were – to judge from what has been excavated so far – opulently appointed and decorated, using materials that came from all over the known world. Archaeological finds in the Assyrian capital of Kalhu, for example, have yielded furniture embellished with ivory. In particular, the tombs of queens buried there, which were excavated in the 1980s, revealed a wealth of intricately worked gold ornaments, not unlike the discoveries made at the royal tombs of the early Ur dynasties. Measuring what has been found against what must have been lost, including perishable materials such as carpets, the phenomenal riches amassed over time can only be guessed at.

Some of that wealth filtered downwards, but we have little idea of the style of living of what we might call the upper echelons of Mesopotamian society, namely those classes immediately beneath the palace and temple élites. Documents show that senior officials were prosperous enough to invest substantially in land and property, and the business of borrowing and lending in silver, in large amounts, is also attested. However, as yet we have no clear idea of the precise size of landholdings and properties.

THE DAILY ROUND, THE COMMON TASK

Lower levels of society are harder to define, except broadly, but once again documentation from the time helps. As noted previously, by the reign of Hammurabi, Mesopotamian society was already divided into three main groups. Nor should we forget that for the bulk of our period and beyond, despite the growth and size of the cities, most people continued to work on the land, and lived in villages that have since disappeared without trace. Some so-called 'census lists' from the seventh century BC indicate that families tended to be small. On average, a farmer would have one wife and two to four children. His landholding would be modest, and he would farm vines and vegetables for his own use, as well as owning a modest amount of livestock. Date orchards were planted close to the rivers, where the water was sweetest, while vegetables and other fruit trees were grown under their canopy.

RIGHT *A detail from the 'Garden Party' frieze (gypsum; c.645 BC) from the North Palace at Nineveh. It is a rare example of the portrayal of a woman in Assyrian sculpture; the queen is shown drinking with her consort, King Ashurbanipal.*

Where the land was not irrigated, there was still enough wild brush and shrubs to provide food for flocks of sheep and goats. Water, however was never far away, and in the marshes rural people could feed themselves on a diet of fish and wildfowl. They also had the means of building to hand, in the shape of the reed-beds. From carvings of their dwellings, it appears that they were not unlike the houses of modern Marsh Arabs (a people of southern Iraq, whose culture is now under severe threat). The reed-beds also provided the raw material for everything from boats to furniture to styluses for pricking out cuneiform.

Agriculture was organized and controlled by the state; this was simply a pragmatic measure, and did not lead to the kind of Stalinist collective farming we might imagine. In any case, the Euphrates was always shifting its course, floods were unpredictable and could wreck people's hard work overnight. Accordingly, all Babylonians were imbued with an awareness of impermanence and so remained adaptable. In this context, it is worth noting that city-states vied with one another to attract labour, and their keen sense of rivalry, which was ingrained and never quite left them even when they became part of a common empire, militated against their accepting any form of totalitarianism. Palace and temple remained the major landowners, and most farmers worked for them.

MESOPOTAMIAN FAMILY LAW

Hammurabi's legal code provides us with a rich vein of information about the domestic organization of society. Marriage was evidently accepted as essentially monogamous, but on practical rather than moral grounds, for polygamy was not unlawful (there is no evidence of polyandry); this was largely to do with inheritance. A man could have a slave-woman as his concubine alongside his wife, and there was no social or moral stigma attached to that, but children of such an arrangement were not considered free unless he formally adopted them, and there might have been some resistance to that from the man's wife and her offspring. A woman cohabiting with a man had no rights as a wife unless she had a written contract. If two families wanted to merge their material interests, marriages might be arranged, between the fathers, or between a prospective bridegroom and the bride's father. If the bride were a minor, she would remain in her father's house, though legally married, until she started menstruating. In a new marriage, the husband would give the wife a cash gift intended to support her in the event of his death; her dowry, though managed by her husband during the marriage, always remained her property. If she died first, it went to her children. If she had none, it was returned to her parental household. Divorce was countenanced, and a woman was as free to sue for it as a man. A woman was protected by the law if her husband sought to get rid of her on any unreasonable grounds. The priestesses of certain gods and goddesses were allowed to marry, but if their cult forbade them children, the husband could father some with an appointed slave-woman. There are still further complexities to the legal statutes governing family matters in ancient Mesopotamia, but the examples cited above give some idea of their scope.

LIFE IN THE CITY

Some ordinary houses dating from Hammurabi's time were excavated in the city of Babylon, in the district known as Merkes, by Robert Koldewey; but the rest of his

> ❛The dress of the Babylonians consists of a linen tunic reaching to the feet with a woollen one over it, and a short white cloak on top; they have their own fashion in shoes, which resemble the slippers one sees in Boeotia. They grow their hair long, wear turbans, and perfume themselves all over; everyone owns a walking-stick specially made for him, with a device carved on the top of it, an apple or rose or lily or eagle or something of that sort ...❜
>
> HERODOTUS: *THE HISTORIES* (c. 450 BC)

city lies below the modern water-table, making it inaccessible. Even were this not the case, the overbuilding of a thousand years has obliterated or permanently interred most of the city prior to the reign of Nebuchadrezzar. Koldewey established that city planners had tried as far as possible to run the streets in straight lines and to have them intersect at right angles. Among the artefacts he found at lower levels were business letters and numerous examples of 'omen literature', stored in jars, as well as a number of shallow, fine-walled but simple bowls, and beakers and vases of various shapes and sizes, as well as early examples of glassware, some imported from Egypt. Koldewey also discovered here clay bells, earthenware model boats, vast storage jars, and shallow basalt bowls for rubbing out grain. Unearthed burials revealed rarely-found bronze swords, knives and lances and exquisite onyx necklaces, together with other ornaments such as rings (some signet rings), bangles and anklets, gold earrings and cylinder seals. Koldewey found evidence of burials '*by the fortification walls, in the streets, and in such parts of the inhabited town as were unappropriated for dwelling-houses at the time of the burial*'. However, he found no evidence of home-burial. The deepest levels he reached, dating to about the time of Hammurabi, revealed 'no sarcophagi. The bodies lay either simply in the earth, or at most were rolled in reed mats or were roughly surrounded by mud bricks. They were almost always laid out at full-length, and often in an attitude that gives an impression that they were left in the same place and situation in which they died.'

More evidence has come to light elsewhere, particularly in Ur, where Leonard Woolley's work in the 1920s revealed a number of private houses and ordinary streets, though most were destroyed in attacks on the city in the period immediately following Hammurabi's demise. But a violent end for these dwellings benefits the archaeologist. Many were burned down, but fire cannot destroy clay or brick, and a wealth of documents and other artefacts relating to daily life were preserved in the ruins. Woolley was able to make several precise identifications: among the streets, which he gave familiar names like Broad Street and Old Street, he found a house belonging to someone called Igmil-Sin, the headmaster of a school, who taught history, mathematics, religion and writing. It contained hundreds of his pupils' clay 'exercise books'; classes were held in the courtyard and guest-room, and other documents found at Igmil's house indicate that he was involved with his temple as a lay official, perhaps a 'churchwarden'.

Another dwelling belonged to Ea-nasir, a merchant trading copper to Dilmun, who ran into financial difficulty and had to sell off part of his house to a neighbour. Thereafter, Ea-nasir dabbled in moneylending, property development and dealt in secondhand clothing, but before long, to judge from apparently unanswered letters to him, he was on the slippery slope. A third establishment was identified as a restaurant or a 'cook-house', not unlike the ones that existed in London in the 17th century, where people could bring their food to be cooked before taking it home. A bronze foundry belonging to one Gimil-Ningishzida, was also found, and in it, oddly, a copy of a Sumero-Akkadian grammar.

City-dwellers often had country property as well, if only a date orchard or a hectare of grain. Rewards for public service frequently took the form of a land grant.

THE LAYOUT OF HOMES

Most houses were two-storey, and built around a courtyard whose floor sloped inwards to a central drain, so that it could be easily cleaned with water – a general design that would be familiar to older Iraqis today. Dwellings varied in size according to the prosperity of the owner – from between 40 and 500 square metres (430–5380 sq ft), with most being between 60 and 200 (646–2150 sq ft). They had reed doors and windows whose frames were of wood. Construction was of brick bound with clay or bitumen, and plastered with clay inside and out. The family dead were buried below the floors or placed in a vaulted tomb at the rear of the house, in a narrow paved yard behind the guest-room, where there was also a small chapel with images of the principal household (or favourite) gods. The dead were buried simply. They had no need of equipment to take with them to the land of Kur, since they were still at home, and still had access to the household goods.

Home burial, which may have originated during Ur III, had not always been the custom. Cemeteries of pre-Sargonid times, like the one in which Leonard

&In every village once a year all the girls of marriageable age used to be collected together in one place, while the men stood round them in a circle; an auctioneer then called each one in turn to stand up and offered her for sale, beginning with the best-looking ... Marriage was the object of the transaction. The rich men who wanted wives bid against each other for the prettiest girls, while the humbler folk, who had no use for good looks in a wife, were actually paid to take the ugly ones ...9

HERODOTUS: *THE HISTORIES* (*c.* 450 BC)

Woolley discovered the royal tombs at Ur, contained thousands of modest plots. Surrounding the final resting places of prominent citizens, these graves revealed that common people were customarily buried with a handful of household goods or weapons to take to the netherworld with them. In Nebuchadrezzar's Babylon, Robert Koldewey found evidence of a necropolis under the principal court of the Southern Palace, containing hundreds of terracotta coffins, originally decorated with a fine blue glaze, and evidently used by the élite.

The houses excavated by Woolley at Ur had other rooms that we would also recognize: kitchens, workshops, store rooms, bathrooms, privies and long, rectangular principal rooms used for both entertaining and as bedrooms. Furniture would have consisted of tables, chairs, stools, chests, cushions, and rugs, of varying quality depending on the owner's affluence. There was no town-planning. City districts grew organically, one house apparently evolving from the next; the streets were a maze where a stranger could easily get lost.

WORK AND PLAY

Cities were frequently divided into quarters devoted to certain trades or professions, as is still the case in several cities throughout the world today. Shops might have been grouped in bazaars or in squares near the city gates, and would have specialized in particular goods – for instance, pottery, leatherware, food, drink, pharmaceutical products, carpets, clothes, spices and scents. In addition, there were barbers and blacksmiths, bath-houses, brewers and perhaps 'bars', and cafés selling grilled fish and lamb, onion, cucumber, dates and apricots. Ordinary city streets also contained modest public temples for day-to-day worship.

The streets were narrow and winding, and the façades of buildings were windowless. The roads and alleyways teemed with water-carriers, peddlers, and messengers, rubbing shoulders with shoppers and businessmen, priests and slaves. Occasionally, in a square or by a temple, you would come across the office or desk of a public letter-writer, while in the evenings you might encounter an 'actor' declaiming one of the epics while his assistant carried round the hat. Life would have been lived on the roofs, where it was cooler, and the city would be at its most animated in the early and late part of the day: the sun at its zenith was far too hot to permit much activity.

The board-game discovered by Woolley in the royal tombs at Ur was a luxury version of a game common throughout the Ancient Near East, and it is from other sources that we recognize it as a cousin of ludo. Scholars have found it hard to pin down exactly what pastimes took place in ancient Mesopotamia; however, as wealth created increased leisure, there must have been a variety of ways in which richer people amused themselves, and an entertainment industry to service their needs. There were certainly musicians and dancers; there is also sufficient evidence of elaborate banquets to suggest the existence of professional chefs.

On the whole, though, games appear to have been linked to the temple and to ritual. Wrestling matches are known to have taken place in celebration of different deities (there are figurines in the National Museum of Iraq and plaques in the Louvre showing them) but we can only surmise the existence of organized athletics, or similar competitive sporting contests. It is, however, possible to hazard a guess that certain forms of sporting activity (as in ancient Greece) might well have been associated with military training, especially in the era of the professional soldier. Some of the wrestlers mentioned may have been younger priests: the priestly caste – which tended to run in families – was large and embraced a wide variety of different offices.

DESPOILING THE ENVIRONMENT

As we know, a burgeoning human population has a negative impact on the environment. In the Ancient Near East, overcutting of oak trees was causing their depletion as early as 10,000 BC, while the high value of cedar prompted intensive felling, from which the once-great forests of Lebanon never recovered. Similarly, overgrazing saw the loss of topsoil in vulnerable regions (as did logging), with sheep and especially goats the principal culprits. Sheep graze to the root level and so destroy the network that holds the soil together; goats eat almost everything that grows. Yet certain plants, such as herbs and scrub vegetation actually thrived on the dung of grazing livestock. Poor irrigation systems during the early period in southern Mesopotamia led to salination of the soil, although steps were taken later to redeem the situation; salt remained present there for ever after, but the problem became manageable. However, silts from soil erosion in the north carried down by the twin rivers and their tributaries could clog watercourses, causing changes of course and flooding of arable land. Silting-up of the irrigation canals was one of the main reasons for the laborious clean-up operations required after every year's harvest.

The region's fauna also suffered terribly as a result of human activity. The Asiatic elephant and the Nile hippopotamus were extinct even before the advent of agriculture. Hunting brought an early end to some species of gazelle, though other antelopes, along with the Asiatic lion, survived until the 20th century.

ABOVE *A bitumen relief plaque from Susa (eighth or ninth century BC) showing a weaver at work. Fanned by a servant and comfortably seated with one leg tucked under her, this elaborately-coiffed Elamite woman spins wool with a spindle. A fish lies on a table in front of her. The wool industry was very important, and concerns were frequently controlled and run by women.*

PART THREE

BABYLONIAN SUNSET

CHAPTER SIXTEEN

THE LAST KING

NEBUCHADREZZAR THE GREAT covered the first decades of his long reign in glory, but there is a dearth of information about his final years. The fact that he built a defensive wall to the north of his capital suggests that he may have had reason to suspect his Median allies of turning against him, but there is no recorded attack from that quarter.

PREVIOUS PAGES *The Fall of Babylon, a mezzotint by the English artist John Martin (1789–1854), created at a time when all things Mesopotamian were very fashionable in England.*

RIGHT *Stele of Nabonidus. Top right are the symbols for Sin (moon), Shamash (sun) and Ishtar (the planet Venus). The original writing beneath has been erased, possibly by followers of Cyrus the Great.*

The end of the Second Book of Kings in the Bible recounts that the governor of Judea, Gedeliah, appointed by Babylon after Zedekiah's fall, was murdered along with his Hebrew and Chaldean entourage, and that, as a result, '*all the people, both small and great, and the captains of the forces, arose and went to Egypt, for they were afraid of the Chaldeans*'. This suggests that Egypt might have been behind the murder, and elsewhere there is a fragmentary text that hints at a Babylonian invasion of that country, but it gives no details.

PRELUDE TO DECLINE

Nebuchadrezzar died in 562 BC and was succeeded by his son, Amel-Marduk (561–560 BC), who seems to have been unpopular at home, and of whom the third-century BC historian Berossus reports that he was restrained neither by the law nor by decency. Amel-Marduk may have been a middle-aged man by the time of his accession; in his short reign he did perform one act of clemency. To cite a subsequent passage from the Second Book of Kings:

'Babylon the creation of Ellil
Babylon that secures the life of the land
Babylon city of abundance
Babylon city whose citizens are overwhelmed by wealth
Babylon city of festivities joy and dancing
Babylon the city whose citizens celebrate ceaselessly
Babylon privileged city which frees the captive
Babylon the pure city.'

HYMN OF PRAISE TO BABYLON FROM THE
TIME OF NEBUCHADREZZAR

And in the thirty-seventh year of the exile of Jehoiachin, King of Judea, in the twelfth month, on the twenty-seventh day of the month, Evil-merodach [i.e. Amel-Marduk] King of Babylon, in the year that he began to reign, graciously freed Jehoiachin from prison; and he spoke kindly to him, and gave him a seat above the seats of the kings who were with him in Babylon. So Jehoiachin put off his prison garments. And every day of his life he dined regularly at the king's table; and for his allowance, a regular allowance was given him by the king, every day a portion, as long as he lived.

We must, as ever, take the Bible's reporting with a pinch of salt, at least as far as Jehoiachin's imprisonment is concerned, but the act of clemency undoubtedly happened, and Jehoiachin must have been relieved after decades of house arrest. A recent discovery by Dr Irving Finkel of the British Museum throws an interesting and very human light on this story. Finkel found a tablet-letter in the museum's collection indicating that Amel-Marduk was himself imprisoned for a time earlier in his father's reign for some act of slander. The letter protests Amel's innocence in tones that are unusually emotional for ancient Mesopotamian writings. Intriguingly, a 12th-century AD Hebrew manuscript relating to this incident suggests that Amel-Marduk may have spent his incarceration in Jehoiachin's company. If this were true, it is easy to see why the new king would free his fellow-sufferer as soon as possible after his father's death. If the Bible can be believed regarding the treatment Jehoiachin received after his release, then quite a close friendship is indicated between the two men. What happened to Jehoiachin after Amel-Marduk's own departure is uncertain.

As for Amel-Marduk himself, he was killed in a palace coup, possibly organized by his brother-in-law Neriglissar, a senior Babylonian general, who may have been with Nebuchadrezzar at the siege of Jerusalem. Neriglissar's reign was also brief (559–556 BC), and we know little of it beyond that he carried out temple restorations in Babylon and Borsippa, as well as conducting an important campaign in Khilakku (Cilicia). There was barely a hint of trouble on the frontiers of the empire, which remained intact after Nebuchadrezzar's death, so Neriglissar's move westwards across the Taurus suggests expansionist ambitions, or at least a move to bring Cilicia, which had been on friendly terms with Babylon, to heel, after the country began making friendly approaches to its western neighbour, Lydia. The political details are complex, but the point is that Neriglissar had the confidence and the means to launch a major campaign and succeed.

The circumstances of Neriglissar's death are obscure; he left as his heir his young son Labashi-Marduk, who was ousted within months in a bloodless coup staged by senior officials, who in his stead installed another general, experienced and well into middle age by the time of his accession. This general, whose name was Nabonidus, denied any personal ambition to be king, but the fact remains that his son, Belshazzar, quickly seized large estates that had been privately owned by Neriglissar.

> ‘Out of his love for me who worships him and have laid hold of the hem of his garment, Sin, the king of all gods, did what he had not done before, had not granted to anybody else, he gave me – a woman – an exalted position and a famous name in the country. He added to my life many days and years of happiness and kept me alive from the time of Ashurbanipal, king of Assyria, to the ninth year of Nabonidus, king of Babylon, the son whom I bore: 104 happy years spent in that piety which Sin, the king of all gods, has planted in my heart. My eyesight was good to the end of my life, my hearing excellent, my hands and feet were sound, my words well chosen, food and drink agreed with me, my health was fine and my mind happy. I saw my great-great grandchildren, up to the fourth generation, in good health, and thus had my fill of old age.’

A PSEUDO-AUTOBIOGRAPHICAL INSCRIPTION ON A MEMORIAL STELE
TO NABONIDUS' MOTHER AT HARRAN

A Deeply Unpopular Ruler

Nabonidus (555–539 BC) was the last king to rule Mesopotamia. Despite his generalship, the records portray him in a non-military light, as a man who was interested in history, antiquity, and restoring temples (in which capacity he completed certain works begun by Nebuchadrezzar and Neriglissar. He was also concerned with promoting the moon-god, Sin, whose worship had fallen into neglect. Nabonidus' mother, Adda-Guppi, of whom he seems to have been very fond, was a high priestess of Sin's cult. His father, Nabu-balatsu-ikbi, was a minor nobleman about whom we otherwise know nothing.

He seems to have concentrated most of his energies in the old south of his country, but must have been an able ruler, since the empire did not fall until the end of his reign; and only then as a result of intolerable pressure. Nevertheless, Nabonidus' championing of Sin did not endear him to the powerful priests of Marduk, while his conduct may not have inspired the confidence of his people. In all likelihood these factors facilitated the Persian invasion that ended his rule; the invaders presented their action as a campaign of liberation.

The fact that Nabonidus was chosen as king by his peers was an indication of his ability. Thirty years before his accession as ruler, he may well have been the commander who negotiated a peace treaty between the Medes and the Lydians. His early years as king were marked by a sound military policy, and he seems always to have retained the loyalty of the army; but still we are not left with the impression that he was popular.

Reasons for this are not hard to find. He was not of Nebuchadrezzar's line, nor was he of noble birth. In themselves these disadvantages might not have mattered. His mother, who lived to the extraordinary age of 104, dying only in Nabonidus' ninth regnal year, was high priestess of Sin at Harran, the northern city that the last king of Assyria had made his final refuge. As high priestesses were usually recruited from

THE WRITING ON THE WALL

Immediately the fingers of a man's hand appeared and wrote on the plaster of the wall of the king's palace, opposite the lampstand; and the king saw the hand as it wrote. Then the king's colour changed, and his thoughts alarmed him; his limbs gave way, and his knees knocked together. The king cried aloud to bring in the enchanters, the Chaldeans, and the astrologers. The king said to the wise men of Babylon, "Whoever reads this writing, and shows me its interpretation, shall be clothed with purple, and have a chain of gold about his neck, and shall be the third ruler in the kingdom." Then all the king's wise men came in, but they could not read the writing or make known to the king the interpretation. Then King Belshazzar was greatly alarmed, and his colour changed, and his lords were perplexed.

This well-known passage from the fifth book of Daniel (verses 5–9) has given rise to a common expression and inspired a famous painting by Rembrandt. Daniel interprets the words – MENE, MENE, TEKEL, UPHARSIN. They indicate diminishing monetary values: MENE refers to the *mina*, TEKEL to the *shekel*, and UPHARSIN to the half-*shekel*, and Daniel glosses the phrase as follows: '*You have been weighed in the balance and found wanting ... Your country will be given over to the Medes and the Persians.*'

The writer of the Book of Daniel, who was composing his text after the event, knew full well that the Persians had seized Babylon, so fulfilling the prophet's interpretation. The crime of Belshazzar, who was never actually king, only regent to his father Nabonidus during the latter's absence in Taima, was to have unwittingly committed sacrilege, using the sacred vessels taken from the temple of Solomon in Jerusalem for the feast ('*for a thousand of his lords*', a relatively modest banquet by Babylonian standards) that the Writing on the Wall brusquely interrupts. But the plundering of defeated enemies' temples was standard practice in Babylonian warfare. Moreover, since the message was written in Aramaic – widespread by Belshazzar's time – he would have been perfectly able to understand it himself. When Rembrandt put this to his friend the Sephardic Rabbi Menasseh-ben-Israel (1604–57), the latter explained that the regent failed to understand it because the words were not written in the order he would have expected. Semantics aside, the story, and those elsewhere in the Book of Daniel relating to dream interpretation, do indicate what great store the Babylonians set by dreams, omens and portents.

RIGHT *Belshazzar taken aback at God's intervention, as imagined by Rembrandt. The painter mistakenly arranged the characters in the damning inscription in columns, rather than right to left, the customary way of writing Hebrew (Aramaic script).*

the nobility, Adda-Guppi – whose praises Nabonidus sings in a pseudo-autobiographical stele he set up for her after her death – was probably herself an Assyrian
aristocrat. It was a long time since Nabopolassar had dealt the death-blow to the
Assyrian empire, but not long enough for the Assyrian hegemony over Babylon to
have been forgotten, especially not by the Chaldeans, who had fought so hard and
so long for their independence. If Nabonidus was of Assyrian stock, it would
certainly not have helped his popularity. It is true that he tried to introduce a series
of governmental and economic reforms, but apparently he did so in such a heavy-
handed manner that even these only served to alienate him further from his people.

One of the first works he undertook was the restoration of his mother's temple,
the Ehulhul, in Harran. One of the texts on the so-called 'Nabonidus Cylinder,'
found at Sippar and now in the British Museum, claims that Marduk instructed him
to do so in a dream, but it is also fulsome in its praise of Sin; and references to
Marduk on inscriptions at Harran itself are conspicuous by their absence. At the
time, Harran was in the hands of the Medes, and Nabonidus could do nothing to
dislodge them, but as the city was at the crossroads of important northern trade
routes serving the northwestern Median empire and the Lydian kingdom (modern
western Turkey), it is possible that Nabonidus' work on the temple was not entirely
dictated by sentimental considerations.

Despite the homage to Babylon contained in the information that Nabonidus
was acting on Marduk's instructions, the restoration work at Harran aroused great
resentment at home. Other stormclouds were also gathering, according to the
cylinder inscriptions:

> At the beginning of the third year [553 BC] they aroused Cyrus, the king ...
> He scattered the vast Median hordes with his small army. He captured
> Astyages, the king of the Medes, and took him to his country as captive. Such
> was the word of the great lord Marduk and of Sin, the luminary of heaven
> and the netherworld, whose command is not revoked. I [Nabonidus] feared
> their august command, I became troubled, I was worried and my face showed
> signs of anxiety. I was not neglectful, nor remiss, nor careless.

It has been suggested that Nabonidus may have tried to oust the Medes from
Harran by sending an embassy to Cyrus, proposing an alliance. If this was the case,
however, clearly nothing can have come of it.

Cyrus, an Achaemenid king, had taken power in Persia and had already made a
successful move against the Medes, seizing their capital, Ecbatana (Hamadan), in 549
BC. Mesopotamia was threatened along its northern and eastern borders. By 549,
Cyrus controlled the entire Median empire. Three years later, he officially assumed
the title of King of Persia.

Meanwhile, apparently insouciant in the face of the Persian threat, Nabonidus
blithely pursued his major rebuilding programmes. Those of his predecessors had
severely depleted the exchequer, and so popular resentment against him grew. His
unpopularity was further exacerbated by an outbreak of plague, and severe inflation:
between 560 and 550 BC, prices rose by 50 percent.

A FATEFUL DECISION

It was at this point, in about 552 BC, that the king, by now probably in his late fifties,
came to an extraordinary decision. Leaving his capable son, Belshazzar, as regent in
the city of Babylon, he abandoned his capital and decamped with his court to the
city of Taima, 560 miles (900 km) to the southwest, in the northern Arabian desert.
There he established what was, to all intents and purposes, a new capital, with regal

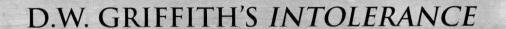

D.W. GRIFFITH'S *INTOLERANCE*

In Hollywood pioneer D.W. Griffith's film *Intolerance* (1916) the 'Babylonian Story' recounts the attack on Babylon by Cyrus the Great of Persia. The peace-loving Prince Belshazzar is betrayed to the Persian king by mutinous priests, despite the efforts of a loyal and ferocious Mountain Girl to save the day. The set was the largest ever created to date, and for the various crowd sequences 16,000 extras were used. The overall budget (US $2 million) was equally impressive for the day; a third was used for the Babylonian sequences.

The story of the fall of Babylon is remarkable for its historical accuracy (up to a point) and for its sympathy towards the Babylonians. The sequences within the city are played on sets worthy of Nebuchadrezzar himself, though it is unlikely that he or his

successors would have had any elephants at his court. In its day, the film was a flop. Its message of pacifism did not go down well in the United States, which was poised to enter the First World War. It is unwieldy, balances its four parallel stories – on the life of Jesus, the St Bartholomew's Day Massacre of 1572, and a 'Modern Story' of social injustice – precariously, and is, at 197 minutes long, a true epic. Interestingly, each of the stories was given its own distinctive tinting; the Babylonian Story had a grey-green tint.

There have been few other feature films, and none of such stature, dealing with Babylon. Domenico Paolella's *Hercules Versus the Tyrants of Babylon* (1964), with Rock Stevens (aka Peter Lupus) and Helga Liné, is an interesting take on the theme.

buildings and temples to match such status. And there he remained for a decade.

Nabonidus had not been forced out of Babylon, and his desertion of his capital at such a dangerous time would not have improved his standing with the people or the priesthood. Most important of all, the Spring Festival could not go ahead in his absence, and so the entire ritual cycle was disrupted and undermined. Furthermore, although Belshazzar was crown prince and controlled the army, he had none of his father's authority and was unable to quell growing opposition. Most damagingly, a pro-Persian faction emerged, perhaps partially funded by Cyrus, which increasingly presented the Persians as liberators.

Various reasons have been put forward for Nabonidus' fateful decision to quit the capital. His obsession with religious reform seems to have become almost a mania, and he made no secret of his disgust at what he saw as the impiety (in their refusal to accept Sin) and even lawlessness of his subjects; certainly the Book of Daniel (while confusing him with Nebuchadrezzar) imputed a period of madness to the king. Might such considerations have persuaded him to depart? Or had he perhaps contracted a disease – leprosy has been suggested – which obliged him to go? Other Hebrew sources suggest a seven-year illness, the result of divine wrath, but these may have derived from propaganda put out by the Marduk faction of the priesthood. Nabonidus' own chronicle states that he was ill in 553–552 BC, but that he recovered.

Perhaps Nabonidus simply did not care about the permanent damage he was doing to his popularity at home. He was evidently neither a vainglorious nor an unintelligent man and so must have realized, if nothing else, how morale-sapping the suspension of the Spring Festival would be. Did he hope, by putting the festival into abeyance, to strike a blow for Sin against Marduk?

Whatever actually occurred, the fact remains that after an absence of ten years, Nabonidus returned to Babylon unopposed and was accepted back without opposition. This is all the more surprising, since he had, in his son Belshazzar, left behind a responsible and unobjectionable representative whom the Babylonians might well have rallied round as an alternative ruler (there is nothing to indicate that he shared his father's crusading zeal for the moon-god). Yet this clearly did not happen.

It therefore seems likely that, in quitting Babylon, Nabonidus had taken a calculated risk for the good of his country. Taima, which was within the empire, stood at the meeting-place of many caravan routes serving Damascus, Saba, the Persian Gulf, the Red Sea, and Egypt. It would have made a good base from which to develop a new trading empire, which could push south along the Red Sea coast and elsewhere, using camel-caravans. Given his earlier interest in Harran, and the fact that international trade flourished during his reign, it may be that his ambitions lay in this direction.

But all this is conjecture, and the last theory, though reasonable and perhaps the most likely, is still open to objection: if Nabonidus knew his history – and he did – he would have realized the sheer folly of any king abandoning his power base, especially in uncertain times. Also, in the ten years he had spent away, he became an old man: would he have had the energy and the ambition to promote such a scheme, given that he must have known how deeply he was disliked at home? But the greatest objection of all lies in the fact that we have no textual evidence for his motives; and that the decade in the wilderness appears to have been entirely fruitless.

BELOW *Nabonidus' promotion of the moon-god Sin and related deities, such as his daughter Ishtar, over the traditional principal god Marduk may well have contributed to his great unpopularity. This third-millennium BC alabaster statue of Ishtar comes from her temple at Mari.*

Among his other achievements was the restoration of the temple at Ur, another seat of the moon-god, and where, in emulation of Sargon, he installed his daughter, Bel-shalti-Nannar, as high priestess, resurrecting the office, which had fallen into desuetude, to do so. The temple at Harran continued to operate for centuries, and as late as AD 300 Roman coins minted there displayed Sin's crescent-moon emblem, a symbol that still has religious significance today. But Nabonidus' faults outweighed his virtues in the public memory, and after the fall of Babylon it was in Cyrus' interests to besmirch the reputation of the king he had defeated. Babylonian supporters of Cyrus busily wrote anti-Nabonidus texts. In one of them, *The Verse Account of Nabonidus*, he is portrayed as a madman, a liar who boasted of victories that had never been his, and a heretic who decried Marduk and foisted on his people instead the god Sin — '*a deity which nobody had ever seen in this country*'. Cyrus' policy was largely one of *laissez-faire* in the countries he conquered: he left the essential infrastructure and certainly the religion alone; and this was one of the reasons why he was so successful.

CYRUS INVADES

Cyrus attacked Babylonia in the autumn of 539 BC. Belshazzar, an able soldier and the army's commander-in-chief, mobilized his forces along the Tigris. But it was a rout. In addition to being an immeasurably stronger force, the Persians were also helped by the defection to their side of Gubaru, the governor of Assyria. Nabonidus had to fall back from Sippar, which fell without a fight, and after a campaign of just 16 days, Babylon was taken, again without putting up any resistance. Nabonidus was taken captive; according to some sources Cyrus spared him and made him governor of Central Persia, though that seems unlikely. Nabonidus would have been around 70 years old, and such a defeat would almost certainly have broken him. His son Belshazzar was killed in fighting at the city of Opis, east of Sippar.

Cyrus himself entered the city of Babylon about a fortnight after it had been taken. There was no looting, nothing was destroyed, and the temples, the gods, private property and the palace were all respected. As soon as order was restored, Cyrus instigated a programme of resettlement, and returned to their home temples in outlying cities the images of gods that Nabonidus had brought into Babylon for safekeeping during the hostilities.

In the face of such magnanimity, it is small wonder that Mesopotamia succumbed. Cyrus pressed home the point by making it clear that he regarded himself as the humble successor to all the established rulers of the country. He praised its heroes, and proclaimed that he himself worshipped Marduk and '*praised his great godhead joyously*'. All the religious ceremonies and cults disrupted by Nabonidus, who had effectively handed victory to Cyrus on a plate, were reinstated. Amid general approval, Cyrus then ordered Nabonidus' name to be chiselled off all his monuments.

A clay cylinder document (the 'Cyrus Cylinder', now in the British Museum), written in Akkadian, has come down to us which, if it can be believed, and we discount Cyrus' own propaganda machine, tells us that the Babylonians accepted the Persian leader unreservedly:

> *All the inhabitants of Babylon, as well as of the entire country of Sumer and Akkad, princes and governors, bowed to him, and kissed his feet, jubilant that he had received the kingship, and with shining faces happily greeted him as a master through whose help they had come to life from death and had all been spared damage and disaster, and they worshipped his name.*

And thus, after many centuries and successive dynasties, indigenous rule over Mesopotamia finally came to an end.

CHAPTER SEVENTEEN

IN SEARCH OF
THE PAST

Most of the existing remains of the city of Babylon lie on the eastern bank of the Euphrates. At its height, it was the greatest city in the known world, and the first historian to take note of it was Herodotus. Alhough we cannot be sure that he actually visited Babylon, his descriptions of it show that he was enthralled by the city.

Herodotus was a Greek traveller and historian who lived in the fifth century BC, between about 485 and 425. The first-century BC Roman orator Cicero called him the 'Father of History', but his other nickname is the 'Father of Lies', on account of his tendency both to fabricate information to make his story more interesting, and to accept at face value whatever he was told. The degree to which this affected his work is still a matter of debate, but Herodotus remains an extremely valuable and entertaining source, and where he is misleading or inaccurate, the work of his successors throughout history is available to alert us to the fact. To his credit, he does tell us that he is only reporting what he was told. Voraciously inquisitive, and an indefatigable traveller, he set out to trace the root causes of the Graeco-Persian wars of 490 and 480–479 BC (the battles of Marathon and Thermopylae were major features of these campaigns). In the process, he delved back into history, and digressed freely according to where his interests led him. His account of ancient Mesopotamia is to be found in Book I in modern editions (and translations) of his *Histories*.

ANCIENT HISTORIANS ON MESOPOTAMIA

Ctesias of Cnidus was a close contemporary of Herodotus. He was physician to the Persian king Artaxerxes II Mnemon (r. 404–358 BC), whom he accompanied on a military expedition in 401 BC against his rebellious brother, Cyrus the Younger. Ctesias wrote works on rivers, and on Persian economics, as well as a long history of Assyria and Persia, the *Persica*, supposedly based on the Persian royal archives.

The first six books of the *Persica* cover the history of Assyria and Babylon up to the founding of the Persian empire; the remaining 17 go down to the year 398 BC. The Greek historian Diodorus Siculus (fl. 45 BC) was strongly influenced by Ctesias, and the second book of his own multi-volume universal history, the *Bibliotheca historica,* leans heavily on his work. The account that Diodorus offers there of ancient Mesopotamia is highly entertaining and enthusiastic, but generally unsound.

The historical value of the *Persica* has been hotly debated, both in ancient and modern times. Many ancient authorities valued it highly, and used it to discredit Herodotus. Nowadays, it is argued that the book has little value as history, since its account of the Assyrian kings fails to match the cuneiform evidence. The Assyrian rhetorician Lucian, writing in the first century AD, thought Ctesias and Herodotus were as bad as each other, and fancifully packed them both off to hell:

RIGHT *An armed Iraqi security guard watches over an ancient Sumerian site that was only discovered in 2000 at Umm al-Aqareb, 186 miles (300 km) south of Baghdad. The settlement there has been dated to 2700 BC, making it one of the oldest archaeological finds in the world. The remains of the town include a cemetery, houses and a palace.*

The people who suffered the greatest torment were those who had told lies when they were alive and written mendacious histories; among them were Ctesias of Cnidus, Herodotus, and many others.

The next historian to write about our period, and who lived shortly after it, was Berossus, who published his *Babylonaica* in around 278 BC. His work as a whole no longer exists, but he is extensively quoted by other historians who came soon after him and did have access to his book, such as Flavius Josephus (*c.* AD 37–100). Berossus was born either shortly before or during Alexander the Great's reign in Babylon, and Berossus (or 'Berossos') is a Greek form of his Akkadian name, which signified: '*Bel is His Shepherd*'. He wrote his work perhaps in response to a commission from the Seleucid king Antiochus I Soter (r. 281–261 BC).

The last of the ancient historians – and there are many more – who should be mentioned here is the Greek Strabo ('squinter'), who lived from about 64 BC to AD 24. His *Geographica* is almost totally lost, but again quotations and references have come down to us through other writers. He himself drew heavily on such scholars as Polybius and Thucydides, but his commentaries are of interest as the *Geographica*, in the course of its 17 volumes, deals closely with the Ancient Near East. From the opinion Strabo had of Herodotus and Ctesias – one echoed several decades later by Lucian – we can infer that the Greeks had by then acquired wider knowledge of Mesopotamian history.

EUROPEAN INTEREST

There then appears to have been a lull in interest (or perhaps any work written has been lost) until we come to the earliest European records of the Ancient Near East, notably that of the 12th-century AD Rabbi Benjamin of Tudela, who travelled in the region and left an account of his experiences. Four centuries later, the London merchant Ralph Fitch (d. *c.*1610) became one of the first Englishmen to visit Mesopotamia. He and his companions also sailed via the Persian Gulf and the Arabian Sea to India and Southeast Asia. In February 1583 he embarked in the *Tyger* for Tripoli and Aleppo, together with fellow merchants John Newbery and John Eldred, a jeweller named William Leedes and a painter, James Story, all financed by the Levant Company. From Aleppo they reached the Euphrates, sailed downriver, crossed southern Mesopotamia to Baghdad, and then made their way down the Tigris to Basra. Eldred stayed there to trade, while Fitch and the others sailed down the Persian Gulf to Ormuz, where they were arrested as spies, at the instigation of the Venetians, who jealously guarded the eastern trade routes. In the autumn they were sent as prisoners to the Portuguese viceroy at Goa. Fitch's journey is mentioned by Shakespeare, some famous lines from 'Macbeth' (Act I, Scene III, 4–10):

> *A sailor's wife had chestnuts in her lap,*
> *And munched, and munched, and munched.*
> *'Give me', quoth I.*
> *'Aroint thee, witch!' the rump-fed ronyon cries.*
> *Her husband's to Aleppo gone, master of the Tiger:*
> *But in a sieve I'll thither sail,*
> *And, like a rat without a tail,*
> *I'll do, I'll do, and I'll do.*

Fitch returned to London in 1591, where his story was recorded, with keen attention, by the founders of the East India Company.

Some 30 years after Fitch's expedition, the Italian nobleman Pietro della Valle (1586–1652) set off, in 1614, at the age of 28, to travel in the east and make a pilgrimage to the Holy Land. He did so at the suggestion of a friend who advised it as a better alternative to suicide – della Valle was suffering from a rebuff in love at the time. He was a cultivated man, well-versed in Latin, Greek, classical mythology and the Bible, to which knowledge he added good Turkish and some Arabic during his first year abroad, spent at Constantinople. Travelling always in high style with a retinue befitting his rank and wealth, he then set off for Alexandria, then Cairo, and reached Jerusalem in time to celebrate Easter in 1616. After Palestine, he visited Damascus and Aleppo, and then made for Baghdad, his curiosity aroused not least by having seen a portrait of the beautiful Princess Ma'ani, who lived there. Travels in Persia followed, from where he would later bring back to Europe the first Persian cats. He then undertook various adventures in India before journeying home via Basra. Della Valle left a memoir of his exploits, *Travels in Persia*, which was published posthumously from 1658 to 1663 and contains interesting accounts of Mesopotamia.

EARLY ARCHAEOLOGICAL EXPEDITIONS

Various other travellers in the 18th century wrote memoirs, but it wasn't until the 19th century that serious archaeological investigation began. Stimulated by their reading of ancient historians, and encouraged by the expansion of the British empire in the Middle East, it was the English who made the first expeditions, though Italian and French scholars were not far behind. The first archaeologists were essentially amateurs, but they approached their task with responsibility and respect. Claudius

BELOW *In 1985, to the great dismay of archaeologists, the Iraqi dictator Saddam Hussein embarked on an extensive rebuilding of the ancient city of Babylon, as an exercise in self-aggrandizement. Seen here is his reconstruction of the Processional Way that led to the Ishtar Gate.*

James Rich (1787–1821), the young British Resident at Baghdad from 1808 to 1821, mapped the country and collected the artefacts which were to form the basis of the British Museum's exceptional collection. He was not always in time to rescue material from the depredations of local townspeople and tribesmen. While exploring Nineveh in 1820, he learned of '*an immense bas-relief, representing man and animals, covering a grey stone the height of two men.*' It had been uncovered two years earlier, and '*all the town of Mosul* [the modern town which abuts Nineveh] *went out to see it, and in a few days it was cut up or broken to pieces.*' Rich wrote two accounts of his work, which aroused great interest in England, and a squib from Byron (from 'Don Juan', Canto Five, 62):

> *But to resume, – should there be (what may not*
> *Be in these days?) some infidels, who don't,*
> *Because they can't find out the very spot*
> *Of that same Babel, or because they won't*
> *(Though Claudius Rich, Esquire, some bricks has got,*
> *And written lately two memoirs upon't) …*

Rich was followed by the French consul in Mosul, Paul-Émile Botta (1802–70), who carried out digs at Nineveh and Khorsabad in 1842 and 1843 – though he believed the latter to be the site of ancient Nineveh. He could be forgiven his mistake, for it was at Khorsabad, ancient Dur-Sharrukin, that he unearthed parts of the palace of Sargon II. He continued work, enthusiastically supported by the French government, until late 1844, when the arduous business began of transporting the huge sculptures he had found. 600 men were employed to drag them to Mosul on specially-constructed carts, after which they were floated on rafts down the Tigris to Basra, a journey of about 930 miles (1500 km), where they were loaded onto ships bound for France. It took two years for them to reach the Louvre.

Botta thought he had extracted everything of significance at Khorsabad and closed his dig, but private local entrepreneurs scavenged the site and the bits and pieces they uncovered were being bought up by the British Museum by 1847. The English also managed to transport two massive *lamassus*, left behind by the French as being unmanageably huge, back to London. They are still in the British Museum.

Austen Henry Layard (1817–94), who was later to carve out a successful career as a politician, spent his younger days as an archaeologist in Mesopotamia. He was the first to adopt a systematic approach. Under the enlightened aegis of Sir Stratford Canning, British ambassador to the Sublime Porte at Constantinople, Layard began a dig late in 1845 at Kalhu (Nimrud), the great city of Ashurnasirpal. Employing local tribesmen but working secretly to avoid stirring up enmities, he immediately struck lucky and subsequent excavations began to reveal much of the glory of the Assyrian emperor's palace. Vast human heads in stone emerged from the sand, to the horror of some locals, who took a while to be convinced that they were not demons.

Off and on, depending on funds and local bureaucracy, Layard continued his work at Nimrud for five years. He was visited there by his friend Henry Rawlinson (1810–95), who had deciphered cuneiform and who was involved in archaeological investigations of his own.

Layard uncovered further palaces and outstanding artefacts, such as the Black Obelisk of Shalmaneser III; but when he turned his attention to Nineveh, he realized that Botta's excavations had not penetrated the mound of Kunyunjik there as fully as they might have. Layard had realised that the Assyrians built their palaces on a foundation of sun-dried brick. He wrote:

GERTRUDE BELL AND THE BAGHDAD ARCHAEOLOGICAL MUSEUM

Born in 1868 in County Durham to a wealthy family, Gertrude Bell first visited Persia in 1892 to visit her uncle, Sir Frank Lascelles, who was British Minister at Tehran. She returned to the Middle East seven years later, travelling widely in Palestine and Syria, and acquired an astonishing mastery of Arabic, Persian and Turkish, as well as Italian, French and German. She made her first trip to Mesopotamia in 1909, visiting the site of Babylon and starting an acquaintance with T. E. Lawrence (later fêted as 'Lawrence of Arabia').

ABOVE *Gertrude Bell – the 'Uncrowned Queen of Iraq'.*

Her first real opportunity to work in Mesopotamia, then still part of the tottering Ottoman empire, came during the First World War. The British had captured Basra as early as November 1914, and Bell was subsequently dispatched there by the Arab Bureau to draw up maps to enable British forces to reach Baghdad, which duly fell in 1917. Bell was the only female political officer in British Intelligence, and her help in the capture of Baghdad earned her promotion to Oriental Secretary. Britons with such intimate knowledge of the area were thin on the ground and few had such detailed knowledge as she. As a result, after the war and the collapse of the Ottoman empire, she was given the task of investigating how the British might best administer the area covered by Mesopotamia. Her recommendation of Arab leadership caused resentment in some circles, but exerted great influence on the drawing of the borders of what, in 1921, became the new country (under British mandate) of Iraq. Faisal I, a staunch ally during the war, became its first king. Bell stayed on as his advisor. She then turned her energies to forming what would later become the Baghdad Archaeological Museum. In the face of European opposition, she insisted (with some success) that finds should remain in Iraq, thereby ensuring an important base for the collection.

Bell returned to Britain in 1925, but could not settle and soon went back to Iraq, where she contracted pleurisy. She recovered, only to learn of the death from typhoid of her younger brother, to whom she had always been devoted.

The museum which she created opened its doors in June 1926. Yet the following month, Bell took an overdose and died, aged 57. Why she took her life is still uncertain, though in London she may have been diagnosed with lung cancer (she had always been a heavy smoker).

Her museum later became the National Museum of Iraq. In 2003, following the US-led invasion of the country and the disastrous looting that ensued, its director, Donny George, ordered its doors sealed with concrete to prevent further depredations. Dr George then left for Syria. The museum now lies sadly derelict, with no date yet set for its reopening.

... in digging for remains, the first step is to search for the platform of sun-dried bricks. When this is discovered, the trenches must be opened to the level of it, and not deeper; they should then be continued in opposite directions, care being taken to keep upon the platform. By these means, if there are any ruins, they must necessarily be discovered ...

By these means, Layard discovered the site of Sennacherib's palace, the largest and possibly the grandest of all the palaces of ancient Mesopotamia.

In 1847, money ran out and Layard returned to London, but as the artefacts unearthed by him began to arrive at the British Museum, interest in the Near East revived, and Layard fanned the flames by publishing *Nineveh and its Remains*. While being a perfectly scholarly treatise, Layard's work was a racy and exciting read as well, a true adventure story that presents the author as a Victorian Indiana Jones. A couple of years later, public interest was increased by the publication of Henry Rawlinson's account of his translations of the texts at Bisitun.

By October 1849, Layard was back at Mosul. Eighteen months later he estimated that he had uncovered 2 miles (3 km) of low-relief sculptured walls in Sennacherib's palace alone. Layard also unearthed Ashurbanipal's library; but by 1852 he had abandoned archaeology for politics, and his position was taken by his assistant, Hormuzd Rassam (1826–1910). An ethnic Assyrian Christian, born in Mosul, Rassam was an archaeologist all his professional life (apart from a disastrous spell in diplomacy, when he failed to defuse a dangerous international incident occasioned by Queen Victoria's rudeness to the Emperor of Ethiopia). Rassam's great achievements at Nineveh and Kalhu eclipse almost everything else in the popular imagination, for it was he who not only discovered the famous sculptures of Ashurbanipal's lion-hunt, but also identified the stone tablets on which is written

'At the northeast corner [of the Principal Citadel] ... there was a great basalt figure of a lion trampling on a man who lay beneath him with his right hand on the flank of the animal and the left on his muzzle. This latter has been chopped away by superstitious hands, and he is marked all over by the stones and flint balls that have been, and are still, flung at him; for he is regarded as the much-feared *djinn* [a demonic spirit in Islamic legend]. On one side the Arabs have dug out a deep hole in his flanks, which is now filled in with cement. The reason of this is as follows. A European once came here, and inquired about the lion, which he had probably read of in the books of earlier travellers. The Arabs showed it to him, and after looking at it attentively, he chose from among the small holes in the basalt the right one, into which he thrust a key and turned it, whereupon his hand was immediately filled with gold pieces. Having accomplished his practical joke the traveller went his way, unable as he was to speak Arabic. The worthy Arabs, however, in order to render the treasure available, hammered this hole in the lion, which must have caused them immense labour, for the stone is extremely hard. '

ROBERT KOLDEWEY: *THE EXCAVATIONS AT BABYLON* (1914)

ROBERT KOLDEWEY

Robert Koldewey was by no means the first archaeologist to dig in Mesopotamia. There had been several important excavations carried out by men such as Claudius Rich, Paul-Émile Botta, Henry Layard and Hormuzd Rassam during the 19th century. Yet Koldewey, though criticized for his neglect of tablets while concentrating on unearthing buildings, was the first to be able to undergo lengthy and systematic work at Babylon.

ABOVE *Despite his preeminence as an archae-ologist, Robert Koldewey never held an academic post in the subject.*

He studied art history and architecture in Berlin and Vienna before joining a dig in Turkey in 1882, and thereafter led many expeditions in Italy and Greece. He first visited Babylon briefly in June 1887, but it was ten years before he returned, equally briefly, in December 1897. On that occasion, he collected examples of 'enamelled brick reliefs' to take back to Berlin with him in order to persuade the Director General of the Royal Collections to sanction a fully resourced expedition. At that time, Babylon lay within the Ottoman empire, which was fostering ties with Germany. In addition, the fact that Kaiser Wilhelm II took a personal interest in archaeogical excavation in Mesopotamia smoothed Koldewey's path.

He started work on 26 March 1899. The Processional Way had been largely opened up, starting at the point where he had found the tile fragments. He worked tirelessly, summer and winter, ignoring the First World War as far as possible, until 1917, by which time his health was broken by his efforts. His condition was not helped by his eccentric insistence on trying to prove that his mind had mastery over his body; among other things, this obsession led to him wearing heavy suits in the blazing summer heat and light ones in the cold of winter. Even so, the year before he died, having published his final excavation reports, he was able to conclude that '*the most important points of this great, illustrious city have been dealt with*'. By great good fortune, he had excavated the most important part only. In terms of the size of the city as a whole, he had only exposed a fraction. What lies beneath Nebuchadrezzar's city, we will never know.

Koldewey excavated the Ishtar Gate from February to November 1902, while in 1903 he uncovered the so-called Vaulted Building, a huge (probable) store room that he mistook for part of the remains of the Hanging Gardens, along with the northeastern corner of the Southern Citadel. In the years that followed, he was able to reveal much of the remains of the Royal Palace, the Great Temple of Marduk, the Esagila, the Etemenanki ziggurat, a series of temples, the massive city walls and the town centre.

Koldewey's contribution, and his application of his architectural training to his work, is of enormous value, since through it we are able not only to understand, but also visualize the city as it would have been under Nebuchadrezzar the Great.

SIR LEONARD WOOLLEY

The famous so-called royal tombs at the ancient city of Ur were excavated by Leonard Woolley in the 1920s. Woolley was born in London in 1880 and started work as Assistant Keeper of the Ashmolean Museum in Oxford. He embarked on his archaeological career in 1906, at the instigation of Sir Arthur Evans (1851–1941; later famous for excavating Knossos), running the dig at the Roman site at Corbridge in Northumberland. Woolley was not formally trained, yet by 1912 he was working alongside T. E. Lawrence at Carchemish, where he stayed for two years. He took charge of the dig at Ur in 1922, leading a joint expedition by the British Museum and the University of Pennsylvania, which put up most of the money.

ABOVE *Leonard Woolley examining a find from the Temple of the Moon God at Ur. In all, he spent 12 years at the site.*

Ur had been known since 1854, when the British vice-consul at Basra, J. E. Taylor, was commissioned by the British Museum to look into some of the ancient sites in southern Mesopotamia. Taylor had noticed a series of mounds about 9 miles (15 km) from the Euphrates, the highest of which was called by the local people Tel al Muqquayar ('The Mound of Pitch'), and decided to start his investigations there. It was an auspicious choice, for soon he was unearthing inscriptions indicating that this was the site of the great city of the Sumerians. The Mound of Pitch was nothing less than the ziggurat of Ur-Nammu and Nabonidus.

Later in the century the University of Pennsylvania sent an expedition to the site, which had not been investigated further owing partly to lack of funds and partly to the fact that it lay in a wild and lawless part of the country. Their work was slight, and after they had left any further attempts were frustrated by the outbreak of the First World War. It was 1922 before another dig could be organized.

Woolley's excavations at Ur lasted for 12 years, until 1934. During that time he was able to discover and send back to the British Museum many hundreds of tablets and precious artefacts, including the famous 'Ram in a Thicket', the 'Standard of Ur', and the wonderful funereal headdress and jewellery of Pu-abi (whom in his book he calls Shub-ad). Woolley's wife Katherine was instrumental in much of the restoration work on these finds, and she also has another curious claim to fame. In 1927 the writer Agatha Christie, recently separated from her husband, was travelling in the Near East. There she met Max (later Sir Max) Mallowan, then a young assistant of Woolley, and was to accompany him on several digs. In 1930 they married. 1936 saw the appearance of Christie's *Murder in Mesopotamia*, set at an archaeological dig in Iraq. Some contemporaries were quick to spot that the character of the wife (and murder victim) was based on Woolley's wife, Katherine. It was no secret that the two women had fallen out in Iraq, after the imperious Lady Woolley interfered in Christie and Mallowan's wedding plans.

The Epic of Gilgamesh. He remained active in Assyria until the early 1880s. Despite suffering occasional setbacks due to racism, Rassam was a lifelong anglophile, married an Englishwoman and ended his days in Brighton. His daughter Theresa became a leading light of the D'Oyly Carte Opera Company.

Somewhat overshadowed by the dramatic discoveries in Assyria, work was also being carried on in Babylon. Between 1849 and 1855 the geologist and naturalist William Loftus (1820–58), working for the British government's Turco-Persian Boundary Commission, was able to undertake limited investigation of the sites of Eridu, Nippur, Susa, Ur and Uruk; while in 1853–4 J. E. Taylor, the British vice-consul at Basra, partly unearthed the ziggurat at Ur. He found clay cylinders at the four corners of the top stage of the ziggurat which bore an inscription of Nabonidus, including a prayer for his son Belshazzar.

NINETEENTH- AND TWENTIETH-CENTURY SCHOLARSHIP

In the late 19th century British influence in the Ottoman empire, which controlled the region, began to wane in favour of Germany, and consequently the archaeological torch passed to the Germans and Americans. German scholars had the backing and active interest of Kaiser Wilhelm II, who ascended the throne in 1888, while the American universities had ample funding at their disposal. The turn of the 20th century saw the major long-term excavation of Babylon by Robert Koldewey (1855–1925). Following the interruption of the First World War, after which Iraq was ruled for a decade by the British under a League of Nations mandate, the 1920s and 1930s witnessed the extensive, and again long-term, excavation of Ur and its surroundings by a joint British Museum–University of Pennsylvania expedition, led by Leonard Woolley (1880 1960).

The 1920s also saw the establishment of a museum for Mesopotamian artefacts in Baghdad. Originally called the Baghdad Archaeological Museum, it was the brainchild of an Englishwoman, Gertrude Bell (1868–1926), an orientalist, archaeologist, diplomat, linguist and spy who had spent many years in the Middle East and had come to regard Iraq as her adopted country. A diminutive chain-smoker, she was so forceful in her role as advisor to the British-appointed King Faisal that she earned the nickname, 'The Uncrowned Queen of Iraq'. The museum opened its doors in the same year she died. It later became the National Museum of Iraq, and housed one of the greatest collections in the world, since Bell had taken care to arrange more-or-less waterproof legislation to ensure that what was found in Iraq stayed in Iraq.

Before the Second World War again threw everything into turmoil, there were expeditions to Kish (Oxford University and the Field Museum of Chicago, 1922–33); Uruk, (from Berlin, 1928–39); a French expedition to Girsu (1929–34); and Eshnunna (Oriental Institute of the University of Chicago, 1930–4).

Work was resumed after 1945, and early in the 1960s the Iraqi Directorate of Antiquities developed a plan designed to save Nineveh from being engulfed by the fast-expanding city of Mosul on its doorstep. The objective was to turn the whole site into a museum. Parts of the city wall and gates were restored. In 1987 the Iraqis were joined by American colleagues and they worked together for three years on the residential quarters of the city. Shattered human remains uncovered at the Halzi Gate bore witness to the last battle for the city, when the Medes sacked it in AD 612.

However, in 1991 work was interrupted by the Iran–Iraq War, and again in 2003 by the US and British invasion. At the time of writing, little serious archaeological work has been possible in Iraq for 18 years.

EPILOGUE

The civilization of Mesopotamia lasted for over 3000 years and had its roots in prehistory. Slightly less time separates us now from Nebuchadrezzer than separated him from the beginnings of his own culture. He was therefore at about the halfway point of human development to date. The peoples of Mesopotamia were no strangers to the destruction of war: cities were razed and people were killed. Nothing can be done about death except to mourn, and try to limit its unnatural causes. As for the cities and the monuments, at the time, at least they could be rebuilt. There is no-one to rebuild them now.

As far as Babylon is concerned, the Iraqi dictator Saddam Hussein (1937–2006) did start a reconstruction programme in 1985, but it seems to have been generally misguided. Much of the reconstruction was on top of existing ancient ruins, burying unexplored and unexcavated monuments and artefacts. Saddam used the wrong materials, and even stamped his name on some of the new thermalite blocks, in emulation of Nebuchadrezzar. The Iraqi leader also had a palace built over ruins in the form of a ziggurat, and in 2003 was about to start work on a cable car over the city.

In 2006, plans to develop further restoration of Babylon were tabled, the aim being to make the place a living museum, with hotels, shopping malls and possibly a theme park. These plans appear for the moment to have been shelved.

Again in 2003, the American forces of occupation were the focus for criticism as a result of the construction by the US 1st Marine Expeditionary Force, under General James T. Conway, of a helicopter landing pad on ancient ruins.

Dr John Curtis, Keeper of the Middle East Collections at the British Museum has described how the occupying forces have also caused damage to the Ishtar Gate. Nine of the brick-relief animal figures on the gate have been damaged by soldiers trying to prise the bricks free as souvenirs. In addition, military vehicles have crushed ancient brick pavements from the second millennium BC, and irresponsible entrenchments and the use of earth-moving machinery have caused extensive harm to the site of the ancient city.

After the initial invasion, there was little or no attempt to protect cultural sites throughout the country. One French Assyriologist recently interviewed described a return visit, in 1998, to a site he had previously been working on in 1990: '*It was unrecognisable. It was like Verdun. Trench after trench after trench. Looting on an industrial scale.*' Looting has since become even more prevalent, encouraged by economic meltdown in Iraq, the decay of the social fabric, and the greed of unscrupulous international dealers and collectors.

Great damage has been done to Baghdad's National Library, where staff work on, despite fires and death threats. The fate of the National Museum is well documented. Pillaging has resulted in the loss of some 15,000 artefacts, not only from our period. Mosques and other Muslim monuments and palaces have not been spared. The museum itself will take decades to recover, if it recovers at all, and yet it housed one of the world's foremost collections.

Iraq contains 42 inventoried museums, and about 12,000 archaeological sites;

everywhere indiscriminate looting and military damage is destroying the archaeological record forever. Meanwhile, the Iraqi government's funding for site protection ran out in mid-2006, and the occupation coalition authorities have never considered such protection a priority. Dr Curtis even discovered sandbags filled with archaeological material, including potsherds, bones and ancient bricks, at a military facility in Babylon – Camp Alpha – occupied by Polish troops from 2003 to 2005. In March 2005, the American contractor Halliburton constructed Camp Babylon for the US Army, causing extensive further damage. Meanwhile at Ur, the birthplace of the prophet Abraham, as early as May 2003 US troops were spraying graffiti on the walls and otherwise vandalizing the city.

All this is interesting in view of the 1954 Geneva and Hague Convention for the Protection of Cultural Property in the Event of Armed Conflict, which, among other provisions, states that an occupying power must take all necessary measures to preserve the cultural property of an occupied country, and is obliged to prevent or arrest '*any form of theft, pillage, or misappropriation of, and any acts of vandalism directed against, cultural property*'.

Yet, despite the generally gloomy picture, there are some grounds for hope. In February 2008 it was announced that the British Army held talks with the British Museum with a view to restoring and protecting what was left of Iraq's shattered cultural legacy. In an interview with the *Art Newspaper*, Dr Curtis, who is behind the British Museum's interest in this initiative, professed cautious optimism. It is at least a start, and if the Iraqi authorities lend their weight to the project, it may even turn out to bear fruit. At present many of the areas under threat are situated in areas too dangerous for archaeologists and Assyriologists to visit.

Meanwhile, archaeology pursues it investigations successfully in the countries around the Mesopotamian core, which in ancient times were influenced by Babylon and by Assyria. Towards the end of April 2008 it was reported that German archaeologists had unearthed a set of carved-stone circles at Göbekli Tepe, near the Syrian border in southeastern Turkey, which date from 9500 BC. They were erected by people who were still hunter-gatherers, but at the moment when agriculture and settlement were about to make their appearance, and begin the process that would lead to our way of life. It would be a great shame, and a supreme irony, if the 'cradle of civilization' were also to become its grave.

One is reminded of the words that end Babylon's greatest epic poem, as the hero returns home and takes solace from what he has achieved in his city of Uruk:

BELOW *A partially completed colossal basalt statue of a lion standing over a prostrate human being. Vandalized over the course of millennia by superstitious locals who regarded it as a* djinn, *it remains* in situ *in Babylon, where Robert Koldewey discovered it in 1903.*

This too was the work of Gilgamesh, the king, who knew the countries of the world. He was wise, he saw mysteries and knew secret things, he brought us a tale of the days before the flood. He went on a long journey, was weary, worn out with labour, and returning engraved on a stone the whole story.

GLOSSARY

ACHAEMENIDS The Persian dynasty, named after its founder, Achaemenes, to which Cyrus the Great, conqueror of the last Babylonian empire, belonged.

AKKADIAN The language of the people who invaded Babylon under Sargon the Great. The term applies both to the people themselves, the Akkadians, and to their city of Akkad (Agade).

AMORITES The people who later invaded Babylon, putting an end to the Ur III dynasty. Their most famous king was Hammurabi, and they established themselves at the city of Babylon.

ANNALS Yearly reports or chronicles of the activities of the Assyrian and later Babylonian rulers.

ARAMAEANS The people who engulfed Mesopotamia at the time of the great Assyrian empire. Their language, Aramaic, gradually supplanted Akkadian.

ASSYRIA The northern part of Mesopotamia, often a separate kingdom from Babylon, sometimes dominating the whole region and beyond. Their language, Assyrian, was a dialect of Akkadian.

BABYLON Name of the city and the state (sometimes Babylonia) which occupied the southern part of Mesopotamia, at certain times dominating the whole region and beyond. Their language, Babylonian, was a dialect of Akkadian.

CHALDEANS Tenacious tribal peoples of the far south, the Sealand. Composed of three principal tribes, they came to take over Babylon and create an empire in the last century of Mesopotamia's power.

CUNEIFORM From the Latin *cuneus* ('wedge'), the symbols of this shape that constituted the written form of Sumerian and Akkadian.

EARLY DYNASTIC Term for three periods, I, II, and III, covering the period from *c.*3000 to 2350 BC.

ENSI Sumerian term for the governor of a city.

JAMDAT-NASR (also JEMDET-NASR)
The period of time, named after the archaeological site which identifies it, covering the transition between the late Uruk and early dynastic epochs (*c.*3100–2900 BC).

KASSITES A people who dominated southern Mesopotamia from the 16th to the 12th century BC.

LUGAL Sumerian word for a king.

MEDES A people of Persian stock, perhaps related to the Elamites, whose alliance with the Chaldeans brought about the end of the last Assyrian empire.

MESOPOTAMIA Literally, 'the land between the rivers' – roughly, the region encompassing Assyria to the north, Babylon to the south, and Sumer in the far south and coastal region.

SUMER The region of southern Mesopotamia which was culturally and politically innovative and dominant before the advent of the Akkadians. Politically, it was a shifting scene of alliances of city-states. Ethnically distinct from the Akkadians, they also had their own unrelated language, Sumerian.

UBAID People and period in prehistoric times, pre-dating the Sumerians (*c.* 5500–4000 BC).

UR III Period of Sumerian revival centred at Ur, after the collapse of the Akkadian state and the Gutian invasion (2112–2004 BC).

URUK PERIOD Period of cultural development centred at Uruk, the second most ancient city (after Eridu) of the region (*c.*4000–3000 BC).

FURTHER READING/MUSEUMS

This short bibliography is arranged in alphabetical order of author and covers the main areas of the history of Mesopotamia. Readers who feel that after finishing this brief survey they would like to learn more, should also feel confident that they will do so from the following books, which also contain their own, sometimes very full, bibliographies. Readers should, however, be aware that some of these books are rare, and some expensive.

Adkins, Leslie: *Empires of the Plain: Henry Rawlinson and the Lost Language of Babylon.* (HarperCollins, London, 2003)

Ascalone, Enrico (transl. Rosanna M. Giammanco Frongia): *Mesopotamia – Assyrians, Sumerians, Babylonians.* (Dictionaries of Civilisation series, University of California Press, Berkeley, Los Angeles, London, 2007)

Baldwin, S. D.: *Nebuchadnezzar's Panoramic Vision of the Six Kingdoms of the World.* (Kessinger Publishing's Rare Reprints, n.d.)

Cameron, George G.: *History of Early Iran.* (Greenwood Press, New York, 1968)

Childe, V. Gordon: *The Most Ancient East.* (Kegan Paul, Trench, Trubner; London, 1928)

Common Bible: Revised Standard Version. (Collins, London, 1973)

Dalley, Stephanie (ed. & transl.): *Myths from Mesopotamia.* (Oxford World's Classics, Oxford, 2000)

Diodorus Siculus: *The Antiquities of Asia: Diodorus Book II.*(transl. Edwin Murphy). (Transaction, Brunswick NY and Oxford, 1989)

Gill, Anton: *Ancient Egyptians.* (HarperCollins, London. 2003)

Guirand, F.: Assyro–Babylonian Mythology: in *Larousse Encyclopaedia of Mythology,* ed. Robert Graves. (Paul Hamlyn, London, 1964)

Griffe, Maurice: *Asia Minor and Mesopotamia – Chronological Table from 3300 BCE to the Present.* (Tableaux Synoptiques de l'Histoire, Le Cannet, n.d.)

Herodotus (transl. Aubrey de Sélincourt): *The Histories.* (Penguin, Harmondsworth, 1965)

Josephus, Flavius (ed. Moses I. Finley, transl. Ralph Marcus and H. St. J. Thackeray): *Selected Writings.* (New English Library, London and New York, 1965)

Koldewey, Robert (transl. Agnes S. Johns): *The Excavations at Babylon.* (Macmillan, London, 1914)

Layard, Austen Henry: *Nineveh and Its Remains.* (Lyons Press, Guilford, Connecticut, 2001; reprint of 1848 edition)

Leick, Gwendolyn: *Mesopotamia – The Invention of the City.* (Allen Lane; the Penguin Press, London, 2001)

Mieroop, Marc Van De: *A History of the Ancient Near East, ca. 3000–323 BC.* (Blackwell History of the Ancient World, Blackwell, Malden, Maine; Oxford, and Carlton, Victoria, Australia)

Mitchell, T. C.: *The Bible in the British Museum – Interpreting the Evidence.* (British Museum Press, London, 2004)

Oates, Joan: *Babylon.* (Thames and Hudson, London, 1986)

Reade, Julian: *Assyrian Sculpture.* (British Museum Press, London, 1983)

Reade, Julian: *Mesopotamia (to 1500 BC).* (British Museum Press, London, 1991)

Roux, Georges: *Ancient Iraq.* (George Allen and Unwin, London, 1954)

Saggs, H. W. F.: *Babylonians.* (Peoples of the Past series, University of California Press, Berkeley and Los Angeles, 2000)

Sandars, N. K. (transl.): *The Epic of Gilgamesh.* (Penguin, Harmondsworth, 1960)

Snell, Daniel C. (ed.): *A Companion to the Ancient Near East.* (Blackwell Companions to the Ancient World, Blackwell, Malden, Maine; Oxford, and Carlton, Victoria, Australia, 2007)

Stevens, E. S. (ed. & transl.): *Folk Tales of Iraq.* (OUP, Oxford, & Humphrey Milford, London, 1931)

Vivien de Saint-Martin, M.: *Ninive: in Le Tour du Monde, Vol. VII.* (Hachette, Paris & London, 1863)

Wallis Budge, E. A.: *Babylonian Life and History.* (By Paths of Bible Knowledge series, The Religious Tract Society, London, 1891)

Wiltshire, Katharine: *The Pocket Timeline of Ancient Mesopotamia.* (OUP Inc., New York, 2005)

Wiseman, D. J. (ed. & transl.): *Chronicles of Chaldean Kings (626–556 BC) in the British Museum.* (Trustees of the British Museum, London, 1961)

Wiseman, D. J.: *Nebuchadrezzar and Babylon – The Schweich Lectures.* (The British Academy, London and OUP Inc., New York, 1985)

Woolley, Leonard: *Excavations at Ur.* (Ernest Benn, London, 1954)

MUSEUM COLLECTIONS

The first four noted are the most important, although the museum in Baghdad is currently (2008) closed.

Baghdad, National Museum of Iraq
Berlin, Vorderasiatisches Museum
London, British Museum
Paris, Louvre Museum

Aleppo, National Archaeological Museum
Ankara, Museum of Anatolian Civilisation
Chicago, Oriental Institute of the University of Chicago
Damascus, National Archaeological Museum
Philadelphia, University of Pennsylvania Museum
Tehran, National Archaeological Museum

INDEX

Figures in *italics* indicate captions to illustrations. and maps

PICTURE CREDITS

Quercus Publishing and its employees have made every effort to trace and identify the source and copyright of all pictures used in this book. Anyone having claim to ownership or copyright of any images not identified correctly is invited to contact Quercus Publishing

akg-images: pages 27 (Iraq Museum; Baghdad/Bildarchiv Steffens); 34 (Iraq Museum; Baghdad/Erich Lessing); 36; 46; 48 (Erich Lessing); 51 (Louvre; Paris/ Erich Lessing); 85 (Delacroix /Louvre; Paris/ Erich Lessing);106-7 (William Blake /Institute of Art; Minneapolis); 123 (Louvre; Paris/ Erich Lessing); 131 & 136 (Bildarchiv Steffens);146 (Iraq Museum/Erich Lessing);161 (Louvre; Paris/ Erich Lessing);185 (Iraq Museum; Baghdad/Erich Lessing).

Bridgeman Art Library: pages 2 (The Stapleton Collection); 9 (Staatliche Kunstsammlungen, Dresden); 21 (Peter Willi); 23 (Ashmolean Museum, University of Oxford); 32 (Museum of Fine Arts, Boston, Massachusetts/Gift of the Guide Foundation and Mrs. Hilary Barrat-Brown; 42, 45 & 47 (Louvre, Paris); 53 (Iraq Museum, Baghdad); 57, 58, 61, 64 & 68 (Louvre, Paris); 74 (private collection); 77 (British Museum, London); 81 (British Museum, London/Boltin Picture Library); 82 (Bibliothèque Nationale, Paris); 94 (British Museum, London/Boltin Picture Library); 96 (Archives Charmet); 97 (private collection); 101(Bibliothèque Nationale, Paris); 106 Stapleton Collection);113 (Stapleton Collection); 117; 118 (Ashmolean Museum, University of Oxford); 119 (Hermitage, St. Petersburg); 120 (British Museum, London); 129 (Louvre, Paris/Lauros/Giraudon); 133 (British Museum, London); 135 (Louvre, Paris/Peter Willi); 139 (Ashmolean Museum, University of Oxford); 141 (Iraq Museum, Baghdad/Giraudon);144 (Louvre, Paris),

145 (Musée de la Poste, Paris/Archives Charmet); 147 (National Museum, Karachi); 149 (private collection); 150 (Louvre, Paris/Lauros/Giraudon); 152 (National Museum, Aleppo/Giraudon); 153 (Louvre, Paris/Lauros/ Giraudon); 162 (British Museum, London); 168 (National Gallery, London),

British Museum: pages 71, 88, 93, 165 & 167

Corbis: pages 1 (Michael Nicholson); 10-11 (News/Cheryl Diaz Meyer); 16 (Picture Desk/ Gianni Dagli Orti); 18 (Gallery Collection); 19 (Picture Desk/ Gianni Dagli Orti); 30 (Werner Forman); 39 (Edge/Michael S.Yamashita); 41 (Bettmann); 43 (Arciad/Mark Fiennes); 53 (Picture Desk/Gianni Dagli Orti); 54 (Bettmann); 64 (Picture Desk/Gianni Dagli Orti); 114 (Documentary/Francoise de Mulder); 137 (David Lees); 156 (Picture Desk/Gianni Dagli Orti); 177 (Documentary/Francoise de Mulder); 179 (Hulton-Deutsch); 182 (Bettmann).

Getty Images: pages 13 (Science Faction/Ed Darack); 25 (Middle Eastern); 55 (Middle Eastern); 86-7(Hulton Archive); 91 (Nineveh National Geographic/Randy Olso); 116 (Time & Life Pictures/Lee Boltin); 124 (Mesopotamian); 125 (Time & Life Pictures/Frank Scherschel); 126 (Assyrian); 130 (Assyrian); 138 (Babylonian School); 143 (Assyrian); 148 (Mesopotamian); 151 (Roger Viollet Collection); 155 (Middle Eastern); 158 (Middle Eastern); 172 (Assyrian School); 175 (AFP/Karim Sahib); 182 (Middle Eastern).

Illustrated London News: page 31
Private collections: pages 10-11; 171

TO THE IRAQI PEOPLE

Author's acknowledgements:

I wish to thank the staff of the Bibliothèque Nationale de France, the British Library, the British Museum, the Institut du Monde Arabe, the Musée du Louvre and the Vorderasiatisches Museum, Berlin.
Also: John Baxter, Marji Campi (particularly), Hilary Ellis, Sir John Hammerton, Richard Milbank, Dr Harold Shukman, Professer Emeritus Geza Vermes and Susan Walby.
I have attended lectures by Dr Irving Finkel and Dr Walter Stephens which provided me with important insights; I am also grateful for indirect input through books, articles, and lectures – from Dr Béatrice André-Salvini, Dr Dominique Collon, and the former director of the National Museum of Iraq, Dr Donny George.
I should also like to acknowledge the support of my agent, Julian Alexander,
and my publisher, Nicolas Cheetham.
Finally, I must express my indebtedness to the authors of the books listed in the Bibliography. No one wishing to pursue this subject further could be in better or safer hands than theirs. Translators from the original languages are credited with their works in that section. I am especially cognisant of the work of Stephanie Dalley, Edwin Murphy, N.K. Sandars and Aubrey de Sélincourt.

Project manager and designer Patrick Nugent
Editor Peter Lewis
Picture researcher Stuart Booth
Indexer Diana LeCore
Proofreader Francine Brody
Cartographer William Donohoe

Metro Books
122 Fifth Avenue
New York, NY 10011

ISBN: 978-4351-2961-0

Printed and bound in China

1 3 5 7 9 10 8 6 4 2